The Book of Genesis

The Book of Genesis

An Introductory Commentary

Second Edition

Ronald Youngblood

BAKER BOOK HOUSE
Grand Rapids, Michigan 49516

Second edition
Copyright 1991 by
Baker Book House Company

First edition in two volumes:

How It All Began: Genesis 1–11 (1980)
Faith of Our Fathers: Genesis 12–50 (1976)

Library of Congress Cataloging-in-Publication Data

Youngblood, Ronald F.
    The book of Genesis : an introductory commentary / Ronald
Youngblood.—2nd ed.
        p.   cm.
    Includes bibliographical references and index.
    ISBN 0-8010-9897-1
    1. Bible. O.T. Genesis—Commentaries.   I. Title.
BS1235.3.Y63   1991
    222'. 1107—dc20   91-146
                                                         CIP

Contents

Part 4 Jacob and Joseph

Preface

"How old is the world?" "Who made the stars?" "Where did I come from?" Questions like these are asked not only by little children but also, at various levels of understanding, by every thinking person. The book you are now about to read does not claim, by any means, to answer such questions fully. I do propose, however, to give responses that I trust will prove helpful in leading the way toward more complete answers. In other words, this book addresses the general topic of how it all began—the universe, the earth, life, sin, redemption, marriage, civilization, society, and much more.

The biblical Book of Genesis has no peer as a source for providing answers to questions like these. Inspired by the Holy Spirit, the first fifty chapters of Scripture deal with the most vital issues that we face in life. And they do so in terms of real people confronting real problems in real historical situations. The following commentary on those remarkable chapters is merely one attempt to get at the questions they pose and the answers they give.

The footnotes and the bibliography at the end of the book indicate but a small sampling of the vast resources available to the reader who wishes to study Genesis in a more extensive way. My personal debt of gratitude to all the students of Genesis who have preceded me can never be repaid. Their work has helped mine beyond measure, and I can only hope that mine will help future students in however small a way.

The present work is a thorough revision of *How It All Began* (a laymen's commentary on Genesis 1–11) and *Faith of Our Fathers* (a similar commentary on Genesis 12–50), two of my earlier studies of the book of Genesis, here combined as one volume. My special thanks go to Allan Fisher and the other editors at Baker Book House, who encouraged me to undertake this task. Such confidence on their part is deeply appreciated. I also wish to express my gratitude to my secretary, Gretchen Entz, for typing the revised manuscript.

Introduction to Genesis

NAME

PURPOSE

AUTHORSHIP

DATE

LITERARY STRUCTURE

OUTLINE

How extraordinary the Bible is! It would be remarkable enough if it were merely a human book. But the fact that it is God's Word makes it all the more amazing. And to think that a loving God has condescended to speak to his often unlovely (and unlovable) creatures through Holy Scripture is enough to stagger the imagination.

Nevertheless, that is exactly what God has done. In the Bible the words may be human, but the voice is divine. The prophets and apostles who spoke and wrote the words of Scripture were "carried along by the Holy Spirit" (2 Pet.1:21) like sailing vessels driven by the wind. Divine authority resides in what they said and wrote because their message is "not the word of men, but . . . the word of God" himself (1 Thess. 2:13). As God's works of creation were made "by the breath of his mouth" (Ps. 33:6), so also God's Word, from beginning to end, is "God-breathed" (2 Tim. 3:16).

In the course of this study, it will be our privilege to see and hear what God is saying to us in the first fifty chapters of his Word. The opening sentences and paragraphs and chapters of any book or set of books are all-important for a proper understanding of what the entire work is saying because they set the stage for everything that follows. It is supremely important, then, that we pay careful attention to Genesis, the book that serves as such a magnificent introduction to the entire Bible. The story told in these chapters has no equal elsewhere in world literature, and the events related in them have no parallel elsewhere in world history. This section of the Bible outlines for us the first steps in holy history and tells us how it all began.

Name

Nearly the entire OT was originally written in the Hebrew language, and Genesis is no exception. The Hebrew title of Genesis is *Bĕrē'šît* (pronounced bray-SHEET), which means "in the beginning." In ancient times a book was almost always named after its first two or three words, a practice still followed in some cases (e.g., hymns and papal encyclicals). With respect to Genesis it was especially appropriate, because Genesis is indeed the book of beginnings.

The Hebrew OT was eventually translated into Greek (beginning about 250 years before the time of Christ) so that people whose native tongue was Greek could have the Word of God in their own language. The Greek translators then gave their own title, "Genesis," to the first book of their OT text. This word, identical to the English title derived from it, is a form of the word *geneseōs* (pronounced geh-NEH-seh-oas), found in the Greek translation at Genesis 2:4 and 5:1 (and, significantly, in Matt. 1:1). Depending on its context the word means "birth," "genealogy," "history of origin," and the like. Again, the Greek and English title is entirely appropriate, because Genesis is indeed a history book of origins, of births, of genealogies—of how it all began.

Purpose

The OT as a whole tells the story of the Hebrew people—who they were, where they lived, what they did, how they acted. The Book of Exodus describes in detail the great redemptive event in their history prior to the first coming of Jesus Christ: their miraculous release from slavery in Egypt, the greatest world power of that time. The Book of Genesis, on the other hand, tells us why the Hebrew people—or, more specifically, the family of Jacob (also known as Israel)—went down to Egypt in the first place.

To put it another way, Genesis was written from the standpoint of the exodus. It is as if the newly-freed Israelite slaves asked their leader Moses, "How did we get here?", and then Moses told them the story of their forefathers, the patriarchs Abraham, Isaac, Jacob and Joseph, culminating with the account of how Joseph, one of Jacob's sons, was sold into slavery in Egypt by his brothers and how the rest of the family joined him there later. That story forms the so-called "patriarchal history" of Genesis 12–50 (or, more precisely, 11:27–50:26).

But that exciting tale would only whet the appetites of the Israelites even further. We can easily picture them as immediately asking another question: "Where did the patriarchs come from?" And another: "What happened before that?" And another—and so on, and so on, and so on! For our part, we can be grateful that God condescended to reveal to his servant Moses the answers to questions that he and his fellow Israelites were asking (we can be fairly sure that Moses shared their insatiable curiosity), because Genesis 1:1–11:26 is the glorious result. And as Genesis 11:27–50:26 is often called the "patriarchal history" because of its clearly defined subject matter, so also is Genesis 1:1–11:26 often called the "primeval history" because of its equally clear theme: It tells us about the beginning of the universe, of the heavenly bodies, of the earth with its seas and lakes and rivers and streams and mountains and hills, of inanimate plant life, of animate life including water creatures and air creatures and land creatures.

Most important of all, Genesis 1:1–11:26 tells us about the beginning of human life and love, of marriage and family, of work and play, of food and drink, of pleasure and delight. And unfortunately—on the darker side—we also learn about the beginning of sin and its consequences: fractured human relationships, alienation from God, divine judgment, and death. All of this, and more, we will find as we make our way through the action-packed and lesson-filled pages of the primeval history found in the first eleven chapters of Genesis. And then, as we continue beyond into the thirty-nine chapters of the patriarchal history, other significant themes surface: God's call to Abraham, his promises to Isaac, his choice of Jacob/Israel as father of the twelve tribes, his protection of Joseph as the one who would save his family—indeed, the entire eastern Mediterranean world—from famine, his settling of Israel in the most fertile region of Egypt. Furthermore, since God's ancient people are our spiritual ancestors (Gal. 3:7), how they responded to him has profound implications for us as well.

Authorship

Until the seventeenth century after Christ, Jewish and Christian scholars alike were virtually unanimous in their opinion that Moses was the author (or at least the compiler) of the first five books of the OT (including, of course, Genesis). That section was known as the "five books of Moses." In order to keep anything from being added to it or subtracted from it, Jewish tradition referred to it as the "five-fifths of the law" (i.e., the "law" of Moses).

But then in 1670 Benedict Spinoza, a Spanish Jew of scholarly repute, published his views regarding the authorship of those five books (known also as the Pentateuch, a word of Greek origin that means "five tools/scrolls"). Spinoza was of the opinion that the Pentateuch was compiled by Ezra (the author or compiler of the OT books of Ezra and Nehemiah, and perhaps the compiler of 1 and 2 Chronicles as well). He felt that no competent author would write about himself in the third person (Moses is almost always depicted in the third person in the Pentateuch) or describe his own death (see Deut. 34:5–8).

Such arguments, however, are not difficult to counter. It was common literary practice in ancient times for authors to refer to themselves frequently in the third person in their writings (as, e.g., Julius Caesar did in his *Gallic Wars*). In fact, Ezra himself, in the book that bears his name, writes of himself sometimes in the third person (e.g., Ezra 7:1–11) and sometimes in the first person (e.g, 7:27–8:1). Also, it is said of Ezra that he was "a teacher well versed in the Law of Moses" (7:6) and that he "had devoted himself to the study and observance of the Law of the LORD, and to teaching its decrees and laws in Israel" (7:10). In short, the Bible describes Ezra as a student and teacher of the law of Moses (i.e., the Pentateuch), not its author or compiler.

As for the argument that no writer could compose his own

obituary after the fact, that is readily granted. But just because Moses did not write Deuteronomy 34 does not mean that he did not write the rest of the Pentateuch. OT books may have a concluding paragraph or chapter that was written by someone other than the main author. For example, Jeremiah 51:64 concludes as follows: "The words of Jeremiah end here"—and then comes the fifty-second chapter of the book. A secretary or other friend of the author often added his own divinely-inspired ending to a biblical book. In Moses' case, it may very well have been Joshua who wrote Deuteronomy 34.

In any event, the arguments of Spinoza and his followers are by no means sufficient to overthrow the long-held, traditional view that Moses was the Pentateuch's author or compiler. Even though the negative opinions of Spinoza and others eventually unleashed a series of attacks against the Mosaic authorship of the Pentateuch on every conceivable basis (style, vocabulary, language, and so forth) that continue unabated down to our own time,[1] conservative scholars have responded forcefully and adequately to all such objections.[2] More to the point, they maintain that Mosaic authorship best accounts for all the evidence and that, in fact, Scripture itself teaches that Moses was the author of all (or at least most) of the various sections of the Pentateuch (see, among many passages that could be listed, Exod. 17:14; Deut. 31:24; Josh. 8:31; 2 Kings 14:6; Rom. 10:5; 2 Cor. 3:15 and—perhaps most impressive of all—the words of Jesus in John 5:45–47).

Although Moses' name is mentioned nowhere in Genesis itself, it follows that if he wrote the Pentateuch he also wrote Genesis. Furthermore Acts 15:1, which describes circumcision as a "custom taught by Moses," probably intends to refer to the detailed account in Genesis 17 where the rite of circumcision is initiated for the Hebrew patriarchs and their descendants, since nowhere else in the Pentateuch are the regulations for circumcision given.

1. See typically J. A. Soggin, *Introduction to the Old Testament*, rev. ed. (Philadelphia: Westminster, 1980), 80–145.

2. See, e.g., U. Cassuto, *The Documentary Hypothesis* (Jerusalem: Magnes, 1961); K. A. Kitchen, *Ancient Orient and Old Testament* (Chicago: InterVarsity, 1966), 112–38; G. H. Livingston, *The Pentateuch in Its Cultural Environment* (Grand Rapids: Baker, 1974), 220–32, 258–68; J. McDowell, *More Evidence that Demands a Verdict* (San Bernardino: Campus Crusade, 1975), 25–169; A. P. Ross, *Creation and Blessing* (Grand Rapids: Baker, 1988), 23–36.

And so, when all is said and done, I concur with the traditional view of the authorship of the first book of the Bible implied in the heading of that book as found, for example, in the RSV: "The First Book of Moses, Commonly Called Genesis."

Date

If Moses indeed wrote Genesis, then it goes without saying that the book was written during his lifetime. By everyone's calculations Moses lived at some time in what archaeologists call the Late Bronze Age (ca. 1550–ca. 1200 B.C.).

The precise dates of Moses' life are tied in with one of the most vexing problems of OT chronology: the date of the exodus. Although many dates for that important event have been proposed, the two most widely held are 1445 B.C. and 1290 B.C. For quite some time, the 1290 date has had formidable archaeological data on its side, relating primarily to evidence for the Israelite conquest of various towns and cities in Canaan (as described in the book of Joshua). But the dating and interpretation of that evidence has recently become increasingly ambiguous,[3] and at the same time other archaeological evidence (primarily from Ebla in northern Syria) has tended to push back the dating of the patriarchal period.[4] These factors in particular have strengthened the position of those who hold to the 1445 date—a date that, in any case, fits better with a literal understanding of the internal biblical chronology than the 1290 date does. According to 1 Kings 6:1, Solomon began to build the temple in the fourth year of his reign over Israel, which was "the four hundred and eightieth year after the Israelites had come out of Egypt." The fourth year of Solomon's reign was about 966 B.C., and 480 years before that would give us a date of about 1445 for the exodus.[5]

Israel's wanderings in the Sinai desert, under the leadership of Moses, would then have taken place during the forty years immediately following 1445 B.C. It would therefore seem safe to assume that Moses—a man suitably qualified for the task in

3. See, e.g., J. J. Bimson, *Redating the Exodus and Conquest* (Sheffield: Almond, 1981); B. G. Wood, "Did the Israelites Conquer Jericho?", *Biblical Archaeology Review* 16 (1990): 45–58.

4. See, e.g., R. Youngblood, "A New Look at an Old Problem: The Date of the Exodus," *Christianity Today*, December 17, 1982, 58–60.

5. See R. Youngblood, *Exodus* (Chicago: Moody, 1983), 10–16.

terms of possessing the necessary education, motivation, energy, and time—wrote the Pentateuch, including the book of Genesis, late in the fifteenth century before Christ.

Literary Structure

No great piece of literature—whether sacred or secular, whether inspired by God or not—comes about by accident. Students in literature courses in high school and college soon learn that poems, short stories, essays, novels, historical accounts, and all other types of formal writing for artistic purposes are carefully crafted and are designed to be esthetically attractive as well as intellectually informative. A good writer will always try to stimulate the eye as well as the mind. He wants to appeal to his readers' sense of order and beauty and symmetry while he is teaching or entertaining them.

This is why students of literature spend so much time analyzing classic examples of prose and poetry in attempts to discover rises and falls in plot, to reconstruct the outline that was in the mind of the original writer, and to understand the literary devices used by the writer to get his main point (or points) across. Whether it be Chaucer's *Canterbury Tales* or Shakespeare's *King Lear* or Poe's *The Pit and the Pendulum* or Melville's *Moby Dick* or Steinbeck's *The Grapes of Wrath* or Haley's *Roots*, an author's work will be better understood and a reader's experience will be more satisfying if the reader takes the time to learn something about literary structure and, more specifically, about the literary structure of the poem or prose account he is reading at the moment. In other words, knowing something about the form of a piece of literature will always help the reader gain a deeper understanding of the contents of that piece.

And this principle holds true for the Bible as well. It is helpful to know that many of Paul's epistles contain a doctrinal section followed by a section that stresses Christian conduct flowing from the doctrines taught (see, e.g., Romans, 2 Corinthians, Galatians, Ephesians, Colossians). To observe that the dramatic poetic dialogues that constitute the heart of the book of Job are sandwiched in between a prose introduction and a prose conclusion will heighten the reader's feelings of suspense and excitement. To perceive that the Book of Deuteronomy is structured along the lines of an ancient political treaty, with the sovereign (God, in this case) demanding certain obligations (based on mutual respect and loyalty) from his people,[6] helps the reader to comprehend more fully the legally binding basis of God's relationships to Israel.

So literary structure, and the order and arrangement implied, is a useful tool to have in hand as we follow any author's line of argument, in the Bible or elsewhere. It will be especially useful to us as we pursue our course of study in Genesis.

As stated earlier, the Greek word *geneseōs* gives the English translation of the book its title. Its Hebrew equivalent, *tôlĕdôt* (pronounced toe-leh-DOTE), proves to be the key to the literary structure of Genesis.

The entire book is divided into two unequal halves: 1:1–11:26 and 11:27–50:26. Each half has five sections, and each section of the Hebrew text is introduced by the phrase "This is the account (*tôlĕdôt*) of . . ." or its equivalent. The first half of Genesis, the so-called "primeval history," exhibits the phrase at 2:4, 5:1, 6:9, 10:1, and 11:10 (the creation narrative of 1:1–2:3 forms the introduction to the primeval history as well as to the book of Genesis as a whole). The second half, the so-called "patriarchal history," displays the same characteristic phrase at 11:27, 25:12, 25:19, 36:1 (repeated for emphasis at 36:9), and 37:2.

Outline

     I. Introduction (1:1–2:3)
    II. Body (2:4–50:26)
       A. The Account of the Heavens and the Earth (2:4–4:26)
       B. The Written Account of Adam's Line (5:1–6:8)
       C. The Account of Noah (6:9–9:29)
       D. The Account of Shem, Ham and Japheth, Noah's Sons (10:1–11:9)
       E. The Account of Shem (11:10–26)
       F. The Account of Terah (11:27–25:11)
       G. The Account of Abraham's Son Ishmael (25:12–18)
       H. The Account of Abraham's Son Isaac (25:19–35:29)
       I. The Account of Esau (i.e., Edom) (36:1–37:1)
       J. The Account of Jacob (37:2–50:26)

---

6. M. G. Kline, *Treaty of the Great King: The Covenant Structure of Deuteronomy* (Grand Rapids: Eerdmans, 1963).

From this basic literary outline we derive the following thematic outline for our own teaching purposes (without, of course, violating the literary outline that comes from Genesis itself):

 I. Creation: Part 1 (1:1–2:3)
  A. Introduction (1:1–2)
  B. Body (1:3–31)
  C. Conclusion (2:1–3)
 II. Creation: Part 2 (2:4–25)
 III. The Fall (3:1–24)
 IV. The Rapid "Progress" of Sin (4:1–16)
 V. Two Genealogies (4:17–5:32)
  A. The Genealogy of Pride (4:17–24)
  B. The Genealogy of Death (4:25–5:32)
 VI. The Extent of Sin Before the Flood (6:1–8)
 VII. The Great Flood (6:9–9:29)
  A. Preparing for the Flood (6:9–7:10)
  B. Judgment and Redemption (7:11–8:19)
   1. The rising of the waters (7:11–24)
   2. The receding of the waters (8:1–19)
  C. The Aftermath of the Flood (8:20–9:29)
   1. A new promise (8:20–22)
   2. New commands (9:1–7)
   3. A new relationship (9:8–17)
   4. A new temptation (9:18–23)
   5. A final word (9:24–29)
 VIII. The Spread of the Nations (10:1–11:26)
  A. The Confusion of Tongues (11:1–9)
  B. The Diffusion of Nations (10:1–32)
  C. The First Semitic Genealogy (11:10–26)
 IX. The Abrahamic Narratives (11:27–25:11)
  A. The Land of Abram (11:27–14:24)
  B. The Covenant of Abram (15:1–17:27)
  C. The Family of Abraham (18:1–21:34)
  D. The Trial of Abraham (22:1–23:20)
  E. The Last Days of Abraham (24:1–25:11)
 X. The Ishmaelite Genealogy (25:12–18)
 XI. The Jacob Narratives (25:19–35:29)
  A. Jacob's Early Years at Home (25:19–27:46)
  B. Jacob's Years in Paddan Aram (28:1–30:43)
  C. Jacob's Return Home (31:1–35:29)

Part 1

Creation and the Fall

1

Creation: Part 1
(1:1–2:3)

INTRODUCTION (1:1–2)

BODY (1:3–31)

CONCLUSION (2:1–3)

The Genesis account of creation is set forth in two parts. The first (1:1–2:3) is written in measured and majestic prose and in a formal—almost liturgical—style. It forms the introduction to the primeval history as well as to the book of Genesis as a whole. Its broad panorama is cosmic in its sweep and includes the visible universe as seen by the naked eye. The second part (2:4–25), on the other hand, zeros in on a small area of the earth's surface (the Garden of Eden) and depicts God's relationships with one human couple (Adam and Eve).

Introduction (1:1–2)

On the western exterior wall of Breyer Hall, the chemistry and geology building at Wheaton College, these words are inscribed:

IN THE BEGINNING
GOD
CREATED THE HEAVENS
AND THE EARTH

On February 5, 1971, Apollo 14 commander Edgar Mitchell deposited on the moon a microfilm packet containing a complete Bible and one verse of the Bible written out in sixteen languages. The words of that verse:

In the beginning God created the heavens and the earth.

After a lifetime of study and synthesis, a distinguished scientist-philosopher of a previous generation asserted that the four fundamental determinations of physics are "time, space, substance, and causality."[1] Permit me to observe that those four basic concepts, and no more, are found in one verse—the first verse—of the Bible:

In the beginning [time] God created [causality] the heavens [space] and the earth [substance].

One could scarcely think of a more suitable way to begin the Bible than with those majestic words, which teach us that God is the Creator of all that exists and that he brought the universe into being at a time so long ago that it staggers the imagination. No one knows for certain, of course, when "the beginning" was. But the OT is far more interested in the fact of creation than in the time of creation, and the simple truth that God's creative activity took place during an indeterminate time known as "the beginning" was joyfully celebrated by poet (Ps. 102:25) and prophet (Isa. 40:21) alike.

The Gospel of John starts with the same three words as does the Bible itself: "In the beginning." The first ten verses of that gospel stress the activity of Jesus Christ in creation. Not only our Redeemer, the Lord Jesus is also our Creator. As John puts it: "In the beginning . . . the Word (Jesus) was with God, and the Word was God" (John 1:1).

But how is that possible? How can anyone say that a person was "with" someone and at the same time "was" that someone?

---

1. B. Bavink, *The Natural Sciences* (New York: The Century Company, 1932), 219.

Although our finite minds cannot completely understand such matters, the first verse of Genesis itself provides us with a helpful clue. It tells us that "God created" (Gen. **1:1**). The noun "God" is plural in the Hebrew text, but the verb "created" is singular in the Hebrew text. The Bible clearly teaches that God is one being, a unity (Deut. 6:4; 1 Cor. 8:4). At the same time, the Bible just as clearly teaches that the one God exists in three persons and is therefore also a trinity (Matt. 28:19; 2 Cor. 13:14). And it would seem that all three Persons were active in creation from the beginning: the Father (Gen. **1:1**; John 1:1-2), the Son (the "Word"; John 1:3, 10), and the Holy Spirit (Gen. **1:2**).

God made everything—with one exception: himself. Everything else had a beginning, but he has always been (Ps. 90:2). In the Bible his existence is never debated; it is always assumed. And no conditions whatever are placed on his existence. "The God who made the world and everything in it . . . is not served by human hands, as if he needed anything, because he himself gives all men life and breath and everything else" (Acts 17:24–25). Although we are totally dependent on him for every breath we take, he is absolutely independent of the universe he has created.

"Create" is a special verb in the OT. It always has God as its subject; it is never used of human activity. You and I may make or form or fashion, but only God creates. In Genesis 1 the verb "create" is used sparingly. We are told that God created "the heavens and the earth" (the universe; **1:1**), "the great creatures of the sea" (animate life; **1:21**), and "man" (human life; **1:27**). Not used indiscriminately, the verb "create" is reserved for the most crucial items in God's program.

Old Testament Hebrew had no word for "universe," so it used "the heavens and the earth" instead. That phrase is one of the biblical ways of saying "all things" (Eccles. 11:5; Isa. 44:24; Jer. 10:16; John 1:3) since everything that exists is either on earth or in the heavens (broadly conceived).

Before we leave Genesis **1:1**, we should remind ourselves that it is not merely a stiff and formal statement about creation. Its teaching is intended to encourage us about who we are and where we come from, and its emphasis is oriented toward life rather than death, as Isaiah 45:18 comments: "God . . . did not create (the earth) to be empty, but formed it to be inhabited." So it is somewhat ironic that the book of Genesis itself, which starts with that majestic phrase "In the beginning God," ends with a phrase that reeks with the smell of death: "in a coffin in Egypt."

Genesis **1:2** concentrates on "the earth" and stresses the world-centered approach of the author. The earth rather than the heavens is the object of his interest at this point. After all, in the words of J. B. Phillips, the earth is the "visited planet." For reasons that are hidden in his own sovereign wisdom, the God who created this incredibly vast universe chose to lavish special attention and care on a tiny planet in a small solar system located in the galaxy known as the Milky Way, itself an island universe shaped like a lens and estimated to be 100,000 light years across. When it is realized that millions of such galaxies exist in the universe proper, we cannot even begin to comprehend the rationale behind God's choice of us to be his "chosen people," belonging to him alone (1 Pet. 2:9).

"Darkness" filled ancient man with nameless horror (Amos 5:18, 20), and "the deep" terrified him as well (Jon. 2:3, 5)—perhaps partially because the Babylonians deified it and worshiped it as a mythological dragon of the watery chaos. But neither darkness nor the deep is to be feared, since both were created by a loving God. The oceans are part of the earth that he made, and he himself says, "I form the light and create darkness" (Isa. 45:7). At the time of creation "the Spirit of God" was there to give life to the lifeless, "hovering over the waters" like a bird that provides for and protects its young (Deut. 32:10–11; Isa. 31:5). The creative power of that same Holy Spirit continues to be exerted today (Job 33:4; Ps. 104:30).

"Formless and empty" in Genesis **1:2** is an English translation of Hebrew *tōhû wābōhû* (pronounced TOE-hoo vah-VOE-hoo), a rhythmic and eye-catching phrase that pictures the situation on earth before it was touched by the creative hand of God (it occurs elsewhere only in Jer. 4:23). As it turns out, the phrase is the key that unlocks the literary structure of the rest of Genesis 1: The acts of separating and gathering on days 1–3 give form to the "formless," and the acts of making and filling on days 4–6 give divine assurance that the heavens and the earth will never again be "empty."

Body (1:3–31)

"And/Then God said" appears a total of nine times in the first chapter of Genesis (1:3, 6, 9, 11, 14, 20, 24, 26, 29) and, when used in conjunction with the phrase "formless and empty" mentioned above, gives us the following outline for Genesis 1:

Days of Forming	Days of Filling
1. "Let there be light" (1:3)	4. "Let there be lights" (1:14)
2. "Let there be an expanse . . . to separate water from water" (1:6)	5. "Let the water teem with creatures, and let birds fly above the earth" (1:20)
3 a. "Let dry ground appear" (1:9)	6 a'. "Let the land produce living creatures" (1:24) a". "Let us make man" (1:26)
b. "Let the land produce vegetation" (1:11)	b. "I give you every seed-bearing plant...and every tree that has fruit within it...for food" (1:29)

The characteristic verbs that tie together days 1–3 are "separate" and "gather"—verbs of formation—while the verbs that unite days 4–6 are "teem" and "fill" and "be fruitful" and "increase"—verbs of filling.

But I would also observe that comparisons between the days can be made horizontally as well as vertically, as the outline indicates. "Light" is the key word on day 1, and "lights" is the key word on day 4. On day 2 God "separated the water under the expanse from the water above it," while on day 5 he said, "Let the water (under the expanse) teem with living creatures, and let birds fly above the earth across the expanse of the sky"—in other words, on day 2 God separated the lower waters from the upper waters and on day 5 he created some animals to inhabit the lower waters and then others to inhabit the upper waters.

Days 3 and 6 are somewhat different from the other days in Genesis 1 since both of them are climactic. Each uses the phrase "And/Then God said" more than once (day 3, twice; day 6, three times). Two additional comparisons can be made between days 3 and 6. On day 3 "dry ground" appeared, and on day 6 God made (1) "livestock, creatures that move along the ground, and wild animals," and (2) "man" to inhabit the dry ground. In addition, day 3 witnessed the covering of the earth with a carpet of "vegetation," while on day 6 God said that he would give to both man and animals "every green plant for food."

These striking horizontal and vertical relationships between the various days can hardly be accidental. On the contrary, they demonstrate the literary beauty of the chapter and emphasize the symmetry and orderliness of God's creative activity. But the obviously careful planning and thought that went into the crafting of such a tightly woven account cause us to raise a question that may help solve a problem or two in the chapter: Is it possible that the order of events in the Genesis 1 story of creation is partly literary and only partly chronological?

Without being dogmatic about it, I would like to suggest that this may be the case. If those English versions that translate the final words in Genesis **1:5, 8, 13, 19, 23,** and **31** as "the first day," "the second day," "the third day," "the fourth day," "the fifth day," and "the sixth day" respectively are correct, then of course the case is closed. Such language demands that the author intends chronological order. But in fact the literal rendering of the Hebrew phrases in question would be as follows: "one day," "a second day," "a third day," "a fourth day," "a fifth day," and "the sixth day." I would point out that the omission of the definite article ("the") from all but the sixth day allows for the possibility of random or literary order as well as rigidly chronological order.

"Nonchronological," needless to say, does not mean "nonhistorical." The Book of Jeremiah, for example, is arranged in topical rather than chronological order, even though it is historical from beginning to end. Similarly, the two historical accounts of the temptation of Jesus by Satan in Matthew 4:1–11 and Luke 4:1–13 arrange the three crucial phases of the temptation in differing orders, indicating that either Matthew's order or Luke's is nonchronological. In fact, Genesis 1–11 itself contains a clear example of nonchronological order. Genesis 10 depicts various peoples "spread out into their territories by their clans within their nations, each with its own language" (10:5), and then Genesis 11:1–9 tells the antecedent story of how that situation came about.

If the Genesis 1 creation account is at least partly nonchronological, several puzzling problems can be easily solved. For example, how can it be that God "separated the light from the darkness" and that he "called the light 'day' and the darkness . . . 'night'" on day 1 (1:4–5) if the sun was not created until day 4? The simplest answer would seem to be that these two days are not related to each other chronologically but that they both refer to the same event—the creation of the sun. Indeed, this would seem to be implied in 1:17–18 where it is stated that God set the sun "in the expanse of the sky . . . to separate light from darkness" (the latter phrase, in fact, is quoted directly from 1:4). In other words, we are told in Genesis 1:4 *that* God separated light from darkness and in 1:18 *how* he did it.

Or, to take another example: How can there be evening and morning (1:5, 8, 13) before the sun is brought into existence? If chronological order is not demanded, that is no longer a problem.

Or again: How can plants—including fruit trees—that require photosynthesis for their very existence survive apart from sunlight (1:12–13)? The answer is best sought along these lines: The creation of the sun preceded the creation of plant life, providing warmth for the soil together with all the other conditions that would foster growth.

Of course, I would not insist dogmatically that the days of creation in Genesis 1 be understood as displaying nonchronological arrangement. I merely suggest it as a possible theory to help explain the difficulties that arise when the reader demands that the order must be chronological.[2]

Let us now turn to a discussion of the details of the individual days in sequence.

Day 1

God had only to speak, and all things came into being (Ps. 33:6, 9; Heb. 11:3). He simply "commanded and they were created" (Ps. 148:5). Among the things he said is one of the choicest statements in Scripture: "Let there be light." These are the first recorded words of God in the Bible, and they are cited in 2 Corinthians 4:6 as an illustration of the spiritual light that illumines the hearts of believers in Christ. Light often symbolizes the nature and glory of God in the Bible (1 John 1:5; Rev. 21:23).

---

2. For additional details, see R. Youngblood, "Moses and the King of Siam," *Journal of the Evangelical Theological Society* 16 (1973): 215–22; for further development of the pros and cons of this subject, see the treatments of R. C. Newman and M. A. Throntveit in *The Genesis Debate*, ed. R. Youngblood (Grand Rapids: Baker, 1991), 36–55.

What God creates is "good" (Gen. **1:4, 9, 12, 18, 21, 25**)—although there is a strange silence on this point in the account of the creation of mankind on day 6. Although fully aware of man's original state of perfection (as the story of the fall of man in Genesis 3 demonstrates), perhaps the author could not bring himself to declare man "good" in the light of his own highly developed understanding of the human propensity for doing evil. Be that as it may, **1:31** stamps the whole of God's creation as "very good," and that summary statement obviously includes man. And just as all that God has made is good, so is he good to all he has made (Ps. 145:9).

When God gave names to the light and the darkness by calling them "day" and "night" (see also **1:8, 10**), he was declaring his sovereignty and rulership over them. To name something or someone in ancient times implied dominion or ownership (2 Kings 23:34; 24:17). Day and night alike belong to the Lord (Ps. 74:16).

Day 2

The "expanse" is the visible atmosphere or sky (Gen. **1:8**), characterized by the layer of clouds that contain the water above it (**1:7**; Ps. 148:4). The older translation, "firmament," gives a false impression of the nature of the expanse. Phrases such as "hard as a mirror" (Job 37:18) and "like a canopy" (Isa. 40:22) are merely highly picturesque ways of describing it.

"And it was so" is the only possible outcome, whether stated (Gen. **1:7, 9, 11, 15, 24, 30**) or implied, to God's "Let there be." He speaks and it is done, whether in heaven or on earth.

"One place" (**1:9**) is a vivid way of describing the location of the "seas" (**1:10**) that surround the dry ground on all sides and into which the lakes and rivers flow. The earth was "founded . . . upon the seas" (Psalm 24:2) and "formed out of water" (2 Pet. 3:5). The waters of the seas are not to cross the boundaries God has set for them (Ps. 104:7–9; Jer. 5:22).

Day 3

Genesis **1:11** teaches that creation, although ultimately a divine act, sometimes took place through secondary means (see also **1:24**). At the same time, the Bible categorically rules out the possibility of evolution on the grand scale overwhelmingly claimed for it by its supporters. Plants and animals alike were to reproduce only within categories called "kinds" (**1:11, 12, 21, 24, 25**) that were carefully distinguished from each other.

Day 4

Although for unbelievers the lights in the sky may be sources of terror (Jer. 10:2), for God's people they serve as signs to mark off periods of time (Gen. **1:14**; Ps. 104:19).

Why are the sun and moon called the "two great lights" in Genesis **1:16**? Perhaps the words "sun" and "moon" are deliberately avoided here since pagan nations in ancient times deified them and worshiped them under those names. The author of Genesis wants his readers to understand that the "lights" are lightbearers to be appreciated, not gods to be feared. In fact, it is the one true God who made them (**1:16**; see also Isa. 40:26). The stars are mentioned here almost as an afterthought, probably because of the emphasis on the specific functions of the sun and moon. Psalm 136:9, however, notes that the stars help the moon "govern the night." Genesis **1:17–18** lists the three main duties of the lights in the sky: to give light, to govern day and night, and to separate light from darkness.

Day 5

Variety and quantity are stressed in the verses encompassing days 5 and 6 (see also Ps. 104:25). Land, sea, and air were to be filled with God's creatures.

The Hebrew word underlying the phrase "creatures of the sea" (Gen. **1:21**) was used in Canaanite mythology as the name of a dreaded sea monster who is often referred to in a literary and figurative way in OT poetry as one of God's most powerful adversaries, whether natural (Job 7:12), national (Babylon [Jer. 51:34]; Egypt [Isa. 51:9; Ezek. 29:3; 32:2]), or cosmic (Ps. 74:13; Isa. 27:1). But in Genesis he is simply the first specimen of animate life created by God—not to be feared as an evil enemy, but to be appreciated because God created him as "good" (see also Ps. 148:7).

The term "winged bird" (Gen. **1:21**) denotes anything that flies, including insects (see Deut. 14:19–20).

God showed gracious and loving concern to the animals by blessing them and making it possible for them to "be fruitful and increase in number" (Gen. **1:22**). He later gave mankind the same command and privilege, both at the time of their creation (**1:28**) and after the flood (9:1, 7).

Day 6

As we noted at **1:1**, God is both a plurality and a unity. After God said, "Let us make man in our image" (**1:26**), he then went on to create man "in his own image" (**1:27**). Though a mystery, the uniplurality of God's nature is taught consistently throughout Scripture.

No distinction should be made between "image" and "likeness," which are in apposition in **1:26** and are synonyms in both OT (5:1; 9:6) and NT (1 Cor. 11:7; Col. 3:10; James 3:9). Since we are made in God's image, every human being is worthy of honor and respect and should not be murdered (Gen. 9:6) or cursed (James 3:9). Just as a coin is stamped with a ruler's image and represents his presence and authority in his realm, so we are all stamped with God's image and should therefore not only represent him faithfully but also acknowledge his dominion over our lives. In light of the ancient practice of conquering rulers to set up statues or images of themselves in the land of the vanquished to serve as reminders of their sovereignty, there may be a physical component intended in our being created in God's image: We are to "rule over" all other living creatures (Gen. **1:26**). But "image" should probably be understood primarily in a spiritual sense here, including such qualities as "knowledge" (Col. 3:10), "righteousness and holiness" (Eph. 4:24). We who believe in Jesus are to be "conformed to the likeness" of Christ (Rom. 8:29), and some day we will be "like him" (1 John 3:2).

Genesis 1 represents the human being as the culmination, the climax, the crown of God's creative activity. God has "crowned him with glory and honor" and "made him ruler" over the rest of his creation (Gen. **1:26**; Ps. 8:5–8). Humankind is a product of divine creation (Gen. 2:7), not of natural evolution.

Genesis **1:27** is by any standard one of the most beautiful verses in the Bible. It is the first bit of poetry in the OT, which is composed of about forty percent poetry and sixty percent prose. The distinctive verb "created" is used three times in this one verse to describe the central divine act of the sixth day. The phrase "male and female" demonstrates that both sexes were present from the beginning, although the man was created first (Gen. 2:22; 1 Cor. 11:8; 1 Tim. 2:13). Matthew 19:4 and Mark 10:6 quote part of this verse.

Among the blessings promised in Genesis **1:28** is the begetting of children, who constitute one of God's greatest gifts to us (Ps. 127:3–5). Another blessing is that of subduing the earth, which has to do with gaining mastery of it and unmasking its secrets rather than exploiting or polluting it.

According to Genesis **1:29–30**, both people and animals were apparently vegetarian before the flood (see 9:3).

The final verse in Genesis 1 declares all of the divine acts of creation to be "very good" indeed. All that is good has our God as its source: "Every good and perfect gift is from above, coming down from the Father of the heavenly lights" (James 1:17).

Conclusion (2:1–3)

Ancient Near Eastern literature, particularly from Mesopotamia and Canaan, provides numerous examples of the use of seven days as a literary framework to circumscribe the completion of a cataclysmic or catastrophic or cosmic event. The pattern in these works runs uniformly as follows: "One day, a second day, so and so happens; a third day, a fourth day, such and such occurs; a fifth day, a sixth day, so and so takes place; then, on the seventh day, the story comes to its exciting conclusion."[3]

Genesis 1:1–2:3 exhibits a subtle and highly sophisticated modification of that literary device. While the extrabiblical poems tell their stories in terms of three sets of two days apiece followed by a seventh climactic day, the Genesis 1 creation account uses two sets of three days apiece, each set having its own preliminary climax, the whole narrative then concluding with a majestic and extended climactic paragraph describing the seventh day. Genesis 1:1–2:3 can be sketched as follows: "On days one, two and three, God gives form to the universe; on days four, five and six, God fills the universe; then, on the seventh day, the Creator of the universe rests from all his work."

As God "rested from all his work" (**2:2**), so also those of us who believe in Christ can share in the rest that Jesus provides (Heb. 4:4, 10). Biblical teaching concerning the Sabbath day finds its source ultimately in Genesis **2:1–3**. Although "Sabbath" does not appear in Genesis 2, the Hebrew word underlying the verb "rested" (**2:2–3**) is the verbal form of the noun "Sabbath."

---

3. For examples, see E. A. Speiser, *Ancient Near Eastern Texts Relating to the Old Testament*, ed. J. B. Pritchard (Princeton: Princeton University Press, 1955), 94; H. L. Ginsberg, *Ancient Near Eastern Texts*, 134, 144, 150.

Genesis 2:3 tells us that "God blessed the seventh day and made it holy, because on it he rested." Exodus 20:8–11, after reminding the Israelites that they were to work six days and rest on the seventh because that is what God did, made the connection between the seventh day and the Sabbath day explicit by paraphrasing Genesis 2:3 slightly: "Therefore the Lord blessed the Sabbath day and made it holy" (Exod. 20:11).

God did not rest until he had "finished" the work he had been doing (Gen. 2:2). In a similar way, Jesus did God's work faithfully (John 9:4) and urged others to do the same while there was still time. And even as he was being crucified for your sins and mine, only when he was absolutely certain that his work of redemption was complete did he say these words in the hearing of all who were at the foot of his cross: "It is finished" (John 19:30).

2

Creation: Part 2
(2:4–25)

MAN IS FORMED (2:4–7)

THE GARDEN OF EDEN (2:8–17)

THE SEARCH FOR A HELPER (2:18–20)

WOMAN IS MADE (2:21–25)

As I pointed out at the beginning of the previous chapter, the Genesis account of creation is set forth in two parts. In Genesis 1:1–2:3, mankind is the culmination of creation, the climax of the divine creative activity, the crowning achievement of God's work. In Genesis 2:4–25, however, the author focuses his attention on mankind right at the outset, causing it to occupy center stage in the drama of creation.

Man Is Formed (2:4–7)

Genesis 1:1–2:3, we remind ourselves, serves as an introduction to the primeval history (1:1–11:26). In a broader sense, of course, it provides an introduction for the entire Book of Genesis.

Genesis **2:4**, on the other hand, leads us into the first of the five main sections of the primeval history, "the account of the heavens and the earth." The sight of that familiar phrase, "the heavens and the earth" (see 1:1), informs us that we are about to read another narrative about creation. And that impression is confirmed when we look at the complete title for the section: "This is the account of the heavens and the earth when they were created."

But what a different account it is when compared to the creation story in 1:1–2:3! The first account has a lofty dignity about it, while the second is much more simple and down-to-earth. The first narrative has stylized expressions and repeated formulas, while the second is lively and full of surprises. The first has the measured cadences of a liturgical hymn, while the second builds to an unexpected but happy climax. In the first story "God" is the transcendent and all-powerful Creator, while in the second "the LORD God" is closely and intimately involved in the life and experiences of the people he has created.

None of these differences amounts to a contradiction in any sense of the word. They are simply differences of emphasis or perspective. The two accounts look at the same or a similar series of events from two distinctive points of view. The one is concerned with the big picture, the other with a few tantalizing details; the one sees the entire forest, the other a few trees.

Even the name of God in the two accounts is different. The supreme Being is uniformly called "God" in Genesis 1:1–2:3, the word itself being used a total of thirty-five times. Thirty-five equals five times seven, and the number seven plays a prominent role in the first creation narrative. Creation is portrayed as taking place in six days followed by a seventh day of rest, as we have already seen. But it is also instructive to note that Genesis 1:1 contains exactly seven words in the original Hebrew text and that 1:2 contains exactly fourteen Hebrew words (two times seven). Other similar examples could easily be pointed out and would serve to show that the author was using the number seven in its symbolic sense of completion or perfection.[1]

But symbolic numbers are not immediately apparent in 2:4–25, and the name of the supreme Being is "the LORD God"

1. See U. Cassuto, *A Commentary on the Book of Genesis, Part I: From Adam to Noah* (Jerusalem: Magnes, 1961), 13–15.

throughout the story. "LORD" is the personal, intimate name of God in the OT and stresses his work as Redeemer (see, e.g., Exod. 6:6–8). "God," on the other hand, is his more formal and impersonal name and emphasizes his work as Creator. Both are names of one and the same God, and the compound name "LORD God" in 2:4–25 is intended to demonstrate that the formal "God" who creates mankind in the first creation account is identical to the personal "LORD" who communes with mankind in the second account. "God" and "LORD" are the two most common names for the Supreme Being in the OT, and each of them is found thousands of times there.

That Genesis 2:4–25 zeros in on a small area of the earth's surface is clear at the beginning of the story. We are told that certain kinds of vegetation (called simply "field shrub" and "field plant") did not yet exist because there were no people to work the land and there was no rain to water it (2:5). The statement that God "had not sent rain on the earth" does not have to be understood in universal terms, because the word translated "earth" often means "land" in the sense of a local geographic region. The reference to the absence of rain, then, probably pertains to the special climate around the Garden of Eden.[2] In any event there were other sources of water available in the form of "streams" coming up from the ground. (The word "streams" was translated "mist" in the older English versions, but increased understanding of the languages of ancient Mesopotamia, from which this word ultimately comes, makes it clear that "streams" is a more accurate rendering.)

The prose description of the creation of man in 2:7, though quite different from the poetic description in 1:27, is equally powerful in its own way. While 1:27 says that God "created" man, 2:7 states that God "formed" man. Since the two verses depict the same divine activity, it is proper to conclude that "create" and "form" are synonyms. God may create *ex nihilo* ("out of nothing"), as he surely did in 1:1. But he may also create by making use of already-existing material, as he did when he formed a man "from the dust of the ground" (2:7). The verb "form" is used specifically of the work of a potter who fashions vessels from clay (see esp. Isa. 45:9).

2. G. L. Archer, *Decision*, February 1973, 5.

The Hebrew text of Genesis **2:7** contains a beautiful play on words: "God formed the man (*'ādam*) from the dust of the ground (*'ădāmâ*)." The pun reminds us that our origins are earthly. As Paul puts it: "The first man was of the dust of the earth," an "earthly man" (1 Cor. 15:47–48). But the Hebrew word *'ādam* can also be read as the proper name "Adam," and in ambiguous cases we must let the context decide between generic "man" and specific "Adam." Paul's citation of the last clause of Genesis **2:7** combines the two possibilities: "The first man Adam became a living being" (1 Cor. 15:45).

Genesis **2:7** teaches that our nature is both physical and spiritual. God not only "formed the man from the dust of the ground"; he also "breathed into his nostrils the breath of life." It was only when this twofold act had been accomplished that "man became a living being." The term "living being" has nothing to do with the ancient Greek concept of a soul inhabiting a body; it is a translation of the same Hebrew phrase that is rendered "living creatures" in 1:20. Hebrew psychology knew nothing of dividing human personality into various parts or compartments. It was remarkably modern in its unified approach to what constitutes a life that is truly human.

Elihu, although a young upstart, nevertheless provides a fine commentary on Genesis **2:7** when he says to Job, "I am just like you before God; I too have been taken from clay" (Job 33:6), and especially when he says two verses earlier, "The Spirit of God has made me; the breath of the Almighty gives me life" (33:4). Since it is God's breath and Spirit that gives us life, if he were to withdraw his life-giving power from us "all mankind would perish together and man would return to the dust" (34:15; see also Ps. 104:29; Eccles. 12:7). Apart from God, says the patriarch Abraham, we are "nothing but dust and ashes" (Gen. 18:27). From a strictly financial standpoint and without the energizing power of God, the chemicals in the average human body are worth less than ten dollars as these words are being written.

No doubt about it: Elihu was right. Though the breath of God can produce ice (Job 37:10) or set a fire pit ablaze (Isa. 30:33), it also can—and does—give us life. To the Lord, and to him alone, we owe our very life and breath (Acts 17:25). In him, and in him alone, "we live and move and have our being" (17:28).

The Garden of Eden (2:8–17)

The place that God prepared for the first man to live in must have been exquisitely beautiful. Its very name, "Eden," is synonymous with "paradise." The original meaning of the word is lost in obscurity. It may have been related to a Hebrew word denoting "bliss" or "delight," or it might have come from a Mesopotamian word that means simply "a plain." In any event, it was in Eden that God planted a garden where the first human couple were to make their first home.

Where was the Garden of Eden located? Genesis **2:8** states that it was "in the east" from the standpoint of the author. Nearly a century ago "Chinese" Gordon, the great British general who was also a devout Bible scholar, made the radical claim that the Garden of Eden was located on one of about a hundred islands in the Indian Ocean just below the equator. Known as the Seychelles, their climate is ideal and their beauty defies comparison. More specifically, Gordon pinpointed the location of the garden in the valley of Mai on Praslin Island. As one British official stated a few years ago: "Whether 'Chinese' Gordon was right or wrong, you must admit that Eden *should* have been here!"[3]

But Gordon was surely wrong in this case, because Genesis **2:14** mentions the Tigris and Euphrates rivers in connection with Eden. This means that the garden must have been somewhere in the land known today as Iraq. While we cannot be absolutely certain about the exact site, the traditional location is in southern Iraq at the confluence of the Tigris and the Euphrates. A tree stump in the area quaintly displays a plaque designating the spot as the home of Adam.

In later generations Eden became proverbial for its beauty and fertility. It is called the "garden of the LORD" in Genesis 13:10 and Isaiah 51:3 and the "garden of God" in Ezekiel 28:13; 31:9. Like most things characterized by spectacular beauty, it had the potential for good and for evil. All kinds of magnificent trees bearing delicious fruit grew in the garden, including the "tree of life" and the "tree of the knowledge of good and evil." The tree of life is obviously desirable in every respect. In the Book of Revelation, for example, the Lord says to believers in the church at Ephesus, "To him who overcomes, I will give the right to eat from the tree of life, which is in the paradise of God" (Rev. 2:7).

3. G. Gaskill, "Armchair Voyage to Paradise," *Reader's Digest*, August 1961, 139–40.

Later in the same book the tree is mentioned again several times, its leaves and fruit being granted to the righteous (22:2, 14) but withheld from the unrighteous (22:19).

And what of the tree of the knowledge of good and evil? For now, we would simply note that its very name is sinister, leaving open the possibility of either good or evil effects on anyone who eats its fruit. The fact of the matter is, however, that God himself predicts only one result for the eater, and that an irreversible, final one: death (Gen. **2:17**; 3:3). A few scholars have felt, therefore, that the tree of the knowledge of good and evil could just as appropriately have been called the "tree of death." The two most crucial trees in the garden would then have been the tree of life, bringing life to its eaters, and the tree of death, resulting in death for its eaters.

It is intriguing, therefore, that a few years ago a Canaanite religious text was discovered in Syria that refers to a "tree of death."[4] This is the only known mention of such a tree in ancient Near Eastern literature. So it is possible that "tree of death" was an alternate name for the tree of the knowledge of good and evil in ancient Israelite tradition outside of the Bible. But even if that should prove to be so, the biblical name is far superior for the purposes of the author of Genesis, as we shall soon see.

Returning now to the Garden of Eden, we note that in addition to the Tigris and the Euphrates two other rivers are mentioned in connection with it: the Pishon (which winds through the land of Havilah), and the Gihon (which winds through the land of Cush). It is theoretically possible to translate "Pishon" and "Gihon" as common nouns ("gusher" and "spurter," or the like) and so avoid the necessity of identifying them with known rivers. But since "Tigris" and "Euphrates" are proper nouns it is quite likely that "Pishon" and "Gihon" are also. Up to now they have not been located, although they would have had to be situated somewhere in southeastern Mesopotamia. As to Havilah and Cush, we know that there was a Cush in Mesopotamia during the days of Nimrod, the ruler of Babylon, Erech and other important cities in that region (10:8–12). So even though "Cush" usually means "northern Sudan" (called "Ethiopia" in ancient times) in the OT, it cannot mean that in **2:13** because of the great distance between Africa and Mesopotamia (modern Iraq). There are two areas

4. M. Tsevat, "The Two Trees in the Garden of Eden," *Eretz-Israel* 12 (1975), 119[*] (English abstract).

called "Havilah" in the Bible (the first is mentioned in 10:7, the second in 10:29; it is doubtless the latter Havilah that was in or near the Garden of Eden).

The Tigris and Euphrates are the two mightiest rivers in Mesopotamia and in fact gave the region its name ("Mesopotamia" means simply "Between the [Two] Rivers"). Both are indeed "great" rivers (Gen. 15:18; Dan. 10:4), and the Euphrates is often called "the River" (1 Kings 4:21, 24) par excellence.

The Search for a Helper (2:18–20)

Fellowship, friendship, and intimacy are basic needs of every human being, implanted in us by God himself: "It is not good for the man to be alone" (**2:18**). But although animals and man both came from "the ground" (**2:7; 2:19**), animals can never provide for man the kind and degree of companionship he really requires. Man's helper must be "suitable for him" (**2:18**).

To allow Adam to perceive this for himself, God brought all the animals to Adam "to see what he would name them" (**2:19**). As Adam gave each animal a name he thereby demonstrated that he was in control of them, that he was their master (see 2 Kings 23:34; 24:17; see also Gen. 1:5, 8, 10). In so doing he began to fulfill God's command given to him earlier: "rule over" them (1:28; see also 1:26).

The name of Adam himself has often been identified with the name Adapa, found in a number of Mesopotamian texts. Such an identification is now unnecessary, however, because several years ago the word "Adam" was found in a cuneiform text from Ebla in northern Syria. It appears in that text as a personal name and is the first such occurrence outside the Bible. This discovery strengthens considerably the traditional view that the biblical Adam was a real person and not simply a personification of mankind in general.

Woman Is Made (2:21–25)

Since none of the animals provided a suitable helper for Adam, God proceeded to make one for him. Genesis **2:21** describes the first case of controlled anesthesia in history: While Adam was sleeping, God took one of the man's ribs and made a woman from it.

In Sumerian, one of the languages of Mesopotamia, the word for "rib" also means "life." Something of that concept is also intended here: The woman comes into being out of the very life of the man. Life begets life.

But surely much more is intended here as well. As many commentators have noted, the woman was not made from one of the bones in the man's head in order to make it possible for her to lord it over him, nor was she made from one of the bones in his foot in order to enable him to trample and crush her. On the contrary, she was made from one of the bones in his side, so that they might share life together in mutual protection and concern and love and care.[5] It is only sin that changed that original divine intention (3:16) and brought about man's subjugation of woman in ways that are often cruel and unjust.

But how perfect was that original pristine relationship! In the Bible's second poem, Adam expressed his unbounded delight:

> This is now bone of my bones
> and flesh of my flesh;
> she shall be called "woman,"
> for she was taken out of man.

As in English, so also in Hebrew the words for "man" and "woman" sound very much alike. Even in themselves they serve to help cement the one-flesh union—monogamy, not polygamy—that was the divine intention for husbands and wives from the beginning. One man would be united to one woman, and they would become one flesh (2:24) forever (Matt. 19:4–6). And in that primeval state of innocence, their nakedness would cause them no shame.

5. W. H. Griffith Thomas, *Genesis: A Devotional Commentary* (Grand Rapids: Eerdmans, 1946), 43.

3

Creation: Late or Early?

THE "DAYS" OF GENESIS 1

OTHER VIEWS OF GENESIS 1:1–2:3

EARLY EARTH, LATE MAN

WHAT GENESIS 1:1–2:25 TEACHES US ABOUT
    CREATION

When did creation take place? How old is the universe? Was the earth created at the same time the universe came into being? When was life created? How long ago did God make the first man?

Until about two centuries ago, Jewish and Christian scholars alike turned to the pages of the OT in their search for answers to such questions. They agreed almost unanimously that all of creation took place about six thousand years ago in six 24-hour days. Using various genealogies and other chronological references in the OT, James Ussher (1581–1656), archbishop of Armagh in northern Ireland, placed the date of creation more specifically in the year 4004 B.C. His contemporary, the Hebraist

John Lightfoot (1602–1675), agreed with him and determined that the creation week was October 18–23 and that Adam was created on the sixth day of that week at nine o'clock in the morning, 45th meridian time.

Although such attempts at precision are no longer taken seriously, the view that creation is relatively late and that it occurred a few tens of thousands of years ago (at the very most) is still held by many students of Scripture—and for understandable reasons. After all, it seems to represent what the text of the Bible actually says, at least when interpreted literally. It also seems to dovetail best with the biblical concept of an all-powerful God, who "spoke, and it came to be" (Ps. 33:9).

In spite of these arguments and others, however, the "late-earth" theory is in the minority in today's scholarly community—even among Christian men and women of science (among, e.g., most of the members of the American Scientific Affiliation, an association of evangelical scientists of national distinction and international reputation). The vast majority of competent scientists are convinced that astronomy and astrophysics have successfully demonstrated the universe to be tens of billions of years old, that geology and paleontology have shown the earth and the earliest forms of life to be billions of years old, and that paleoanthropology and archaeology have proved that hominids (manlike creatures, though not necessarily human beings in the biblical sense) have been on the earth for millions of years.

Needless to say, proponents of the "early-earth" theory do not agree with each other in detail any more than the "late-earth" theorists agree among themselves. Estimates change as new evidence accumulates and as new methods of evaluating that evidence are developed. But the following approximate figures represent the current consensus:

Universe—14.5 billion years old

Earth—4.6 billion years old[1]

Life—3.8 billion years old[2]

Hominids—5.0 million years old[3]

1. *Newsweek*, April 19, 1976, 10; similarly, see H. J. Van Till, *The Fourth Day* (Grand Rapids: Eerdmans, 1986), 140–141, 151, 180, 236.

2. *Newsweek*, August 6, 1979, 77; see also D. Wonderly, *God's Time-Records in Ancient Sediments* (Flint: Crystal Press, 1977), esp. 1–3, 48–65.

3. *Newsweek*, May 21, 1979, 59–60.

(Man in the biblical sense is doubtless much more recent, as we shall attempt to show later in this chapter.) These figures are derived not from only one system of measurement or calculation but from numerous converging lines of evidence resulting in similar conclusions arrived at independently of each other. One author has this to say in a discussion of a particular group of measurement methods: "To get a value of 6,000 years for the age of the earth one would have to assume an error of 99.9998 percent for *each of the major radioactive methods*. Inasmuch as the different methods employ different techniques and . . . different assumptions, an error of such magnitude as this is quite incredible."[4]

In any event, the likelihood that the "early-earth" theory is substantially correct suggests that it might be well for us to take a closer look at the Genesis account of creation. Since the works of God (as revealed in nature) and the Word of God (the Bible) do not conflict when each is properly understood, and since the "early-earth" theory gets the better of the argument over the "late-earth" theory in terms of hard scientific data, perhaps the historical narratives of Genesis 1–11 should be understood in something other than the traditional sense. Once scientific facts have been established as precisely as is humanly possible, "the redemptive thinker will . . . strive to interpret the biblical revelation in a way which is consistent with scientific truth."[5] And since the Bible is undeniably the finest and greatest piece of literature ever penned, I would agree that "the language of the Bible is more like the language of literature than that of science."[6]

The "late-earth" theory is based primarily on (1) a literal interpretation of the "days" of Genesis 1, (2) a literal interpretation of the genealogies of Genesis 5 and 11 (often also including an insistence that there are no gaps in them), and (3) a rereading of selective scientific data to harmonize with said literal interpretations. I wish to discuss here the nature of the "days" of Genesis 1, leaving for chapter six a treatment of the genealogies.

4. D. England, *A Christian View of Origins* (Grand Rapids: Baker, 1972), 105.

5. C. S. Evans, *Preserving the Person* (Downers Grove, Ill.: InterVarsity, 1977), 142.

6. A. F. Holmes, *All Truth Is God's Truth* (Grand Rapids: Eerdmans, 1977), 47. For arguments pro and con with respect to the "early-earth" theory, see the treatments of S. R. Schrader and D. A. Young in *The Genesis Debate*, ed. R. Youngblood (Grand Rapids: Baker, 1991), 56–85.

The "Days" of Genesis 1

The necessity of a literal interpretation of the word "day" in the first chapter of Genesis is more apparent than real, since there have been dissenting voices throughout the history of the church. For example, Augustine referred to the days of creation as "ineffable," believing that 24-hour days were unworthy of an omnipotent God and considering the word "day" to be a figure of speech in Genesis 1. In this connection we do well to remind ourselves that the omnipotence of God is not the point at issue here, because the task of the interpreter is not to try to discover what God *could* do, since a sovereign and all-powerful God "does whatever pleases him" (Ps. 115:3). It is rather the interpreter's task to find out, if possible, what God *did in fact* do, and that can be learned only through painstaking and patient study of the inspired Scriptures coupled with a teachable willingness to give up our earlier ideas, no matter how deeply cherished or long held.

A careful examination of the use of "day" in Genesis 1:1–2:3 indicates that the word means at least three different things in that passage: (1) twelve hours (1:5, 14, 16, 18); (2) twenty-four hours (1:5, 8, 13, 14, 19, 23, 31); (3) an unspecified length of time (2:2, 3). So it is clear that it need not be interpreted literally in the first part of the creation narrative even by the standards of Genesis itself. But what about that sixth day—the day on which man and woman were created? Genesis 2:4–25, I have argued, tells essentially the same story as Genesis 1:1–2:3 but focuses on a restricted area of the earth's surface (Eden). Allowing for the instantaneous creation of the land animals, man, and woman, we must nevertheless take note also of Adam's activity on the sixth day. During the time between his creation and Eve's, God (1) put him in the garden "to work it and take care of it"; (2) gave him a command with respect to the trees in the garden; (3) brought "all the beasts of the field and all the birds of the air" (hundreds—or thousands—of different "kinds"?) to see what he would name them, a monumental task that Adam successfully undertook (by no means a casual procedure, naming was a serious matter that was done carefully and thoughtfully in ancient times); and (4) observed that Adam had gradually realized that none of the birds or animals was a "suitable helper" for him and that he had had time to become lonely (as reflected in Adam's joyful exclamation in 2:23). That all of this took place within 24 hours is difficult, if not impossible, to believe.

Finally, what about the seventh day—the day on which God "rested from all his work"? Christian theology has traditionally taught that God's rest from his initial creative activity is still in effect and will continue forever. The seventh day, then, is everlasting.

It would seem that Augustine was right all along: Genesis tells us nothing about the time span of creation. The "days" are literary and timeless, not literal and time-bound.[7] This understanding of the "days" lends further support to our interpretation of Genesis 1:1–2:3 as given in chapter one. At the same time it has negative implications for competing interpretations, to a sampling of which we now turn.

Other Views of Genesis 1:1–2:3

The Gap Theory

Those who hold this position teach that a perfect creation (1:1) was followed by a universal catastrophe that destroyed it (1:2; or, between 1:1 and 1:2), and that in turn was followed by a perfect re-creation (1:3–31). The gap between 1:1 and 1:2 (or between 1:1 and 1:3) gives sufficient "scope for all the geologic ages."[8] Geology needs time, and the gap theory provides it—billions of years, if necessary.

While the gap theory has been attacked from many different angles, it has one especially fatal flaw: It cannot stand up to the statement in Exodus 20:11 that "in six days the LORD made the heavens and the earth." In other words, "the heavens and the earth" of Genesis 1:1 were created during the six days, not prior to an indefinite period of time before the days began.

The Geologic-Era Theory

Proponents of this view hold that the "days" of Genesis 1 are not to be understood as literal 24-hour days but are to be interpreted metaphorically as geologic "eras" or "ages." They are "days" from God's standpoint, since "with the Lord a day is like

---

7. For arguments pro and con with respect to whether the days of creation were 24 hours long, see the treatments of T. E. Fretheim and R. C. McCone in *The Genesis Debate*, ed. R. Youngblood (Grand Rapids: Baker, 1991), 12–35.

8. *The Scofield Reference Bible* (New York: Oxford University Press, 1909), 3 n. 2.

a thousand years, and a thousand years are like a day" (2 Pet. 3:8). Many late-nineteenth- and early-twentieth-century geologists within the church taught and popularized this theory. But geologic ages tend to overlap with each other and are not capable of the sort of rigid division implied by the words "And there was evening, and there was morning—the first day" (Gen. 1:5; see also 1:8, 13, 19, 23, 31). Also, while it is true that the Hebrew word for "day" is somewhat elastic, we should probably not press it to denote so lengthy a period as a geologic era.

Progressive Creationism

This view inserts periods of millions or billions of years between the days of Genesis 1 and assumes that God's creative activity took place in a series of steps separated by eons. In so doing, it tries to preserve the advantages of the traditional interpretation of 24-hour days on the one hand and those of the geologic-era theory on the other. An approach that bears at least an oblique relationship to this view is that of "threshold evolution," which teaches that Genesis 1 neither affirms nor denies the possibility of biological evolution within the "kinds" but that these great divisions of the plant and animal kingdoms cannot be violated by the evolutionary process since each had to be created separately by God.

But although progressive creationism has undoubted strengths it has its weaknesses as well. The gap theory assumes one gap; progressive creationism must assume several gaps and, in so doing, multiplies the difficulty. Also, while it preserves the advantages of the 24-hour-day and geologic-era theories, it combines or compounds their disadvantages at the same time, so that nothing is gained in the process.

It will be observed that all of these theories, and many others like them, tend to view the "days" of Genesis 1 as time-bound, as related to time in some way. But as we tried to show earlier, the use of "day" in 1:1—2:3 is by no means uniform. For that and other literary reasons, it is best to consider the days as indefinite and timeless.

In any event, however, both Genesis and geology place the emergence of mankind at the very end of the sequence of events. Science tells us that manlike creatures began to appear on the earth at least five million years ago. But the biblical account, as related in Genesis 1:26—11:26, cannot be interpreted to allow for the creation of Adam that far back in time. Does that mean, then, that the estimates of science are wrong in this case?

Not necessarily.

Early Earth, Late Man

Genesis 1:27 states that man was created "in the image of God." Genesis 2:7 adds that God "formed the man from the dust of the ground and breathed into his nostrils the breath of life" and that "the man became a living being." These descriptions of the origin of biblical man indicate that God did something highly extraordinary at the end of the creation sequence. By a special act of creation, God made man from dust and in the divine image. Whatever hominids (Cro-Magnon, Neanderthal, and earlier) may have existed prior to the time of Adam, they had only animal intelligence and were not bound to God in a covenant relationship. Recent prolonged studies of various primates have shown that they possess remarkable intelligence and ingenuity, as well as a rudimentary creativity. Even in the wild they make tools from twigs to obtain food, greet one another with kisses and embraces, show off when old and mimic when young. In captivity they can be trained to communicate in various ways. A gorilla named Koko, for example, has been taught more than 1,000 signs of the American Sign Language (a system of communication routinely used by the deaf), and her trainer, Penny Patterson, has reported that Koko has even invented a few signs of her own. Lana, a chimpanzee, mastered a vocabulary of one hundred words formed by pressing, in predetermined order, combinations of colored keys bearing nine geometrical symbols on a computer keyboard. With it she composed grammatically correct sentences that answered researchers' questions or made requests for treats. Perhaps most amazing of all, another chimpanzee, named Moja, drew a simple design with chalk on a blackboard and, when asked what it was, made the American Sign Language sign for "bird."[9]

If primates can demonstrate such a degree of brainpower, it should not surprise us that pre-Adamic hominids had similar skills. Six hundred carefully fashioned knifelike tools, unearthed in the last decade and used by early hominids, have been firmly

9. *Newsweek*, March 7, 1977, 70–73.

dated at 2.6 million years old.[10] An engraved bone 135,000 years
old was excavated several years ago in the rich archaeological
region of the Dordogne in France. Called the oldest "work of art"
yet discovered, it is a complex expressive form carved by a pre-
Neanderthal hominid.[11]

Such skills and capacities in these pre-Adamic creatures, however, are proof neither of humanity in the biblical sense nor of
moral and spiritual sensitivity. Adam and Eve, the first "man"
and "woman" in the biblical sense of those terms, date back to a
few tens of thousands of years ago at best. Scientists are free to
date pre-Adamic hominids to much earlier periods.[12] Compared
to such hominids, who were part of the early earth, biblical man
is relatively late in time. And we are all the spiritual descendants
of the biblical Adam himself, through whom "sin entered the
world" (Rom. 5:12).

What Genesis 1:1–2:25 Teaches Us about Creation

Although the first two chapters of Genesis do in fact speak volumes to the scientist, their main interest is theological. They are
more concerned with the "who" and "why" than they are with
the "how" and "when." They give us "a doctrine of a Creator
rather than a doctrine of creation."[13] They introduce us to God,
and to man, and to God's relationship with man. Here are a few
of their major teachings:

1. God is outside the universe and above it as its Creator.
   Against materialism, which teaches that matter is everything and eternal, Genesis teaches that God is eternal,
   above matter, and the Creator of matter (which is therefore neither eternal nor everything). Against pantheism,
   which teaches that everything is God or that God is everything, Genesis teaches that God is separate from his creation and above it. Against dualism, which teaches that a
   struggle rages between two equally matched gods or principles, one evil and the other good, Genesis assumes the
   existence of one good God who declares each of his cre-

10. *Newsweek*, December 24, 1973, 102.
11. *Newsweek*, December 18, 1972, 70.
12. G. L. Archer in *Decision*, February 1973, 5, and *Decision*, February 1980, 14.
13. D. F. Payne, *Genesis One Reconsidered* (London: Tyndale, 1964), 23.

ative works to be "good" and stamps the whole creative sequence "very good." Against polytheism, which teaches that there are many gods who are often at odds with each other, Genesis teaches that there is only one beneficent God.

2. God created all the denizens of the universe. He both formed it and filled it: "The earth is the LORD's, and everything in it, the world, and all who live in it" (Ps. 24:1). God even made those beings and things whom man called God's enemies: "the deep," denied divine status and equated with "the waters" (Gen. 1:2); "the great creatures of the sea," created by his mighty hand and pronounced "good" (1:21); "two great lights" and "the stars," God's celestial rivals whom people often worshiped in preference to him (1:16); and animals of all kinds, God's creatures great and small, to be effectively controlled by man rather than deified by him.

3. God made man and woman as the crown and climax of his creative activity, as his highest and finest creations, as the particular objects of his special providence and care. Everything else was made in a beautiful and orderly pattern, each in its time being prepared for eventual dominion by mankind.

4. Man was created as totally distinct from the animals. He was not to mate with them, worship them, or relate himself in any other degrading way to them. On the contrary, he was to exercise lordship over them and make them his servants.

5. Man found his only suitable counterpart in woman, who together became the physical and spiritual progenitors of the entire human family.

> O Lord my God, when I in awesome wonder
>   Consider all the worlds thy hands have made,
> I see the stars, I hear the rolling thunder,
>   Thy power throughout the universe displayed,
> Then sings my soul, my Savior God, to thee,
>   "How great thou art! How great thou art!"
> —Stuart K. Hine

4

The Fall
(3:1–24)

THE TEST

REALITY AND SYMBOL

PASSING THE BUCK

GRACE IN THE MIDST OF JUSTICE

Some time ago a friend, with justifiable pride, showed me a snapshot of a beautiful little girl: her two-month-old niece. After doing the appropriate (and, in this case, spontaneous) oohing and aahing, I said to my friend, "Wouldn't it be a wonderful thing if everyone in the world stayed as innocent and lovable and trusting as your little niece is right now? What a paradise this world would be!"

She agreed, of course—and then both of us quickly returned to the harsh realities of our workaday situations, knowing full well that even in the best of circumstances our lives are beset with problems and difficulties and heartache and pain and grief, and that all of these can be traced ultimately to the most basic evil in the world: human sin.

And my friend and I also realized—sadly, to be sure—that her niece has been "a sinner from birth," just as the psalmist confessed of himself (Ps. 51:5). We knew that as she grew up into childhood and then womanhood her life would increasingly demonstrate her fundamentally sinful nature in a number of different ways. We knew that even this lovely little baby girl was by no means exempt from the verdict laid down long ago by the apostle Paul: "All have sinned" (Rom. 3:23).

Where did this awful thing known as "sin" come from? What is its origin?

Genesis 3 gives us a vivid picture of how sin entered the world, a picture that we shall examine in detail. We would observe in passing, however, that even a chapter describing the fall of mankind into sin can bear the marks of a literary craftsman of the first order. The ebb and flow of the events outlined in Genesis 3 have a striking symmetry all their own: (1) The serpent sins (3:1–5), then the woman, and finally the man (3:6); (2) next, the Lord confronts them with their sin by speaking to them in the reverse order: first the man (3:9–12), then the woman (3:13), and finally the serpent (3:14); (3) the Lord concludes this phase of his response to them by judging them in the same order in which they had sinned: first the serpent (3:14–15), next the woman (3:16), and last of all the man (3:17–19). The chapter ends with one of the saddest scenes in all of Scripture: the Lord banishes the man and his wife from the Garden of Eden (3:22–24), where he had originally put him (2:8).

Having briefly analyzed the literary structure of the chapter, we now turn to a topical discussion of what Genesis 3 teaches us about the fall of mankind into sin.

The Test

It was just as true then as it is now: God may test us, but he never tempts us. James 1:13 tells us that God does not "tempt anyone."

Testing and tempting may be distinguished from each other in two ways. First, the subject of testing is always God (ultimately), while the subject of tempting is always Satan (ultimately). It is Satan who tempts; God never tempts anyone. Second, the objects or purposes of testing and tempting differ from each other. The object of temptation is the fall of the person being tempted.

When Satan tempts us, he hopes that we will fall into sin. But that is not true of testing. The purpose of tempting is to make us worse, while the purpose of testing is to make us better.

Look, for example, at Deuteronomy 8:2: "God led you all the way in the desert these forty years, to humble you and to test you in order to know what was in your heart, whether or not you would keep his commands." And follow that up with 8:16: "He gave you manna to eat in the desert, . . . to humble and to test you so that in the end it might go well with you."

That is why God tests us—so that in the end it might go well with us, so that positive results might be the outcome, so that we might grow in grace and in the knowledge of him, so that we might be better people after the period of testing is over.

And that is why God tested Adam and his wife in the Garden of Eden: to strengthen their faith and trust in him.

Reality and Symbol

I believe that the fall of man actually took place in history and as described in Genesis 3. At the same time, the various elements in the story symbolize profound spiritual truths that are deeply meaningful to us today.[1]

First, *the serpent* symbolizes temptation and sin. In Revelation 20:2 (see also 12:9) he is called "that ancient serpent, who is the devil, or Satan." It is he who brought evil into the world of mankind by placing in the woman's mind doubts concerning God's providence. He said to her, "Did God really say . . . ?" (Gen. 3:1). The serpent was crafty, and the woman succumbed to temptation. The suggestion to doubt God worked on her mind and heart, and she fell into sin.

The apostle Paul warns us that the same thing can easily happen to us today. "I am afraid that just as Eve was deceived by the serpent's cunning, your minds may somehow be led astray from your sincere and pure devotion to Christ" (2 Cor. 11:3). None of us is immune from the clever wiles of Satan, who "prowls around like a roaring lion looking for someone to devour" (1 Pet. 5:8).

Second, *the Garden of Eden*, the most ideal and idyllic place on the face of the earth, is a symbol of fellowship with God. It was there that God "put the man he had formed" (Gen. 2:8); it was there that God gave him satisfying work to do (2:15); it was

---

1. See esp. G. Vos, *Biblical Theology* (Grand Rapids: Eerdmans, 1948), 37–51.

there that God walked "in the cool of the day" (**3:8**); it was there that God "made garments of skin for Adam and his wife and clothed them" (**3:21**).

Eviction from the garden, then, implied alienation from God and exclusion from fellowship with him. Because of man's sin, God "banished him" from the Garden of Eden (**3:23**), and his relationship to God would never again be the same.

Third, *the tree of the knowledge of good and evil* plays a crucial role in Genesis 2 and 3, and as such it symbolizes the period of testing. God used the tree as a means of testing Adam (2:17), as a means of strengthening his faith and confirming his obedience. The serpent, on the other hand, used the same tree as a means of tempting the woman (**3:1–5**), as a means of causing her to fall into sin. In allowing herself to be deceived by the serpent, she disobeyed God and then caused Adam to do the same (**3:6**).

As we observed in chapter one, the Hebrew language had no word for "universe," so instead it used the phrase "the heavens and the earth" (1:1; 2:1, 4). Similarly, Hebrew could not express the concepts of "moral knowledge" or "ethical discernment" apart from using the phrase "good and evil" or the like (see esp. Deut. 1:39; Isa. 7:15–16). By eating the fruit of the tree of the knowledge of good and evil, Adam and his wife left the state of moral innocence in which they had been created and entered a state of moral responsibility to which God had not called them. No longer did they share a childlike faith in God; they now had reached the age of accountability, of moral adulthood. Like disobedient children, they had sinned against their loving Father.

And how clever Satan was in bringing them to such a sad and sorry state of affairs! He had told the woman that if she ate the fruit she would become "like God, knowing good and evil" (Gen. **3:5**)—and, in a horribly perverted sense, that is exactly what happened (**3:22**). All the trees in the garden were "pleasing to the eye and good for food" (2:9), but the serpent succeeded in convincing the woman that the tree of the knowledge of good and evil had fruit that, in addition to being "good for food and pleasing to the eye," was "also desirable for gaining wisdom" (**3:6**).

Satan has the demonic ability of taking things that are not necessarily intrinsically evil and twisting them for his own diabolical purposes. When he tempted Jesus for forty days in the desert, he took something that was potentially "good for food" and said to our Lord, "Tell this stone to become bread" (Luke 4:3). He then took something that was "pleasing to the eye" and showed Jesus "all the kingdoms of the world," promising to give him "all their authority and splendor" (4:5–6). Finally, Satan played on the universal human desire for power and "wisdom" and dared Jesus to throw himself down from "the highest point of the temple" (4:9). But Jesus deflected each of Satan's fiery darts and rendered them useless by quoting, each in its turn, a verse of Scripture appropriate to the temptation. In successfully defeating the devil on this and other occasions, our Lord remains to this day the only person in history "who has been tempted in every way, just as we are—yet was without sin" (Heb. 4:15).

But, totally unlike Jesus Christ, Adam and his wife failed their test miserably. While still in their innocent state they had two options available to them. They were (1) *able to sin* or (2) *able not to sin*. Certain theologians during the Middle Ages made the intriguing suggestion that if Adam and his wife had passed their test by obeying God, he would doubtless have confirmed them in righteousness and made them *not able to sin*. It is inconceivable that God would have relentlessly put them through an endless series of tests, each one a bit harder then the previous one. Such activity might characterize an ogre, but surely not a loving heavenly Father. The first human couple, however, did not succeed in passing the most elementary test that God gave them. The result? They became *not able not to sin*—and that universal tendency to disobey God at every opportunity became their awful legacy to the whole human race. In its quaint but devastatingly correct way, the *New England Primer* described for generations of children in colonial America the human predicament as follows: "In Adam's fall / we sinnéd all."

Fourth, *the tree of life*, the garden's only other tree that is given a symbolic name in the Genesis account, exemplifies life in the fullest sense of that term. Life means different things to different people, of course. To take just one example, for some of us life equals wealth; but Jesus is careful to remind us that "a man's life does not consist in the abundance of his possessions" (Luke 12:15). On the contrary, life in the biblical sense is better described in qualitative than in quantitative terms. Of his followers Jesus said, "I have come that they may have life, and have it to the full" (John 10:10).

The tree of life in Genesis symbolizes that kind of life. Only that kind of life is worth living forever, without interruption.

And Adam and his wife forfeited that kind of life when they sinned against God. Having eaten the fruit of the tree of the knowledge of good and evil, they were no longer allowed to eat the fruit of the tree of life (Gen. **3:22–23**).

Fifth, if life is symbolized by the tree of life, death is symbolized by *the return to dust*. When God formed a man from the dust of the ground he "breathed into his nostrils the breath of life, and the man became a living being" (2:7). After man sinned, the very ground from which he had been taken was cursed because of him (**3:17**), and death returned him to its dust (**3:19**). Freshly dug graves the world over still open wide their mouths, eventually to receive us all—"ashes to ashes, and dust to dust"—and all because of our sinful rebellion against God. "The wages of sin is death" (Rom. 6:23).

A garden and its trees, a serpent and dust—real entities, one and all. But how familiar and vivid are the spiritual truths they symbolize! Here is how the Book of James summarizes much the same story: "Each one is tempted when, by his own evil desire, he is dragged away and enticed. Then, after desire has conceived, it gives birth to sin; and sin, when it is full-grown, gives birth to death" (James 1:14–15).

Passing the Buck

Genesis 4 teaches us that the flames of sin, once kindled, spread like wildfire. Even in Genesis 3, however, the initial stages of sin's tendency to stain everything it touches stand out in bold relief.

In their state of innocence "the man and his wife were both naked, and they felt no shame" (2:25). But no sooner had they sinned than "they realized they were naked . . . and made coverings for themselves" (**3:7**). They even used their nakedness as an excuse to hide from God (**3:10**). What had originally been a morally neutral quality was transformed by sin into a cause for shame and fear.

And sin changes trust into fear as well. A healthy dose of remorse would have done Adam a world of good when God confronted him with his sinful deed, but Adam chose to blame it all on his wife (**3:12**). In turn, she chose to blame the serpent (**3:13**). In these earliest days of man's relationship toward God, flight from responsibility quickly became a stampede.

In order to give Adam a chance to respond, God asked him,

"Where are you?" (**3:9**)—not because he could not find him, but because he wanted Adam to respond in joyful obedience.

With the same desire, God calls to us today.

Grace in the Midst of Justice

Because God is just, he must judge sin; and because God is loving, he gives grace to the sinner. It is not surprising, then, that grace and justice intermingle in each case as God judges the serpent, the woman, and the man.

Though all were judged, only the serpent was cursed—and that is just. He initiated the temptation that led to human sin, and his judgment is therefore the most severe. Dust, the symbol of death, would be his food, and he would crawl on his belly in abject misery as long as he lived.

But he would in fact live. An element of grace pervades all of life, however miserable. Ultimately, the offspring of the woman would crush the serpent's head, and there is far greater grace in that fact.

Traditionally, Genesis **3:15** has been called the *protevangelium* ("first gospel"). As early as the second century A.D., scholars of the caliber of Justin Martyr and Irenaeus taught that the woman's offspring referred to Christ, who would some day defeat Satan himself.[2] Although the passage teaches that truth in a general way, the apostle Paul understood the whole body of believers as involved in crushing Satan (Rom. 16:20; see 16:18–19 for evidence that Paul was reflecting on the context of Gen. 3). With her risen Lord the church shares the privilege of fulfilling the prophecy of Genesis **3:15**.

Just as the serpent is cursed in what constitutes his nature as serpent, so also the woman is judged in what constitutes her nature as woman. Her labor would be increased in childbearing (**3:16**). In addition, however, she would now submit herself to the will of her husband, even though earlier he had submitted himself to hers (**3:6**). In all of this there is justice.

But grace shines forth as well, because the woman would "give birth to children." We think here of Carl Sandburg's definition of a baby: "God's opinion that the world should go on." Through the miracle of childbirth the human race, sinful though it is, would

2. H. P. Ruger, "On Some Versions of Genesis 3.15, Ancient and Modern," *The Bible Translator* 27 (1976): 106.

continue. In grateful acknowledgment of God's blessing in this regard, "Adam named his wife Eve, because she would become the mother of all the living" (**3:20**). The Hebrew word for "Eve" looks very much like the Hebrew word for "living."[3]

As in the case of the woman, so also in the case of the man: God judges him in connection with the role that characterizes him as man. He would be the breadwinner for the family, but he would be forced to wrest food from the soil by the sweat of his brow (**3:19**). He would literally work himself to death, and in doing so his "toil" (**3:17**) would match the "labor" of his wife.

Again, however, we notice signs of grace in God's judgment on the man. Certainly, he would have to work hard; but three times God says to him, "You will eat" (**3:17, 18, 19**). The food produced by the man would sustain the lives produced by the woman, and it would sustain their own lives as well.

But perhaps there is another lesson to be learned here. If it is true that "an idle mind is the devil's workshop," if it is true that too much leisure time gives us too many opportunities for practicing old sins and inventing new ones, then there is yet another element of grace in working long and hard.

Nevertheless, Genesis 3 ends on a somber note. Man's last and most vivid memory of the garden from which he had been driven was that of a portal flanked by cherubim, reminiscent of the awe-inspiring, winged human-headed bulls of Assyro-Babylonian sculpture that guarded the entrances to temples and palaces in ancient Mesopotamia.[4] The cherubim at Eden kept man from eating the fruit of the tree of life and served to remind him that his legacy was death caused by sin. And if he considered the cherubim his enemies, it was only because he had forgotten that his own worst enemy was himself. All of us share the question of the apocryphal writer: "O Adam, what have you done? For though it was you who sinned, the fall was not yours alone but ours also who are your descendants" (2 Esdras 7:48[118]). The apostle Paul summarizes: "In Adam all die" (1 Cor. 15:22).

As the late cartoonist Walt Kelly used to express it through one of his characters in the comic strip Pogo:

We have met the enemy, and he is us.

---

3. The Hebrew word for "Eve" also looks very much like one of the Semitic words for "snake"—ironic indeed in light of her fateful encounter with the serpent in 3:1–5.

4. J. D. Davis, *Genesis and Semitic Tradition* (Grand Rapids: Baker, 1980), 78–84.

5

The Rapid "Progress" of Sin (4:1–16)

Two Brothers (4:1–7)
Murder—and More (4:8–16)

Sin on a rampage—that is the main theme of the first half of Genesis 4. Once sin was unleashed in the world, there was no stopping it. Everyone on earth fell under its sinister power, and it tainted everything it touched. Following the evil example of Adam and Eve, their descendants sinned against God in open rebellion. "Since they did not think it worthwhile to retain the knowledge of God, he gave them over to a depraved mind, to do what ought not to be done. They have become filled with every kind of wickedness, evil, greed and depravity. They are full of envy, murder, strife, deceit and malice. They are gossips, slanderers, God-haters, insolent, arrogant and boastful; they invent ways of doing evil; they disobey their parents; they are senseless, faithless, heartless, ruthless" (Rom. 1:28–31).

What a frightening description—and indictment—of sinful

mankind! Our earliest ancestors had the unparalleled potential of deepening their relationship with a loving heavenly Father, but they chose to exchange "the knowledge of God" (Rom. 1:28) for "the knowledge of good and evil" (Gen. 2:9, 17).

Two Brothers (4:1–7)

"Knowledge" and "knowing" are key terms in Genesis 3 and 4. "Knowing good and evil," Adam was driven from the Garden of Eden (3:22–23). When God asked Adam's son Cain where his brother Abel was, Cain replied, "I don't know" (**4:9**). And knowledge in a very special sense is the opening motif of Genesis 4.

"Adam lay with (lit. "knew") his wife Eve" (**4:1**). The Hebrew verb "know" is almost never used in a casual sense. Far from reflecting merely knowledge by acquaintance, it nearly always refers to knowledge by experience. Unlike the casual sense, which tends to be shallow and fleeting, biblical knowledge is deep and lasting. For that reason "know" is often used to mean "have sexual intercourse," the most intimate experience a husband and wife can share.

When Eve, "the mother of all the living" (3:20), had given birth to Cain she said, "With the help of the LORD I have brought forth a man" (**4:1**). Cain's name sounds very much like the Hebrew verb here translated as "brought forth." The same verb is used by Melchizedek in 14:19 and by Abram in 14:22 when they called God the "Creator of heaven and earth." The God who created everything that exists, the God who brought forth the heavens and the earth, helped Eve to bring forth a baby boy.

Eve's second son was named Abel, a Hebrew word that signifies a lack of permanence or meaning. The same word is found at the beginning and near the end of Ecclesiastes, pointing to one of the major themes of that book: "Meaningless! Meaningless! . . . Everything is meaningless" (Eccles. 1:2; 12:8). In Abel's case his very name reminds us that his life itself was soon to be cut short.

The classic confrontation between the farmer and the shepherd is merely incidental in the story of Cain and Abel. The narrative focuses, rather, on the nature of the offering that each man brought to the Lord. Properly understood, sacrifice is always the gift of life or the choicest product of one's livelihood. Much is often made of the fact that Abel's offering was an animal sacrifice while Cain's was a gift of plants, and this is sometimes connected with the supposed contrast between the "garments of skin" (Gen. 3:21) that God made for Adam and Eve and the coverings of "fig leaves" they made for themselves (3:7). It is then implied that God demands blood sacrifices and that man far too often responds with bloodless offerings.

But the Cain and Abel story stresses an entirely different matter. The issue at stake is not the nature of the offering but the heart attitude of the offerer.[1] Cain brought "some of the fruits of the soil" (4:3) to the Lord, apparently random samples of what he had grown. On the other hand, Abel brought "fat portions from some of the firstborn of his flock" (4:4). He cared enough to give the very best he had, and so the Lord "looked with favor" on both him and his offering. But because of Cain's careless and indifferent attitude while bringing his offering, God "did not look with favor" (4:5) on either him or his gift. Unlike Cain, Abel was motivated by faith in God: "By faith Abel offered God a better sacrifice than Cain did. By faith he was commended as a righteous man, when God spoke well of his offerings" (Heb. 11:4).

So the account of the contrast between Cain's and Abel's offerings is a foreshadowing of the teachings of the OT prophets, who consistently emphasized inward motivation over against outward performance and ritual (Isa. 1:11–17; Jer. 7:19–20; Hos. 6:6; Amos 5:21–24; Mic. 6:6–8). Samuel's words to Saul come immediately to mind: "Does the LORD delight in burnt offerings and sacrifices as much as in obeying the voice of the LORD? To obey is better than sacrifice, and to heed is better than the fat of rams" (1 Sam. 15:22). It is as true today as it was in Samuel's time that "man looks at the outward appearance, but the LORD looks at the heart" (16:7).

No wonder, then, that God "did not look with favor" on Cain and his offering! Of course, Cain could have taken the divine hint by expressing a heartfelt desire to humbly obey God from that time forward. But instead he "was very angry, and his face was downcast" (Gen. 4:5).

God's gracious and loving response to Cain's anger is coupled with a stern warning, making it clear that the choice is Cain's to

---

1. For arguments pro and con with respect to this matter, see the treatments of H. H. Hobbs and J. D. Heck in *The Genesis Debate*, ed. R. Youngblood (Grand Rapids: Baker, 1991), 130–47.

make. If Cain does what is right the next time, says the Lord, he will be accepted and blessed. If he refuses to do so, however, sin is close at hand, waiting to gain the mastery over him.

The image of sin crouching at the door (**4:7**) is indeed a vivid one. In the original Hebrew text the phrase in question would be literally translated as follows: "At the door, sin is a croucher." In Akkadian (the language of ancient Assyria and Babylonia) the same word translated here as "croucher" can refer to an evil demon who is depicted as lurking at the entrance of a building to threaten the people who are inside.[2] What a picture of sin! Waiting to pounce on its unsuspecting victims, sin is like an evil demon "crouching at your door; it desires to have you" (**4:7**). Only the grace of a loving God, available to Cain for the asking, could save him from so fearful a menace.

But Cain would have none of that. He turned his back on God—and slid deeper and deeper into sin.

Murder—and More (4:8–16)

Cain's selfish attitude when he brought his offering to the Lord turned into anger when he realized that God did not look with favor on him. His anger was then replaced by jealousy toward his brother Abel. After deciding to get rid of Abel once and for all, Cain invited him to accompany him on a pleasant walk in the fields—out where God could not see him, Cain thought—and then he attacked and killed Abel (**4:8**).

Cain's murder of Abel was all the more monstrous not only because it was the first one recorded in history but also because it was committed by a man against his brother (see Gen. **4:8, 9, 10, 11**; 1 John 3:12). It was also premeditated, since Cain carefully chose the time and place. And it was committed against an innocent man, a "righteous" man, as Jesus reminds us (Matt. 23:35; see also Heb. 11:4; 1 John 3:12). Jesus even called Abel a "prophet" (Luke 11:50–51), perhaps in the sense that Abel continues as God's spokesman "even though he is dead" (Heb. 11:4).

Just as Paul expressed his fear that we could be deceived by Satan as Eve was (2 Cor. 11:3), so also John warned us not to follow Cain's example: "Do not be like Cain, who belonged to the evil one and murdered his brother . . . because his own actions were evil and his brother's were righteous" (1 John 3:12).

---

2. E. A. Speiser, *Genesis*, 3d ed. (Garden City, N.Y.: Doubleday, 1983), 33.

Trying to cover up his brother's murder, Cain lied to God. When asked where Abel was he said, "I don't know" (Gen. 4:9)—a deliberate and blatant falsehood. Then he asked with a spirit of indifference and lack of concern, "Am I my brother's keeper?"

Those words have provided a rationale down through the centuries for people who have refused to get involved with the problems and difficulties experienced by their neighbors. Like the priest and the Levite in the parable of the good Samaritan, whenever they see human misery and suffering they pass by "on the other side" (Luke 10:31–32). They have little or no sense of responsibility toward others. They are totally unlike the apostle Paul, who said concerning his own ministry, "I am obligated both to Greeks and non-Greeks, both to the wise and the foolish" (Rom. 1:14). Far from wanting to destroy life as Cain did, Paul declared, "I have become all things to all men so that by all possible means I might save some" (1 Cor. 9:22).

On Mount Zion in modern Jerusalem stands a small museum that contains the remains of several of the six million Jews who were put to death by the Nazis during World War II. Included among the shocking exhibits are lampshades made of human skin and soap made of human fat. The museum itself is called the Chamber of Destruction, and the relics it contains are disquieting reminders of man's inhumanity to man. Outside the building is a simple plaque inscribed with a brief quotation from Genesis 4:10: "Listen! Your brother's blood cries out . . . ."

Cain had nothing to gain by lying to God, because his brother's blood gave him away. One of Adam's illustrious descendants, Judah, might have been thinking of the story of Cain and Abel when he said to his own brothers who had plotted to kill their brother Joseph, "What will we gain if we kill our brother and cover up his blood? Come, let's . . . not lay our hands on him; after all, he is our brother, our own flesh and blood" (Gen. 37:26–27).

From time immemorial the blood of Abel has been a most fitting symbol of the death of the innocent and righteous sufferer. Although Abel was righteous in a relative sense, nevertheless he too was a sinner in need of God's grace and mercy, and therefore his shed blood carries no redemptive significance. As such it forms a powerful contrast to the blood of another righteous sufferer, to "the precious blood of Christ, a lamb without blemish or defect" (1 Pet. 1:19). In the final analysis, it is Jesus' "sprinkled blood that speaks a better word than the blood of Abel" (Heb. 12:24).

Cain had disobeyed God, and disobedience always brings divine judgment (Deut. 28:15). The ground had been cursed by God at the time of Adam's fall, but hard work and painful toil would nevertheless make it possible for man to grow food for himself and his family (Gen. 3:17–19). Now, however, Cain himself would be under a curse and would be driven from the very ground that he had soaked with his brother's blood (**4:11**). Previously, Cain had worked the soil and it had produced food enough and to spare (**4:2–3**). But now, though he might labor long and hard, the ground would no longer yield its crops for him (**4:12**). The irony is obvious: The ground that had received the blood of Cain's dead brother would never again provide Cain with the livelihood he had enjoyed. Far from being the settled farmer he had always been, he would become "a restless wanderer on the earth" (**4:12, 14**).

Thus for Cain disobedience brought restlessness and wandering. Other descendants of Adam would experience the same fate, and the "wandering Jew" would become a common motif in the history of the human race. The united witness of the people of Israel as they reflected on their turbulent past was summed up in a single sentence: "My father was a wandering Aramean" (Deut. 26:5). If judgment on fields and flocks would begin the long list of God's curses for his people's disobedience (28:15–24), banishment and wandering and lack of repose would end that same list (28:64–68).

One would have thought that by this time Cain might have begun to feel a slight twinge of remorse, murderer that he was. But, incredible as it seems, he still did not ask God to forgive him for the death of Abel. His response to divine judgment was totally self-seeking: "My punishment is more than I can bear" (Gen. **4:13**). He was being driven out from God's presence and protection, and he was afraid that whoever found him would kill him (**4:14**).

A question that is often asked about Genesis **4:17** is this: "Where did Cain get his wife?" A similar question can be asked of **4:14**: "Who were the people of whom Cain was so afraid?" The answer that is frequently given to the first question is that Cain married his own sister. Of course, that is entirely possible since when mankind first appeared on earth it would have been necessary for close relatives—even brothers and sisters—to intermarry.

But we cannot dispose of the second question quite so easily. The context (**4:13–17**), which speaks of "the land of Nod" and of "building a city," seems to presuppose considerable numbers of people. It would place a severe strain on the passage to insist that all of them were additional children of Adam and Eve. The very fact that Cain had to keep on the move appears to mean that he feared far more people than the members of his immediate family.

A possible solution to this difficulty has already been suggested in chapter three. If the theory of pre-Adamic hominids—who made razor-sharp weapons with which they killed animals—is correct, perhaps they are the enemies that Cain feared so much. Having much more intelligence than they, Cain and his family may have ultimately subdued them. But all such speculation takes us far beyond the evidence at our disposal.[3]

In any event, the Lord graciously promised Cain that he would not be killed, and he put a mark on him "so that no one who found him would kill him" (**4:15**). Perhaps the mark was some kind of tattoo, and the Lord may have placed it on Cain's forehead (see Ezek. 9:4 for a possible parallel). Although we cannot be sure of the details, we can certainly marvel that the Lord would promise to protect so violent a man as Cain.

This section of the narrative ends with Cain settling down in a land called Nod, east of Eden (**4:16**). The name of his new home would continually remind him of the curse that had been placed on his life, since Nod in Hebrew means "wandering."

How sad and sorry a tale this is! Cain's failure to give God his heart along with his offering made it impossible for God to look on him with favor. Cain then became angry at God and jealous of his brother. As the jealousy grew and festered, it gave way to murder, forcing Cain to tell a lie to cover it up. When his falsehood was found out and God announced judgment, Cain responded not with remorse over what he had done but with complaints about overly severe punishment and with selfish concern about his personal well-being. Alienation from God was the final, awful result: "Cain went out from the LORD's presence" (Gen. **4:16**).

3. For arguments pro and con with respect to the existence of hominids before the time of Adam, see H. W. Seaford, Jr., and G. Kufeldt in *The Genesis Debate*, 148–65.

6

Two Genealogies (4:17–5:32)

THE GENEALOGY OF PRIDE (4:17–24)

THE GENEALOGY OF DEATH (4:25–5:32)

LONGEVITY AND THE PRE-FLOOD PATRIARCHS

GENESIS 5 AND THE AGE OF THE HUMAN RACE

Wh_en God created man as male and female he said to them, "Be fruitful and increase in number; fill the earth and subdue it" (Gen. 1:27–28). As the crown and climax of God's creative activity, man was not intended to play a minor role in the ongoing purposes of God in the world. On the contrary, the divine plan thrust the human race onto center stage in the drama of history. God gave them a mandate of fruitfulness and increase and dominion. The author of Genesis now turns to that mandate.

He does so by giving two illustrations of how the descendants of Adam and Eve branched off into various family trees. The first illustration is a genealogy that serves to demonstrate how the cancer of sin was transmitted through Cain to the generations that followed him. The second is a genealogy that summarizes the time gap between the creation of the human race and the flood.

The Genealogy of Pride (4:17–24)

This section begins just as the previous section (4:1–16) did. The language is the same—only the characters are different: "Cain lay with [lit. "knew"] his wife, and she became pregnant and gave birth" (**4:17**). As God had promised, the human race would continue to propagate itself.

Although archaeologists have uncovered human settlements that go back to the earliest stages of civilization, the remains of ancient Jericho include the oldest ruins of a "city" found to date. An eminent British archaeologist, the late Kathleen Kenyon, excavated Jericho and found the fortified walls (including a massive defensive tower) of a Neolithic (New Stone Age) city at the lowest level of the site. Conservative dating for the building of that city estimates it at about 7000 B.C.

Cain doubtless lived before that time, and he built a city called Enoch (after the name of his son). Either its remains have been entirely obliterated or archaeologists have not yet found it. Of course it is possible that our dating methods are faulty and that archaeologists have indeed found Cain's city but have failed to recognize it as such. In any case, the existence of a city in Cain's time implies the presence of substantial numbers of people (see chapters three and five for a possible explanation of who those "people" were).

Adam's line through Cain contained exactly seven generations (Adam, Cain, Enoch, Irad, Mehujael, Methushael, Lamech). This fact serves as a subtle reminder of the importance of the number seven in these early chapters of Genesis (see chapter two). "Seven" signifies "completion" in such cases, as in the Lord's statement that anyone who killed Cain would "suffer vengeance seven times over" (**4:15**).

Each of the seven names in the genealogy of Adam through Cain is matched by a similar or identical name in Adam's line through Seth (though not in the same order) in Genesis 5 (see below).

Adam	Adam (5:1)
Cain	Kenan (5:12) ·
Enoch	Enoch (5:21)
Irad	Jared (5:18)
Mehujael	Mahalalel (5:15)
Methushael	Methuselah (5:25)
Lamech	Lamech (5:28)

The similarity between the two sets of names, which is even closer in the original Hebrew text, is probably to be accounted for by the selective nature of each genealogy. Both of them highlight the names of prominent family members and doubtless include gaps (as we shall see later).

Lamech, the seventh man in this genealogy, "married two women, one named Adah and the other Zillah" (4:19). Tempting though it might be to ascribe an element of perfection to such an arrangement ("from A to Z"), in the Hebrew alphabet "Adah" does not begin with the first letter and "Zillah" does not begin with the last. While the OT nowhere condemns polygamy in an explicit and unambiguous way, it everywhere illustrates the sorrow and suffering that come to the family of a man who has more than one wife. Genesis 2:24 clearly states that God's original ideal for marriage was that it was to be a holy ordinance in which two people (not more than two) of the opposite sex (not of the same sex) were to "be united" and "become one flesh." Lamech's action in marrying more than one woman further illustrates a willful disobedience of God's commands and the continued downward slide of the human race into ever-multiplying forms of sin.

Adah and Zillah each gave birth to two children. The only daughter among the four was Naamah, about whom we have no further information. But the names and occupations of the other three children tell an interesting story in their own right.

Lamech's three sons had very similar names—Jabal, Jubal and Tubal-Cain—all of which have as their basis a Hebrew root that is action-oriented and means "bring, carry, lead." Jabal was the ancestor of the nomadic shepherd way of life, of those who "live in tents and raise livestock" (4:20). Representing the artistic side of mankind, Jubal was the forerunner of musicians who played string or wind instruments, "the harp and flute" (4:21). Tubal-

Cain represents the world's toolmakers (the Hebrew word "Cain" means "metalsmith") as he "forged all kinds of tools out of bronze and iron" (**4:22**).

The mention of bronze and iron so early in human history presents something of a minor problem. The oldest known bronze artifacts date to about 3500 B.C., and the use of iron appears later still (ca. 1800 B.C.) and then only among the Hittites for several centuries (until ca. 1200 B.C.). I would suggest three possible solutions to this problem: (1) Adam is to be dated to a relatively late period; (2) early copper- and iron-smelting methods were lost and then rediscovered much later; or (3) there are one or more time gaps in the line of Cain as recorded here. In my judgment a combination of (2) and (3) provides the most likely answer to the question raised.

The account of Cain's line concludes with a brief poem sometimes called "The Song of the Sword." Though its form may be beautiful, its content is barbaric. In retaliation for a wound he has received, Lamech decides to kill the young man who inflicted the wound. While God had promised to avenge Cain's death seven times (4:15), Lamech threatens vengeance seventy-seven times—and for only a wound (**4:23–24**).

So ends the "genealogy of pride"—pride that led to disobedience in marrying more than one wife, pride that carried with it the ever-present danger of self-glorification in the building of cities and the development of the arts and crafts, pride that spawned violence and the wanton destruction of human life. If humility is one of the most basic of all virtues, pride is one of the most deadly of all sins.

The Genealogy of Death (4:25–5:32)

All is not lost, however. A second "written account of Adam's line" (**5:1**) traces his descendants through a son named Seth. In contrast to the line of Cain, which was characterized by pride and self-indulgence, the text specifically states in connection with Seth's line that "at that time men began to call on the name of the LORD" (**4:26**). In contrast to the description of Cain's descendant Lamech as a sinful man, two of the men in Seth's genealogy—Enoch and Noah—are said to have "walked with God" (5:22, 24; 6:9). For these reasons the two genealogies are sometimes called "the sinful line" and "the godly line" respectively.

The story of Adam's line through Seth is introduced in much the same way as Cain's genealogy was: "Adam lay with (lit."knew") his wife" (**4:25**; see **4:17**). Eve gave birth to a son whom she named "Seth," a word that sounds much like the Hebrew verb translated "granted" in the statement giving the rationale behind the name: "God has granted me another child in place of Abel, since Cain killed him" (**4:25**). Thus the text reminds us that Cain's line was the line of a murderer, while the genealogy of Seth holds out the promise of something far better. During the days of Seth's son Enosh people began to call on the name of the Lord, and that practice would often be followed by the best of Seth's descendants in the future (12:8; 26:25).

The opening verses of Genesis 5 take us back to the creation of the human race by using the language of 1:26–28. Just as God created man in his own image and likeness, so also Adam became the father of a son "in his own likeness, in his own image" (**5:3**). Such proverbs as "like begets like" and "like father, like son" gain a great measure of their power from biblical texts like these.

Unlike the seven-name line of Cain, the genealogy of Seth contains exactly ten names from Adam through Noah. In this respect, and structurally as well, it resembles the genealogy in 11:10–26, which also contains exactly ten names (this time from Noah's son Shem through Abram).

Each of the main paragraphs of the Genesis 5 genealogy follows the same basic pattern: "When so-and-so had lived x number of years, he became the father of such-and-such. And after he became the father of such-and-such, so-and-so lived y number of years and had other sons and daughters. Altogether, so-and-so lived z number of years, and then he died."

The doleful refrain, "and then he died," repeated over and over again throughout the chapter, has prompted me to entitle this section "the genealogy of death." Even virtuous persons, however long their lives, must eventually die. God's judgment on Adam because of his sin extended universally to the entire human race.

Well, not quite all of the human race. In this very chapter we note the fact that Enoch's paragraph does not end with the phrase "and then he died." Rather it ends by telling us that "then he was no more, because God took him away" (**5:24**). He was translated from this life to the next without passing through the portals of death. As Hebrews 11:5 puts it: "By faith Enoch was taken from this life, so that he did not experience death; he could not be found, because God had taken him away. For before he was taken, he was commended as one who pleased God."

The verb "take (away)" is used in a special sense in these verses. On rare occasions God "takes" one of his choice servants to himself with an immediacy that eliminates the experience of death. The only other clear example in the OT is that of Elijah, who was "taken" (2 Kings 2:10) directly to heaven "in a whirlwind" (2:11). But it may well be that two of the Psalms express the same confident hope (Pss. 49:15; 73:24).

So although everyone else in Genesis 5 "died" (including Noah; see Gen. 9:29), Enoch "was no more, because God took him." Similarly, although everyone else in Genesis 5 "lived" (see, e.g., **5:26**), Enoch "walked with God" (**5:22, 24**). The author is telling us that there is a vast difference between walking with God and merely living. Adam and Eve could have walked with God in the garden and so lived, but instead they chose to disobey God, and so they died. To walk with God is to be righteous and blameless (6:9; 17:1); to walk with God is to please him (Heb. 11:5).

Enoch is the shining exception to the otherwise unrelieved gloom of Genesis 5. What a contrast he presents to his numerical counterpart in Cain's line! Lamech, the seventh in the genealogy of Cain, is the epitome of evil. But "Enoch, the seventh from Adam" (Jude 14) in the genealogy of Seth, "was commended as one who pleased God" (Heb. 11:5). The very length of his life was perfection itself: "365 years" (Gen. **5:23**), 365 being the number of days in a full year. Many years ago Robert Ripley observed in a "Believe It Or Not" column that although Methuselah was the oldest man in the Bible he was outlived by his father Enoch, since Enoch never died!

Longevity and the Pre-Flood Patriarchs

As it turns out, Enoch's 365 years is the shortest life span in Genesis 5. Everyone else named in the chapter lived at least twice as long. In fact everyone except Lamech (**5:31**) lived to be about 900 years old (including Noah; see 9:29). How are we to understand these extraordinarily long life spans? Are the numbers to be taken literally, or did the author of Genesis have something else in mind in recording them for us?

Bible scholars today interpret these large numbers in many different ways. Some take them at face value, claiming either that (1) climatic conditions before the flood were ideal and were conducive to long life, or that (2) the pace of human life and the rate of human metabolism was much slower in those days, enabling people to live much longer, or that (3) the ravaging effects of sin on human longevity had not yet developed to their full extent before the flood, or that (4) God in his sovereignty determined that certain special people should live unusually long lives and made it possible for them to do so. Others suggest that the solution to the problem lies in a combination of two or more of these proposals.

The main difficulty with all such suggestions, however, is that paleoanthropologists have not yet uncovered any ancient skeletal remains that even remotely approach such advanced ages. If anything, scientific investigation has taught us that people had briefer life spans in the earliest periods of time than they do today. (Of course, this is not to deny that God could have supernaturally extended life in special cases if he had chosen to do so.)

Other scholars understand the numbers symbolically or take them to be literary devices or figures of speech. For example, they observe the striking similarity between **4:24**, which says that "if Cain is avenged seven times, then Lamech seventy-seven times," and **5:31**, which tells us that the Cainite Lamech's namesake "lived 777 years." It is hard to read those numbers in other than a symbolic way, given the frequency of the number seven in the early chapters of Genesis.

Similarly, scholars have noted that every number in Genesis 5 is either a multiple of five or a multiple of five to which seven has then been added. Seven is the number of completion or perfection (as we have seen), and not necessarily in a strictly quantitative sense. In the case of Methuselah, whose number is the largest in the chapter, the age is a multiple of five to which fourteen (twice seven) has then been added.[1] This means—so the theory goes—that Methuselah's age is doubly perfect and therefore will never be exceeded in any way.

Several other ancient genealogies from sources outside the OT resemble Genesis 5 in several significant ways. Known as the

---

1. U. Cassuto, *A Commentary on the Book of Genesis, Part I: From Adam to Noah* (Jerusalem: Magnes Press, 1961), 259–60.

Sumerian king lists, they seem to summarize the lengths of reign of various important kings of Sumer prior to the flood. Two of them in particular—the Weld-Blundell 62 text and a Greek variant preserved by Berossus—form close parallels to Genesis 5 in three ways.

1. Like Genesis 5, these two lists include exactly ten names. When we remember that the Genesis 11 genealogy also has ten names and that Genesis itself exhibits a literary structure that contains exactly ten sections (see the introduction for details), we are perhaps justified in concluding that the most ancient accounts of man's origins favored the number ten as a convenient literary device, especially in genealogical narratives.

2. As in Genesis 5, the last name in the two Sumerian lists is that of the man who survived the flood (as we know from the Mesopotamian flood stories). Weld-Blundell 62 calls him Ziusudra (the Greek equivalent in the Berossus text is Xisouthros). In the Gilgamesh epic, the Babylonian parallel to the biblical flood narrative, he is known as Utnapishtim. Ziusudra and Utnapishtim find their historical counterpart in the biblical Noah.

3. Genesis 5 exhibits unusually long life spans, and the two Sumerian lists display incredibly long reigns for their kings. The very names of Ziusudra and Utnapishtim translate roughly as "Life of Distant Days," reflecting the idea that long ages ago important people used to live and reign for periods of time that were exponentially greater than those we now experience. Three of the men in the Berossus list are said to have reigned for 64,800 years apiece, while three in Weld-Blundell 62 are stated to have been on the throne for a staggering 72,000 years! Such figures reduce even Methuselah to a babe in arms by comparison. By exaggerating figures beyond all reasonable belief, the Sumerian texts make it possible for us to characterize the Genesis 5 account as a model of restraint.[2]

2. For arguments pro and con with respect to whether the pre-flood patriarchs lived for hundreds of years, see the treatments by J. A. Borland and D. L. Christensen in *The Genesis Debate*, ed. R. Youngblood (Grand Rapids: Baker, 1991), 166–83.

Genesis 5 and the Age of the Human Race

If the ten numbers in Weld-Blundell 62 are totaled, the Sumerian kings in that list would have reigned for 456,000 years. The figures in Genesis 5, however understood, yield only a fraction of that amount. But the Sumerian lists, since they claim to report the lengths of reign of important kings, may provide us with an additional clue or two for a proper understanding of Genesis 5.

Most conservative scholars today have given up the traditional assumption that Genesis 5 represents an exact chronology, and the Sumerian king lists have added support to this newer understanding. The frequent occurrence of ten names in ancient family or regnal lines suggests selectivity rather than the inclusion of every generation. Only the most important names were entered, and the omission of unimportant names from ancient genealogies was the rule rather than the exception.[3] To take a classic example, Matthew 1:8 states that Joram was "the father of Uzziah" (also known as Azariah). But 1 Chronicles 3:10–11 shows clearly that Joram was in fact the great-great-grandfather of Uzziah.

This in turn demonstrates that words like "father," "son," and "beget" are much more flexible in the Bible than we might at first imagine. For example, Zilpah, Leah's maidservant, is said to have given birth to her great-grandchildren (Gen. 46:17–18). All of this implies that there might very well be time gaps of substantial size in Genesis 5.

Furthermore, the names in Genesis 5 might represent families or dynasties rather than individuals. Just as "Israel" or "David" in the OT can be the name of a family or tribe or dynasty as well as the name of an individual, depending on the context, so also any of the names in Genesis 5 could be understood in a sense other than that of an individual person. Maybe all that Genesis 5 intends, then, is to give us the names of important pre-flood dynasties together with the lengths of reign of their rulers. Needless to say, such an interpretation would have implications for a proper understanding of the life spans of ancient men and women and would lend more credence to the dating methods of the paleoanthropologists.

3. On this whole section, see esp. W. H. Green, "Primeval Chronology," in *Classical Evangelical Essays in Old Testament Interpretation*, ed. W. C. Kaiser (Grand Rapids: Baker, 1972), 13–28.

In addition, the fact that Genesis 5 and 11 display a beautiful symmetry that suggests careful and intentional arrangement would seem to show that no continuous chronology is presupposed by them and that we should not try to calculate the date of Adam's creation from them (except in the most general way; see chapter three for details).

Finally, the OT gives cumulative totals of years for such historic periods as "the length of time the Israelite people lived in Egypt" (430 years; see Exod. 12:40) or the time span between the exodus and the laying of the foundations of Solomon's temple (480 years; see 1 Kings 6:1). But no such totals are given for the time between creation and the flood or between Noah and Abraham.[4]

Taking such data into consideration, one recent evangelical student of Genesis came to this conclusion: "Prior to the time of Abraham, there is no possible way to date the history of what we find in Scripture. . . . When the Bible itself reaches back and picks up events and genealogies in the time before Abraham, it never uses these early genealogies as a chronology. It never adds up these numbers for dating."[5]

Although the figures in Genesis 5 give us no chronological information, they are marvelously consistent within themselves. Apart from Noah and his three sons (**5:32**), none of the men in Genesis 5 survived the flood. In fact Methuselah (whether the name of a man or a dynasty) died in the very year of the flood itself: The figures in **5:25**, **5:28**, and 7:6 add up to precisely 969.

The birth of Noah, whose name sounds like the Hebrew word for "comfort" (see **5:29**), is ominous in its import as well. The Lord had cursed the ground because of man's sin soon after creation (3:17). Genesis **5:29** echoes that curse and prepares us for a second divine judgment on mankind that would prove to be even more devastating than the first.

4. O. T. Allis, *God Spake By Moses* (Nutley, N.J.: Presbyterian and Reformed, 1951), 22.

5. F. A. Schaeffer, *Genesis in Space and Time* (Downers Grove, Ill.: InterVarsity, 1972), 124.

Part 2

The Flood

7

The Extent of Sin Before the Flood
(6:1–8)

SONS OF GOD AND DAUGHTERS OF MEN (6:1–3)

THE NEPHILIM (6:4)

SIN AT ITS WORST (6:5–8)

Was Lamech, in his polygamy and selfishness and pride and violence (Gen. 4:19–24), the wickedest man who ever lived? We cannot say for sure, of course—but he would obviously be a prime candidate for that unenviable designation. In any case, sin in its worst forms reached epidemic proportions in the days before the flood. And although the godly walk of Enoch (5:21–24), the expectant spirit of the second Lamech (5:28–29) and the blameless life of Noah (6:8–9) might delay divine judgment for a time, it could not postpone it indefinitely.

Sons of God and Daughters of Men (6:1–3)

As the population of the earth continued to increase, more and more marriages would take place. In this connection we are told that the "sons of God" married the "daughters of men."

Who were these pre-flood "sons of God"? Two main interpretations have been held down through the centuries.[1]

Angels

The phrase "sons of God" frequently refers to angels in the Bible. For example, in Job 1:6 and 2:1 we read that "the angels (lit. "sons of God") came to present themselves before the LORD." Satan was among them, and since Satan is a fallen angel there can be no reasonable doubt about the meaning of "sons of God" in the opening chapters of Job.

Although Psalm 29:1 is not quite so clear an example, most commentators assert that angels are in view in that passage as well: "Ascribe to the LORD, O mighty ones (lit. "sons of God"), ascribe to the LORD glory and strength." When read in the light of its context, this verse seems to be encouraging the angels to praise and worship God after the pattern or in the spirit of Isaiah 6:1–3.

"Sons of God" in such passages is not to be understood literally, of course. Although other ancient religions had highly developed theogonies (mythological stories about the origins of gods who had wives, children, and other relatives), the religion of the OT teaches that there is only one God, who is eternal and has neither family nor rivals. In fact, the Hebrew language did not even have a word for "goddess." When it wanted to refer to a female pagan deity it had to use its word for "god," as in 1 Kings 11:33 where the text mentions "Ashtoreth the goddess (lit. "god") of the Sidonians."

When "sons of God" means "angels," then, it uses the word "son" not in the sense of physical offspring but in the sense of a "member of a group." Just as "sons of the prophets" means "members of a prophetic guild," so also "sons of God" can mean "members of the divine council" or the like. God is sometimes pictured figuratively as having celestial "advisors" in his court, "advisors" with whom he sometimes talks and shares information, as in Genesis 3:22: "The man has now become like one of us, knowing good and evil."[2]

Another point in favor of interpreting "sons of God" as "angels" in Genesis 6 is the NT teaching concerning fallen angels. First Peter 3:19–20, which talks about "the spirits in

1. For detailed discussion of the two interpretations, see the essays by F. B. Huey, Jr., and J. F. Walton in *The Genesis Debate*, ed. R. Youngblood (Grand Rapids: Baker, 1991), 184–209.

2. G. L. Archer, *Decision*, May 1979, 14.

prison who disobeyed long ago when God waited patiently in the days of Noah while the ark was being built," is often thought to refer to such angels. The passage, however, is difficult at best and does not lend itself to confident conclusions.

Second Peter 2:4 would seem to be more to the point: "God did not spare angels when they sinned, but sent them to hell, putting them into gloomy dungeons to be held for judgment." But this verse appears to refer to a rebellion against God that took place before the fall of mankind in Genesis 3—indeed, a rebellion that was severely judged by God. Since nothing is said in Genesis **6:1–3** about judging angels, we would be overstepping our bounds if we insisted that 2 Peter 2:4 and Genesis 6 referred to the same event.

A third NT passage that some claim is related to Genesis 6 is Jude 6: "The angels who did not keep their positions of authority but abandoned their own home—these he has kept in darkness, bound with everlasting chains for judgment on the great Day." But this verse is much more similar to 2 Peter 2:4 than it is to Genesis **6:1–3**. Its references to judgment and darkness are out of keeping with the context at the beginning of Genesis 6.

To summarize, then, Genesis **6:1–3** bears only a superficial resemblance to the NT texts described here. It is not at all clear that the Genesis passage portrays fallen angels or disobedient spirits. If the "sons of God" in **6:2, 4** are indeed angels, that identification will have to be confirmed on other grounds.

At this point the identification begins to break down. Since this would be the first mention of angels in Scripture, why would the author not simply call them "angels" in order to avoid all ambiguity? While it is true that ancient mythologies often include stories about gods cohabiting with women, the Genesis account is not mythical in form or intention and is set forth as sober history.

Jesus' response to the Sadducees in Luke 20:34–36 seemingly delivers the decisive blow against the angel interpretation: "The people of this age marry and are given in marriage. But those who are considered worthy of taking part in that age and in the resurrection from the dead will neither marry nor be given in marriage, and they can no longer die; for they are like the angels." Jesus tells us here that angels do not marry, and his statement would flatly contradict Genesis **6:2, 4** if the "sons of God" in that passage are angels.

Men

In the OT the phrase "sons of God" is never used unambiguously to refer to human beings. Equivalent expressions, however, are fairly common. A few examples will suffice.

In Deuteronomy 14:1 Moses said to the people of Israel, "You are the children (lit. "sons") of the LORD your God." Due to their sin the text says that they are "no longer his children (lit. "sons")" (Deut. 32:5). Elsewhere the psalmist says to God that under certain circumstances he "would have betrayed this generation of your children (lit. "sons")" (Ps. 73:15). Isaiah 43:6 quotes God as saying, "Bring my sons from afar." And in Hosea 1:10 the people of Israel are called "sons of the living God."

The NT evidence is, if anything, even stronger. In Luke 3:38 Adam is called "the son of God." Christians are referred to as "children of God" (1 John 3:1, 2, 10). But the most impressive passage is the section from Luke 20 that we quoted earlier. There we read that people who are considered worthy of taking part "in the resurrection from the dead will neither marry nor be given in marriage, and they can no longer die; for they are like the angels. They are God's children (lit. "sons of God")" (Luke 20:34–36). The text itself tells us that people, though not angels, are nevertheless "sons of God."

From the standpoint of biblical usage, then, there can be no objection to interpreting "sons of God" in Genesis 6 as "men." In fact, such an understanding is much to be preferred in the context of the passage. A brief paragraph about angels would be an abrupt interruption in the flow of the story. But if the "sons of God" are men, who are the "daughters of men" (Gen. **6:2, 4**)?

"Sons of God" in this passage means, more specifically, "godly men." Since they chose to marry "daughters of men" rather than daughters of God (i.e., godly women; see, e.g., Isa. 43:6)—a live possibility for them, it would seem—that choice proved to be unwise. The "sons of God" are no doubt the descendants of Seth, whose line is summarized in Genesis 5. They chose either to marry sinful women within their own lineage or to intermarry with members of the wicked line of Cain. Although my personal preference is the latter, the results were disastrous in either case, as we shall see. Genesis 6:1–2 describes the intermarriage of the Sethites of Genesis 5 with the Cainites of Genesis 4.

The Lord's response to this unhappy state of affairs is also subject to more than one interpretation. The key verb in **6:3** can be translated in at least two ways: (1) "My spirit will not *remain in* man forever," or (2) "My Spirit will not *contend with* man forever." If the former is correct, then the text is saying that man's life span will be limited to 120 years from this point on because God will not allow the breath of life to remain in him indefinitely. If the latter is correct, then the text states that 120 years will be the period of grace between the time of God's pronouncement and the arrival of divine judgment. The former is contradicted by the genealogy in Genesis 11:10–26, while the latter is substantiated by 1 Peter 3:20: "God waited patiently in the days of Noah while the ark was being built."

The teaching of Genesis **6:3** is solemn indeed. It reminds us that though God is merciful and patient, though he is compassionate and slow to become angry (Exod. 34:6), the Holy Spirit's convicting influence can be stifled and quenched by our willful rejection and rebellion. Eventually, if we continue to harden our hearts against him, he will stop speaking to us altogether. At that point—the point of no return—judgment becomes inevitable.

The Nephilim (6:4)

According to Numbers 13:33 the Nephilim were the ancestors of Anak and his descendants, some of whom settled in the vicinity of Hebron (Judges 1:20). They were people of great size and strength (Num. 13:28–33), and earlier English versions translated "Nephilim" in Genesis **6:4** as "giants."

Although the word itself appears to be a proper noun and is therefore the name of a tribe or people, in Hebrew it means literally "fallen ones." As such it fits the context admirably because it describes the moral and spiritual depravity of the human race just before the flood. Though the Nephilim were "the heroes of old, men of renown" (Gen. **6:4**), they were wicked sinners in the eyes of a holy God. The depths of evil into which they had fallen, starkly portrayed in the next few verses of Genesis, had made them ripe for judgment.

Sin at Its Worst (6:5–8)

In the days before the flood, sin had become pervasive and all-encompassing. Its evil tentacles reached into every nook and cranny of a person's life, and no one was ever free of its influence. The description in Genesis **6:5** of the awfulness of sin would be hard to match anywhere else in Scripture. Man's wickedness had become so great that "every inclination of the thoughts of his heart was only evil all the time." It is not merely that he harbored a somewhat sinful thought once in a while. On the contrary, his depravity was total: *Every* tendency of his *innermost* thoughts was *only* evil *all* the time.

Genesis 8:21 quotes a portion of **6:5** and observes that "all the time" means "from childhood" on. Original sin among human beings began with Adam and Eve, but each of us participates in original sin in another sense as we begin to exhibit sinful traits soon after we are born. David confessed that fact after he had committed adultery with Bathsheba: "I have been a sinner from birth, sinful from the time my mother conceived me" (Ps. 51:5; see also 58:3).

"The LORD saw how great man's wickedness on the earth had become" in the days before the flood (Gen. **6:5**). And he witnesses our evil actions and motivations today as well. At this very moment he "looks down from heaven on the sons of men to see if there are any who understand, any who seek God" (Ps. 14:2). But his verdict is the same as it was in the days of Noah: "All have turned aside, they have together become corrupt; there is no one who does good, not even one" (Ps. 14:3). The cancer of sin rages through us and strikes at the very core of our being. "The heart is deceitful above all things and beyond cure" (Jer. 17:9).

Before the flood man's "heart was only evil," and therefore God's "heart was filled with pain" (Gen. **6:6**). Man's sin is always God's sorrow. The Lord was "grieved" that he had made mankind in the first place. Our God is a loving heavenly Father, and his heart breaks when we disobey him. To cause him such grief is the height of ingratitude in the light of all that he has done for us in Christ. That is why Paul said to us, "Do not grieve the Holy Spirit of God" (Eph. 4:30).

As we stated earlier in this chapter, mankind before the flood had sunk to such depths of moral and spiritual degradation that God had no alternative but to punish them. Having passed the point of no return, they were ripe for divine judgment. When God is grieved by man's sin, his heart is filled with pain because he loves us. But the grief that man's sin brings to God's heart also has its darker side—in cases like the one described here, it issues in divine judgment. Though God loves the sinner, he judges his sin.

Scripture teaches that God responds negatively to sin but positively to repentance. When we forsake our sin and turn to him in genuine remorse, he forsakes his intention to judge us and turns to us in love. The reverse is also true, however, as Jeremiah so clearly outlined both alternatives: "Then the word of the LORD came to me: . . . 'If at any time I announce that a nation or kingdom is to be uprooted, torn down and destroyed, and if that nation I warned repents of its evil, then I will relent and not inflict on it the disaster I had planned. And if at another time I announce that a nation or kingdom is to be built up and planted, and if it does evil in my sight and does not obey me, then I will reconsider the good I had intended to do for it'" (Jer. 18:5, 7–10).

God's judgment of pre-flood mankind was not inevitable—at least not at first. As long as his Spirit contended with them (Gen. **6:3**) they had the opportunity to repent. But when God's deadline for repentance had passed, he announced that he would "wipe mankind . . . from the face of the earth" (**6:7**). He doubtless did so reluctantly, since they were the crown of his creative activity. But they had defaced the divine image in which they had been made. It was beyond restoration, and God decided to destroy all mankind. Human sin had so tainted the entire created order that all the animals and birds would die as well. No life of any sort would remain.

"But Noah found favor in the eyes of the LORD" (Gen. **6:8**). Noah's life was the one point of light shining bravely through the awful darkness about to engulf the world. Although he was a "righteous man" (6:9), he and his family would survive the waters of the flood—not because of his goodness, but because of God's grace (see similarly Dan. 9:18).

And so it is with us today. We who are Christians would do well to remind ourselves often that the Lord has "saved us, not because of righteous things we had done, but because of his mercy" (Titus 3:5).

8

Preparing for the Flood (6:9–7:10)

RIGHTEOUSNESS IN THE MIDST OF CORRUPTION (6:9–12)

THE COMMAND TO BUILD THE ARK (6:13–22)

THE COMMAND TO ENTER THE ARK (7:1–5)

ENTERING THE ARK (7:6–10)

This is the account of Noah" (**6:9**) is the title of the third major section in the primeval history recorded in Genesis 1–11. By far the longest of the five sections that constitute that history, it tells the story of the flood that destroyed sinful mankind in the days of Noah. It describes the divine judgment on the human race that came because of their rebellion against God.

Needless to say, biblical events did not take place in an historical vacuum. The people of the OT were very much a part of the times and places in which they lived. Genesis 1–36, for example, has Mesopotamia as its historical and cultural background for the most part, while chapters 37–50 find their home in the land of Egypt.

Although Genesis 1–2 bears only a superficial resemblance to various Mesopotamian creation stories, we have already noted several similarities between Genesis 5 and the Sumerian king lists (see chapter six). Genesis 6–9 has parallels, however, from Mesopotamia—both Sumerian and Babylonian—that are closer still.

Of all the Mesopotamian flood stories, the eleventh tablet of the Babylonian *Epic of Gilgamesh* (named after its main character) bears the most striking resemblances to Genesis 6–9. They include (1) a divine warning of the impending flood, (2) the building of a ship coated with pitch, (3) the gathering of representative animals and birds to save them from the flood, (4) the ship's coming to rest on a mountain, (5) the sending out of birds to reconnoiter, and (6) the offering of a sacrifice after leaving the ship.

Differences between the Babylonian and biblical stories, however, are equally impressive: (1) the Babylonian ship is in the shape of a cube, while Noah's ark has the general proportions of modern ships and is therefore much more seaworthy than its Babylonian counterpart; (2) the order of sending out the birds is different in the two accounts; (3) the Babylonian flood lasts fourteen days, while the biblical flood lasts more than a year; (4) the Babylonian flood has only two survivors (Utnapishtim and his wife), whereas eight survive the biblical flood; (5) the two Babylonian survivors achieve immortality after the flood, while Noah and his family eventually die; and (6) the Babylonian account is grossly polytheistic (the gods "cower like dogs" next to a wall and "gather like flies" above a sacrifice),[1] while the Genesis account knows only the one true God.

Although the Gilgamesh epic is older than the present form of the Genesis story, both may be dependent on a still earlier account. The superintending influence of the Holy Spirit preserved the sober historical character of the biblical flood story and kept it from being tainted by the polytheism that so debased the Babylonian narrative.

1. See E. A. Speiser in *Ancient Near Eastern Texts Relating to the Old Testament*, ed. J. B. Pritchard, 2d ed. (Princeton: Princeton University Press, 1955), 94–95.

Righteousness in the Midst of Corruption (6:9–12)

Noah's godly life is described in three complementary ways in Genesis **6:9**. Like John the Baptist (Mark 6:20) and Simeon (Luke 2:25), Noah was a "righteous" man, satisfying the standards established for him by a holy God. Like Abraham (Gen. 17:1) and Job (Job 1:1), Noah was "blameless," giving his contemporaries no excuse to criticize his conduct. And like Enoch (Gen. 5:22, 24), Noah "walked with God," exhibiting in word and deed the closeness of his fellowship with the Lord.

Although Noah's three sons—Shem, Ham, and Japheth—had already been mentioned earlier in the account (5:32), their names and their relationship to their father appear again in the context of his righteous life (**6:10**). The reference to them here would seem to be superfluous unless we assume its purpose to be that Noah's sons shared his moral and spiritual ideals. That in turn would help to explain why Shem, Ham, and Japheth, as a part of their father's godly family, were saved from the flood along with Noah himself.

The rest of mankind, however, was very wicked indeed. Three times in **6:11–12** we are told how "corrupt" the earth had become. In Genesis 1 God saw how good, how "very good" (1:31), his entire creation was. In Genesis 6 God sees how thoroughly corrupt "all the people on earth" (**6:12**) have become as a result of the entrance of sin into the human heart. Because violence and evil reign everywhere, God has decided to destroy all mankind and to make Noah and his family the ancestors of a new humanity.

The Command to Build the Ark (6:13–22)

An enormous ship was the vehicle that God chose to use to save the righteous few. The Hebrew word translated as "ark" in the flood story is used in the OT almost exclusively to refer to Noah's ship. It appears elsewhere only in Exodus 2, where it is translated as "basket" (Exod. 2:3, 5). As the ark saved Noah and seven others from a watery grave, so the basket saved the baby Moses from a similar fate. And both the ark and the basket were coated with pitch (Gen. **6:14**; Exod. 2:3). If Moses was indeed the author of both Genesis and Exodus, these striking similarities between the story of his own deliverance and that of Noah must have impressed him deeply.

The wood that the ark was made of was probably cypress, although we cannot be sure. It had three decks, which in turn were divided into rooms. One interpretation of Genesis **6:16** pictures the ark as having a series of small windows running the entire length of the vessel eighteen inches from the top. The windows would admit light and air, while an overhanging roof would keep the rain from coming in. The door in the side of the ark was its only entrance and exit.

The ark's dimensions were truly remarkable for its time. It was "450 feet long, 75 feet wide and 45 feet high" (Gen. **6:15**). Modern ocean liners rarely exceed twice the length of Noah's ark. To compare it with something perhaps more familiar to us, we observe that the ark was half again as long as a football field.

What did the ark look like? Only its dimensions are given to us, so we are free to speculate concerning its shape. It probably did not resemble modern ships because such construction requires the skills of expert shipwrights. Nor would a simple rectangular shape have been suitable, since then Noah would have been forced to provide the vessel with a maze of supporting beams and braces, drastically reducing the living space available for himself, his family and all the animals. In any case a rectangular ark would not have been buoyant enough to carry its huge load and would not have floated evenly in the water without a massive keel.

Meir Ben-Uri, an Israeli scholar, developed an attractive theory concerning the shape of the ark. He believed that it was a long flattened box, its two ends shaped like lozenges. A straight line joining any two of the acute angles in the cross section of a ship built in such a shape would be exactly parallel to the surface of the water when the ark was afloat. The obtuse-angled bottom of the ship would have served as a rudimentary keel as it provided stability and kept the ark from capsizing. Ben-Uri said that such a ship would have weighed about 6,000 tons and have had a carrying capacity of about 15,000 tons.[2] There would have been plenty of room for Noah's family, the animals, and enough food for all of them during the year they spent on board.

But whatever the shape of the ark, its declared purpose was to provide sanctuary for eight people and thousands of animals throughout the crisis of the flood. The devastating power of the

2. *The Jerusalem Post*, October 10, 1967.

floodwaters would totally destroy all other life "under the heavens" (6:17; see 2 Pet. 3:6). Every creature that had "the breath of life" in it would die, but the Lord would "keep alive" Noah, his three sons, Noah's wife and his son's wives (Gen. 6:19–20). The story of Noah's salvation from the flood is used in the Bible to typify God's deliverance of all who trust in him (Heb. 11:7; 2 Pet. 2:5), and it also provides a beautiful symbol of baptism (1 Pet. 3:20–21).

The story also illustrates another important biblical principle. While God bestows his saving grace and love on individuals, he is concerned about their families as well (see, e.g., Gen. 17:7–27; Deut. 30:19; Pss. 78:1–7; 102:28; 103:17–18; 112:1–2; Acts 2:38–39; 1 Cor. 7:14). Acts 16:31 summarizes this principle: "Believe in the Lord Jesus, and you will be saved—you and your household."

God announced in advance that he would establish his covenant with Noah (Gen. 6:18), a covenant that Noah would fully understand only after the flood was over (9:8–17). It would include the promise that such a destructive flood would never again wipe out all mankind. But implicit in its provisions would also be the divine mandate to "be fruitful and increase in number," "to fill the earth and subdue it" (1:28; see 9:1, 7). The same command that God gave when he created mankind would also be necessary if the earth was to be repopulated after the flood.

Noah was also to lead into the finished ark a minimum of two of every "kind" (see chapters one and three) of bird and animal in order to restock the earth after the floodwaters receded. Two is intended as a minimal figure, as 7:2–3 makes clear: "Take with you seven of every kind of clean animal, a male and its mate, and two of every kind of unclean animal, a male and its mate, and also seven of every kind of bird, male and female, to keep their various kinds alive throughout the earth." Whether "seven" in these verses means literally "seven" or "seven pairs" or even "several" (see 1 Sam. 2:5; 2 Kings 4:35), it is clear that although only two of every kind of unclean animal may have been needed, many more than two of every kind of clean animal were required. This is because the unclean animals had only to reproduce themselves after the flood, while the clean animals would not only have to reproduce themselves but would also be needed for the burnt offerings that Noah would sacrifice (Gen. 8:20).

Only animals that were ceremonially clean could properly be offered to God.

Apparently all the animals would "come to" Noah voluntarily (**6:20**). It would seem that he would not have to hunt them down or look for them in remote places. Their natural instinct for self-preservation, energized by a special act of God, would bring them unerringly to Noah's ark.

The story emphasizes Noah's obedience in fulfilling every order that God issued to him. We are told over and over that he "did everything just as God commanded him" (**6:22**; see also **7:5, 9, 16**). Because he was righteous, he obeyed whenever God spoke and did whatever God told him to do, however strange or unusual the command may have seemed to him. In so doing he anticipated the quality of prompt obedience that would later characterize his descendant Abraham (12:4; 17:23; 21:14; 22:3).

The Command to Enter the Ark (7:1–5)

For the second time in the story, Noah is said to be "righteous," again in contrast to nearly everyone else (**7:1**; see **6:9**). And as his righteousness led him to obey God, so also God would single out him and his family for salvation because the Lord had found him righteous.

The number seven continues to figure prominently in the Genesis narrative. In addition to the seven (or seven pairs) of every kind of clean animal discussed above, seven was the number of days between the Lord's command to enter the ark and his sending of rain on the earth (**7:4**). It goes without saying that the floodwaters came in seven days as a result of the rain just as God had said they would (**7:10**).

"Forty days and forty nights" would be the amount of time that the rain would continue to fall (**7:4**, 12). That length of time, whether understood literally every time it occurs or figuratively in some cases, was often used as the temporal backdrop for critical periods in the history of God's people. Moses stayed on Mount Sinai forty days and forty nights (Exod. 24:18), and there the Lord gave him the two stone tablets of the covenant on which the ten commandments were written (Deut. 9:11). Jesus fasted forty days and forty nights in the desert (Matt. 4:2), and there the devil tempted him three times (4:3–11).

After the Lord told Noah that the rains were about to fall he repeated his earlier words of judgment: "I will wipe from the face of the earth every living creature I have made" (Gen. **7:4**). Those are the last recorded words of God to Noah until after the flood itself, more than a year later. God's final speech before the flood begins with the words, "Go into the ark" (**7:1**); his first speech after the flood begins with the words, "Come out of the ark" (8:16). The text of Genesis represents the year between those two speeches as a time when God is silent, a time of patient waiting for Noah and his family.

Entering the Ark (7:6–10)

Noah reached the advanced age of 500 years before Shem, Ham, and Japheth were born (5:32), and he was 600 years old "when the floodwaters came on the earth" (**7:6**). If the 120 years of 6:3 were the period of grace between the time of God's pronouncement in that verse and the arrival of divine judgment (as we argued in chapter seven), then the period had to begin before Noah's 500th year. At any rate, Noah's sons were able to assist him in building the ark only after the 120 years were already well under way. In fact it would seem that God's command to Noah to build the ark was not issued until after all three sons were born (**6:10–13**), reducing the amount of time traditionally allowed for its construction and making the feat itself all the more amazing.

Noah and his family entered the completed ark "to escape the waters of the flood" (**7:7**). What were other people doing just before the floodwaters came?

In a graphic description of his second coming, Jesus gave us a vivid portrayal of the situation in those early days: "As it was in the days of Noah, so it will be at the coming of the Son of Man. For in the days before the flood, people were eating and drinking, marrying and giving in marriage, up to the day Noah entered the ark; and they knew nothing about what would happen until the flood came and took them all away" (Matt. 24:37–39). The tragedy of repeatedly defying God, of toying with his patience continually and persistently, is that eventually the time of repentance passes by and it becomes too late to seek his forgiveness. When the flood came, everyone outside Noah's immediate family was beyond hope and doomed to destruction.

As it was then, so it will be when Jesus returns: "The Lord is not slow in keeping his promise, as some understand slowness. He is patient with you, not wanting anyone to perish, but everyone to come to repentance. But the day of the Lord will come like a thief. The heavens will disappear with a roar; the elements will be destroyed by fire, and the earth and everything in it will be laid bare" (2 Pet. 3:10).

Seven days after Noah's family and the birds and animals entered the ark, the floodwaters inundated the earth.

9

Judgment and Redemption
(7:11–8:19)

THE BEGINNING OF THE FLOOD (7:11–16)

THE FLOODWATERS CONTINUE TO RISE (7:17–24)

THE FLOOD CEASES (8:1–14)

LEAVING THE ARK (8:15–19)

T he biblical flood story provides unforgettable illustrations of divine judgment and divine redemption. Judgment stands out in bold relief in the account of the relentless rising of the waters (7:11–24), a section that divides into two parts: the beginning of the flood (7:11–16) and the continuing of the flood (7:17–24). Redemption is stressed in the account of the gradual receding of the waters (8:1–19), a section that also divides into two parts: the cessation of the flood (8:1–14) and the exit from the ark (8:15–19).

Before looking at each of the four subsections in detail, it will be useful for us to examine the chronological framework in which the flood narrative itself is set. Since "Noah was six hundred years old when the floodwaters came on the earth" (7:6), his age will be the year-date in a series of shorthand notations as I list the critical events in their proper order, much as Noah might have entered them in the ship's log. For example, "2/17/600" will be our way of writing "the six hundredth year of Noah's life, on the seventeenth day of the second month" (**7:11**).

2/17/600: The great flood begins as water pours down from above and bursts forth from below (**7:11**).

For 40 days and 40 nights the rain continues to fall (**7:4, 12**) and the waters continue to rise (**7:17**).

For a total of 150 days the waters flood the earth and the ark floats on them (**7:24; 8:3**).

7/17/600: The ark comes to rest on the mountains of Ararat at the end of exactly 150 days (**8:4**).

10/1/600: The tops of the mountains become visible as the waters gradually recede (**8:5**).

After 40 days Noah sends out a raven from the ark, and the bird flies back and forth until it finds a dry nesting place (**8:6–7**).

Sometime later (probably seven days, since **8:10** mentions "seven more days") Noah sends out a dove that returns when it finds no dry place on which to land (**8:8–9**).

After seven more days Noah sends the dove out again, and it returns the same evening carrying a freshly plucked olive leaf (**8:10–11**).

After waiting another seven days Noah sends the dove out once more, and this time it does not return (**8:12**).

1/1/601: The floodwaters have now receded to the extent that the surface of the ground is dry (**8:13**).

2/27/601: The water has now dried up entirely, and the earth is completely dry (**8:14**).

Even though some of the sevens and tens and forties in this chronological sketch may be figurative or round numbers rather than precise numbers, the first and last dates clearly demonstrate that the great flood lasted for over a year.

The Beginning of the Flood (7:11–16)

Anyone who has ever experienced even a minor flood knows something of the devastating force generated by water that breaks free of whatever was holding it back. But we can only dimly imagine what it must have been like on the day when "all the springs of the great deep burst forth, and the floodgates of the heavens were opened" (**7:11**). The incredible power and speed of massive quantities of water gushing out of subterranean springs and pouring down from the skies above caught everyone by surprise—everyone, that is, but "Noah and his sons, Shem, Ham and Japheth, together with his wife and the wives of his three sons" (**7:13**). By entering the ark on the day the flood began, they and the animals they had gathered escaped with their lives.

The story of the onset of the great flood is a masterpiece of brief but vivid description. Upheavals beneath the ocean floor are portrayed as the bursting forth of springs, and the falling of torrential rains is compared to the opening of floodgates. We are served notice right from the start that this was no ordinary flood.

The biblical flood account gave rise to the use of untamed and unleashed waters as a literary symbol of sudden and overwhelming judgment in the writings of OT poets. The psalmist in his agony cried out to God: "Deep calls to deep in the roar of your waterfalls; all your waves and breakers have swept over me" (Ps. 42:7). A poet in the same tradition voices his complaint to the Lord: "Your wrath lies heavily upon me; you have overwhelmed me with all your waves" (88:7). The ancient Israelites were reminded by their flood narrative that water can crush as well as cleanse.

Five main categories of animate life are mentioned in the Genesis 1 creation account: sea creatures, birds, wild animals, livestock, and creatures that move along the ground (Gen. 1:21–25). Pairs of all the members of each category—except, of course, the sea creatures—went into the ark with Noah (**7:14–15**). The flood was so widespread that only the sea creatures could remain outside the ark and survive. After the floodwaters had receded completely, however, they would once again fall under human dominion together with all the other animals (9:2).

The paragraph that describes the beginning of the flood concludes by telling us that the animals entered the ark "as God had commanded Noah. Then the LORD shut him in" (**7:16**). Why the sudden shift in the divine name in the space of such a few words?

We observed in chapter two that in the OT "LORD" is the intimate, personal name of God and emphasizes his work as Redeemer, while "God" is his more formal and impersonal name and focuses on his work as Creator. The compound name "LORD God" that occurs so often in Genesis 2 shows us that both names are titles of one and the same God.

Thus in **7:16** God as Creator issues commands to Noah, but God in his role as the redeeming Lord gently closes the door of Noah's ark and shuts him in. The ark is the vehicle of salvation for Noah and his family. Much later, Jonah would state a basic truth after he himself was delivered from a watery grave: "Salvation comes from the LORD" (Jon. 2:9).

The Floodwaters Continue to Rise (7:17–24)

The previous section was the only major paragraph in the flood story that used both of the most common OT names for God. In contrast, the section now before us is the only major paragraph in the flood narrative that omits the name of God entirely. The reason is clear: as soon as Noah and his family are safely in the ark, God unleashes the full fury of his wrath on the rest of mankind. He turns his back on them, and the floodwaters are free to do their awful work of judgment. The people outside the ark had sinned once too often against God, and he left them to their own devices.

The language used in these verses is vigorous indeed and leaves no doubt as to its intention. We are told repeatedly that the waters increased and rose greatly, that they covered all the high mountains, that every living thing that moved on the earth "perished," "died," "was wiped out." The flood was so massive and extensive and prolonged that "only Noah was left, and those with him in the ark" (Gen. **7:23**).

At their greatest height, the floodwaters covered the highest mountains "to a depth of more than twenty feet" (**7:20**). Since the ark was "45 feet high" (6:15), the waters were deep enough to allow the ark to float freely and to keep it from scraping bottom.

When God had first created man, he had breathed "into his nostrils the breath of life" (2:7). But just as God, because of human sin, had banished the first couple from the garden where the tree of life was located, so also now, because of human sin, God sends the great flood in order that every living thing that has "the breath of life in its nostrils" will die (**7:22**). As the ground was cursed because of mankind's original sin (3:17), so also now the earth and all its creatures great and small are judged because of mankind's disobedience and rebellion against God (**7:21–23**). The fatal effects of the sin of human beings are experienced by all other living creatures as well.

It will be useful for us at this point to summarize a number of principles of divine judgment as illustrated by the flood.

1. *God's judgments are not arbitrary.* Our God is not capricious in his decisions to judge his creatures. Divine judgment is always related to human wickedness. The Lord was determined to wipe mankind from the face of the earth because of their violent and corrupt behavior. Their conduct caused him grief and filled his heart with pain, and so he decided to put an end to all the people on earth (6:5–13).

2. *God always announces his judgments beforehand.* Once having made a decision to judge his sinful creatures, God warned them of the impending judgment. He did not sneak up on them unawares and judge them without first telling them of his plans. Far from being a distant and hidden God who conceals his desires from his people, he proclaimed to them in no uncertain terms and in a variety of ways (Heb. 1:1–2) what he intended to do. In the case of the flood the Lord revealed to Noah that he was going to destroy the earth and every living creature on it (Gen. 6:13).

   Although God sometimes announced coming judgment directly, he more often did so through his chosen servants. While the ark was being built, Noah, "a preacher of righteousness" (2 Pet. 2:5), proclaimed a message of condemnation to the world of his day. In so doing, he witnessed to the vitality of his own faith (Heb. 11:7); himself warned, he also warned others.

3. *God always grants time for repentance.* If God merely warned sinful people of impending judgment and then immediately carried it out, the warning would be no more than a cruel charade. On the contrary, however, our patient and loving God is generous in giving us plenty of time to repent. Though the Holy Spirit "will not contend with man forever" (Gen. 6:3), he will nevertheless contend and plead with him for a considerable period of time. In the case of the flood it was "a hundred and twenty years" (6:3), an ample length of time indeed when we think of the depths of sin that depraved human ingenuity had plumbed during those days.

4. *God always follows through on his decision to judge unless man repents.* Apart from man's sincere remorse for his sinful deeds and apart from his willingness to confess them, God always implements his warnings of judgment. He said that he would send rain on the earth for forty days and forty nights (7:4), and he did so (**7:12**). He said that he would wipe from the face of the earth every living creature he had made (7:4), and he did so (**7:23**). Our God can be counted on to fulfill every promise he makes, even when they are promises of judgment. When God's people refuse to respond to his warnings, divine judgment is both inevitable and irreversible.

5. *God's judgments always result in death.* His announcements of impending judgment are serious indeed, and although death may not be the immediate result of his judgments it is always the ultimate result. In the case of the flood, there is scarcely room for doubt that both spiritual and physical death are intended. The animals and birds may have experienced only physical death, but wicked mankind surely experienced both. Just as eternal life is a gift from God, so also "the wages of sin is death" (Rom. 6:23)—eternal death.

6. *God judges because he is just.* "Do not be deceived: God cannot be mocked. A man reaps what he sows" (Gal. 6:7). For God not to judge sin would be to make a mockery of justice. Since God is love, he grants salvation to the righteous; because he is just, he judges the sinner. The flood stands forever as a vivid reminder of the latter principle.

In the words of Sir Thomas Browne: "That there was a Deluge once seems not to me to be so great a miracle as that there is not always one."

The Flood Ceases (8:1–14)

"Water, water everywhere," cried the ancient mariner—and the ark floated on its surface (Gen. **7:18**). For five long months Noah and his family and all the animals rode out the flood (**7:24**). During that entire time they saw no dry land at all. They must have had the sinking feeling that God had forgotten them.

"But God remembered Noah" (**8:1**). Just when all seemed lost, God paid attention to Noah and lavished his loving care on him—for that is what the verb "remember" means in Scripture. To remember in the biblical sense of that term is not merely to recall to mind or to refresh one's memory. To remember someone means to express concern for him, to visit him with gracious love.

"God remembered Rachel," and she gave birth to a son whom she named Joseph (30:22). Though even a mother may forget the baby at her breast, the Lord never forgets his children (Isa. 49:14–15). At Calvary the dying criminal asked Jesus to remember him, and Jesus assured him that he would (Luke 23:42–43). When God remembers his people, he remembers them "with favor" (Neh. 5:19; 13:31).

Genesis **8:1** functions as the hinge of the flood story, the fulcrum on which the story is balanced. Up to this point things were getting progressively worse, but from this point on things gradually improve. And the reason they improve is because "God remembered Noah."

In a very real sense, the period after the flood marks a new beginning for the human race. It is again the first day of the first month of the first year of a man's new life (**8:13**). And in a remarkable way the events of Genesis 8 parallel the events of Genesis 1 in their literary order:

8:1: God "sent a wind over the earth" (see 1:2; the Hebrew word for "wind" is the same as the word for "Spirit").

8:2: "The springs of the deep and the floodgates of the heavens had been closed" (see 1:7: God "separated the water under the expanse from the water above it").

8:5: "The waters continued to recede . . . and . . . the tops of the mountains became visible" (see 1:9: "Let the water under the sky be gathered . . . , and let dry ground appear").

8:6: Noah "sent out a raven, and it kept flying back and forth" (see 1:20: "Let birds fly above the earth").

8:17: "Bring out every kind of living creature that is with you—the birds, the animals, and all the creatures that move along the ground" (see 1:25: "God made the wild animals . . . , the livestock . . . , and all the creatures that move along the ground").

Genesis 9 continues the series by giving us three more parallels:

9:1: "God blessed Noah and his sons, saying to them, 'Be fruitful and increase in number and fill the earth'" (1:28 says almost exactly the same thing).

9:2: "The fear and dread of you will fall upon all the beasts of the earth and all the birds of the air, upon every creature that moves along the ground, and upon all the fish of the sea" (see 1:28: "Rule over the fish of the sea and the birds of the air and over every living creature that moves on the ground").

9:3: "Just as I gave you the green plants, I now give you everything" (see 1:30: "I give every green plant for food").

Although other instructive and helpful comparisons could be made between Genesis 1 and Genesis 8, the events in question are not set forth in the same literary order in the two accounts. But the above examples illustrate the fact that Genesis 8 and 9 were deliberately structured with chapter 1 in mind. The story of what took place as the floodwaters began to recede is the account of a "new creation" that parallels the account of the original creation in Genesis 1.

God remembered not only Noah and his family but also all the animals "that were with him in the ark" (**8:1**). Thousands of years later an angel of God said to Paul, who was in a sailing vessel on the storm-tossed Mediterranean, "God has graciously given you the lives of all who sail with you" (Acts 27:24). As the salt of the earth and the light of the world, God's people can sanctify those around them as well as influence them for good.

The Lord sent a wind to make the waters recede (Gen. **8:1**), but he can accomplish the same result simply by speaking a word of command (Isa. 44:27; Nah. 1:4). During a furious storm on the Sea of Galilee, Jesus rebuked the winds and the waves, and all became calm. Failing to recognize his deity, his disciples exclaimed, "What kind of man is this? Even the winds and the waves obey him" (Matt. 8:24–27). For God the Father and God the Son, mastery over wind and wave is routine (Matt. 14:22–33).

Noah's ark eventually "came to rest on the mountains of Ararat" (Gen. **8:4**). The kingdom of Ararat (called Urartu by the

Assyrians in later times) is mentioned in Isaiah 37:38 (par. 2 Kings 19:37) and Jeremiah 51:27. Urartu was an extensive and mountainous kingdom, including much of the region north of Mesopotamia and east of modern Turkey and encompassing the headwaters of the Euphrates as well as Lake Van and Lake Urmia. The landing site of Noah's ark was probably in southern Urartu rather than in northern Urartu. In any event, the peak known today as Mount Ararat, in northeastern Turkey on the Soviet border, has no better claim than any other mountain to be the place where the ark settled, since Genesis **8:4** states only that it came to rest somewhere on the "mountains" (plural) of Ararat (see chapter ten).

Noah sent out birds from the ark four times to find out whether there was dry land in the vicinity. The third and fourth times produced positive results: First, the dove returned carrying a "freshly plucked olive leaf" in its beak (**8:11**), proving to Noah that the waters had receded from the earth sufficiently enough to enable plants to grow again; and second, when the dove went out seven days later, it did not return to Noah because it had found its own nesting place (**8:12**), perhaps at the mouth of a cave for protection and shelter (Jer. 48:28).

Small wonder, indeed, that the dove should sometimes serve as a symbol of the Holy Spirit in the NT (Matt. 3:16), or that a dove carrying an olive branch in its beak should be a modern symbol of peace!

After removing the covering of the ark to get an accurate idea of the ground's dryness, Noah still had to wait for almost two more months before the earth would become completely dry, making it possible for him, his family, and the animals to leave the ark in comfort and safety (Gen. **8:13–14**).

Leaving the Ark (8:15–19)

The Lord broke his yearlong silence by commanding Noah and his family to come out of the ark. All other human life had perished in the flood, and Noah's descendants would form the seed bed for the new human race.

Though the rest of mankind had been judged, Noah and his family had been redeemed. God had brought his faithful children through the fearful trial of the flood by telling them specifically how to escape it and survive. Throughout the long ages of history the Lord has always rescued those who trust in him, because "God did not appoint us to suffer wrath but to receive salvation through our Lord Jesus Christ" (1 Thess. 5:9).

The animals shared Noah's deliverance, and as they had entered the ark with him, so also they left the ark with him. They too had been saved from the flood, and now they could once again fulfill the command to multiply and be fruitful and increase in number.

God would soon bless Noah and his sons with a similar command. But before that blessing was spoken, the aged patriarch would worship the Lord by building an altar to him and sacrificing offerings on it. Worship and fellowship would blend in joyful celebration as a redeemed man and a redeeming God communed together.

10

The Flood: Universal or Local?

THE UNIVERSAL-FLOOD THEORY

THE LOCAL-FLOOD THEORY

One of the most intriguing and difficult questions that every serious student of the Bible must try to answer for himself sooner or later is this: How extensive was Noah's flood? Did the floodwaters cover the entire globe, or was only a portion of the ancient Near East under water?

Some readers of the Book of Genesis would consider the above distinction irrelevant. They believe that the biblical flood story is to be understood as a parable and, therefore, that the flood never really took place at all. The story has merely theological meaning, they say; it teaches us that God takes sin seriously and judges all who disobey him.

Others claim that the biblical flood narrative is a myth or legend, a kind of fairy tale, related to other similar myths both ancient and modern. Such stories represent a mentality that is unsophisticated or primitive or childlike, we are told; their authors believed that a worldwide flood did in fact take place, but they were mistaken; at best, a local flood grew in the telling and was eventually exaggerated to a magnitude out of all proportion to its original size. But in any event, say the proponents of this view, whether the flood actually happened is not important; what really matters is what the story tells us about God (or the gods) and his (or their) relationship to ancient mankind.

Needless to say, we who believe that the great flood occurred in space and time—that it was a genuine historical event of profound importance—must categorically reject the parabolic and mythical views. The text of Genesis offers no evidence that the flood story is either a myth or a parable. Furthermore, Noah is connected to the historical Adam by the Genesis 5 genealogy and to the historical Abraham by the Genesis 11 genealogy (see also Luke 3:34–38).

Thus in this chapter our task will be to set forth the main arguments pro and con with respect to the two dominant views held by evangelical believers today: (1) Noah's flood was geographically worldwide; (2) Noah's flood was geographically restricted to a portion of the ancient Near East.

The Universal-Flood Theory

Ten rather formidable arguments can be marshaled in favor of the idea that the great flood covered the whole earth. I will examine each of these in turn, first defending them and then challenging their validity.

1. *The depth of the waters as described in Genesis demands that the flood be worldwide.* "All the high mountains under the entire heavens were covered. The waters rose and covered the mountains to a depth of more than twenty feet" (Gen. **7:19–20**). The ark was "45 feet high" (**6:15**), so "more than twenty feet" probably refers to the draft of the ark. The world's highest mountains were covered by enough water to keep the ark from scraping bottom and grounding, no matter where it drifted.

Arguing that the admittedly universal language of the flood story demonstrates conclusively that the flood itself was universal in extent may turn out, however, to be self-defeating for several reasons.

First, universal language is often a literary device that is best interpreted phenomenally or optically—that is, from the limited standpoint of the eyewitness who writes the account. The biblical flood narrative, with its carefully recorded chronological notations and other details, reads like a logbook kept by Noah himself.[1] If so, the "high mountains" were mountains that he knew of or had heard of or could see, the low-lying eminences of Shinar or Babylon (see 11:2) rather than the lofty peaks of the Zagros or Caucasus ranges, or—even less likely—the Himalayas. After all, height is a relative matter. If Noah was accustomed to living in the plains, "high mountains" for him were not necessarily alps. We may also apply the same principle to the other universal terms in the narrative: the "entire heavens" would mean all the heavens that Noah knew (the sky within his immediate perception or vision); "all" would mean only everything that he could perceive; the "earth" would mean only the earth that Noah experienced, better translated as "land" (the Hebrew word for "earth" in the Genesis flood story means "land"—a much more limited term than "earth"—in eighty percent of its OT occurrences, and there is no reason that it could not mean "land" throughout the flood story as well); and so forth.

Second, universal language is often the language of hyperbole, the language of deliberate exaggeration for literary effect. Joel 3:2 refers to "all nations," but the context limits the phrase to the nations surrounding Jerusalem and Judah (see also Gen. 41:57; 2 Chron. 36:23; Dan. 2:37–38). Note especially Colossians 1:23, which states that the gospel "has been proclaimed to every creature under heaven."

An excellent modern example of hyperbolic language used to describe a flood by those who experienced it is the devastating deluge that struck Tunisia in 1969. The actual facts are these: The flood ravaged eighty percent of the land, more than 250,000 Tunisians fled their homes, 100,000 temporarily lost their homes to the floodwaters, at least 542 died, and 14 percent of the country's cattle and sheep were drowned. The flood was caused by torrential rains that poured down for two months with scarcely a break. And how did the flood victims themselves describe the disaster? It was "the flood of a thousand years," said one. "It was like the end of the world," said another.[2] If such language can be

---

1. A. C. Custance, *The Flood: Local or Global?* (Grand Rapids: Zondervan, 1979), 25. For detailed arguments pro and con with respect to the universality of the flood, see S. A. Austin and D. C. Boardman, *The Genesis Debate*, ed. R. Youngblood (Grand Rapids: Baker, 1991), 210–29.

2. *Newsweek*, December 22, 1969, 34.

used to vividly portray the Tunisian flood of 1969, how much more is such language appropriate to describe the vastly greater flood of Noah's day!

Third, the chronology of the biblical flood story will not support a depth of more than a few hundred feet of water. One scholar has estimated (generously, we believe) that it took 324 days for the floodwaters to run off and completely dry up. At the reasonable runoff rate of four inches per day, the flood would have been only 108 feet deep—terribly destructive, to be sure, even at that. If we double the rate of runoff, the flood would have been 216 feet deep—still more destructive. For the sake of the argument, let us now assume that the present Mount Ararat (more on this later) was the site of the ark's landfall. Ararat's 17,000 feet divided by 324 days yields a daily average runoff rate of 52 1/2 *feet*—caused only by a "wind" sent by God (**8:1**)! Water moving at that speed would doubtless have so severely damaged the earth's surface that it would have been virtually impossible to cultivate it for quite some time. And if we insist on understanding the universal language of the account literally, we would observe that the highest mountain known is Everest, forcing us to double the 17,000-foot figure and making the runoff problem twice as difficult.

Fourth, it has been calculated that if the Genesis flood story uses literal language throughout, to cover the highest mountains would require eight times more water than the world now contains. Question: Where did all those floodwaters run off to? An attempt to drain off so much water, especially in such a relatively short period of time, would seem to be impossible.

Other questions immediately suggest themselves: If our entire planet was at one time covered with a sheath of water several miles thick, would astronomers not be able to detect its effects on astral history caused by the temporary increase in the earth's mass? Would not that much water have left visible marks on the earth's surface as well? Would not the indiscriminate mingling of fresh water and salt water all over the world have caused irreparable damage to nearly all forms of marine and freshwater life?

2. *Water always seeks its own level, and since the highest mountains in the Near East were covered, the highest mountains in the rest of the world were covered also.* The highest mountains

in the Near East are well over 10,000 feet tall, and therefore the flood must have been worldwide.

The validity of this argument, however, is closely tied to that of the previous one. We would of course agree that water always seeks its own level. But it may well be that the area covered by Noah's flood included mountains rising to only a few hundred feet, as the most plausible runoff rate of the floodwaters would seem to indicate. One or more of the extensive natural basins in the ancient Tigris-Euphrates flood plain would have been a suitable locale.[3] The region would most likely have included at least the southeastern part of Urartu (Ararat), where the mountains in ancient times may have been considerably lower than they are even today. In summary, until we can pinpoint the place where the ark landed (and we may never be able to do so) we will not be able to draw any conclusions about the universality of the flood based on the truism that water always seeks its own level.

3. *The flood lasted for over a year and was therefore universal.* While such a length of time is entirely in keeping with a worldwide flood, a local flood would have lasted for a few weeks at most.

One could argue just as strongly, however, that a universal flood—especially a flood during which the waters rose to a height of tens of thousands of feet—would require far longer than a year. The two months of rain during the 1969 Tunisian flood turned normally placid rivers into raging cataracts that crushed everything in their path. In the days of Noah, "the waters flooded the earth for a hundred and fifty days" (**7:24**). If the floodwaters covered the whole earth they rose at least a hundred feet per day during those five months. Such swiftly rising waters would have generated powerful currents that would have smashed the ark to smithereens against a cliff wall or mountainside. It will do no good to observe that "God remembered Noah" (**8:1**) and thus preserved the ark from such a calamity, because the sentence of which that phrase is a part is connected with the receding of the waters rather than with their rising. Obviously, then, a yearlong period of time is more suitable to a local flood—admittedly

3. For a similar suggestion, see B. Ramm, *The Christian View of Science and Scripture* (Grand Rapids: Eerdmans, 1954), 239.

widespread and extensive—than to a universal flood. In the type of localized area described earlier, the floodwaters would have risen a couple of feet per day at the most during the five-month period and would not have threatened a huge ark in the least.

4. *The geology of the flood implies its universal extent.* The "springs of the great deep" (**7:11**) burst forth and continued to flood the continents of the world for five months, at the end of which the springs were closed (**8:2**). Such massive geologic upheavals imply a worldwide deluge and cannot be easily harmonized with the idea of a more localized flood.

The fact is, however, that we simply do not know the duration of the geological phenomena described in Genesis **7:11**. It is entirely possible—indeed, contextually quite probable— that the verbs in **8:2** should be understood not in the past tense but in the pluperfect: "The springs of the deep and the floodgates of the heavens had been closed, and the rain had stopped falling from the sky." If that is so, the time span for the rising of the waters is reduced (perhaps considerably), making the theory of a local flood once again more attractive than that of a universal flood since reducing the time span increases the speed at which the waters must rise.

Proponents of a universal flood generally claim that all observable stratigraphic phenomena find a satisfactory explanation in the tremendous pressures built up during such a deluge. Some assert that even the world's oil deposits came into being during Noah's flood.[4] But most Christian geologists insist that although there is evidence for extensive local flooding in ancient times, no geological evidence whatever exists to prove the universal-flood theory. And if a worldwide flood is the best way to account for the origin of oil, how was Noah able to coat the ark "with pitch inside and out" (**6:14**) before the flood? The pitch Noah used was most likely "a natural derivative of crude petroleum."[5]

5. *The size of the ark compels us to assume that the flood was universal.* The ark's dimensions (**6:15**) are better calculated to serve the needs of tens of thousands of animals from all over the

---

4. H. M. Morris and J. C. Whitcomb, Jr., *The Genesis Flood* (Philadelphia: Presbyterian and Reformed, 1961), 434.

5. T. C. Mitchell, "Bitumen," in *The New Bible Dictionary*, ed. J. D. Douglas (Grand Rapids: Eerdmans, 1962), 159.

world than those of "only eight people and a few animals from the Near East."[6]

It would appear that the ark was indeed an enormous vessel (see chapter eight), although we would readily admit that we have no way of knowing for certain just how long Noah's cubit (his basic unit of measurement) actually was. If it was considerably shorter than the cubit of later times, then the ark was much smaller than we have traditionally thought. But such speculation is fruitless, except insofar as a smaller vessel and its animal cargo would have been much more easily serviced by eight people than a larger one would have.

A much more serious problem, however, for the universal-flood theory arises in connection with the animal cargo itself. How would tens of thousands of species from all over the world get to the ark from their distant habitats? How would large land animals from other continents cross the oceans? Once in the ark, how could a mere eight people feed them and care for them? How could those people—or, for that matter, a much larger group of people—provide the special diets and varied environments necessary? Although very few animals hibernate, it has been suggested that practically all of the animals on the ark did so during the yearlong flood, freeing Noah and his family to perform other tasks. But if that is so, what are we to make of Genesis **6:21**: "You are to take every kind of food that is to be eaten and store it away as food for you and for them"? It would seem that the animals in the ark were to masticate rather than hibernate during their year-long voyage. It would also seem to be much more likely that, no matter what the size of the ark, eight people cared for a smaller number of animals during a local flood than that eight people cared for thousands upon thousands of animals during a world-wide flood.

6. *No ark of any size would have been necessary unless the flood was universal.* If the impending flood was local, Noah and his family (and whatever animals would have been threatened with extinction) would have had plenty of time to move to a safe place out of reach of the floodwaters. They would also have been spared the enormous amount of labor involved in building the ark.

6. J. C. Whitcomb, Jr., *His*, May 1958, 38.

The ark, however, was more than simply a ship in which to ride out a flood. It was just as much a part of Noah's witness to his friends and neighbors as were his actual words. It served as a graphic warning to them that they could choose either to heed or to ignore.[7] A migration by Noah and his family would not have had nearly the same powerful effect. In fact other people might have joined them out of curiosity and escaped the flood in the bargain. The ark proved to be the best way to make absolutely certain that only Noah and his family would survive.

7. *Second Peter 3:5–7 assumes that Noah's flood was universal.* Since creation (the subject of v. 5) was universal, and since the coming judgment (the subject of v. 7) will be universal, the flood (the subject of v. 6) was also universal. If that were not so, the comparison would break down.

While verses 5 and 7 speak of the heavens and the earth in a clearly universal sense, verse 6 tells us only that "the world of that time was deluged and destroyed." It almost seems as though Peter deliberately chose a different word (*kosmos*, here translated "world") in verse 6 to differentiate it from the earth (and heavens) of verses 5 and 7. If Noah's flood is understood as being local, then the "world" of 2 Peter 3:6 would mean the "world of mankind" or the like in its broader biblical context.[8] This leads us immediately to the next argument often used in support of a universal flood.

8. *Since all mankind was destroyed, the flood must have been worldwide.* A local flood would have destroyed only a part of mankind, and the text of Genesis insists that all sinful people were destroyed and that only Noah and seven others survived.

Two possible responses come to mind in this connection. From Noah's perspective, "all sinful people" or its equivalent could be understood to refer to all the people who lived in the section of the ancient Near East with which he was familiar. Or, if we date the flood early enough (see below), "all sinful people" or its equivalent could in fact mean all the people on earth, since it is generally conceded that the most ancient civilizations emerged in the Near East.

7. Custance, *The Flood*, 33–35.
8. W. F. Arndt and F. W. Gingrich, *A Greek-English Lexicon of the New Testament* (Chicago: University of Chicago Press, 1957), 447.

In either case, from the standpoint of the writer's intention, the purpose of the flood was to destroy all sinful mankind. It cannot be proved that the writer had in mind anyone other than the inhabitants of the ancient Near East. And Noah's flood did not need to be worldwide in order to destroy them.

9. *Flood stories are found in cultures all over the world, and that proves that the flood was universal.* There are about 150 such stories, and they come from nearly every part of the world. If Noah's flood was local, why should flood stories of all sorts be so widespread?

We note immediately that not all of the flood stories have the same value or importance. Some of them are merely local adaptations of the Genesis flood story, the latter having been taught to this or that group of people by Christian missionaries. Others bear little or no resemblance to the Genesis flood account. But a substantial number still seem to be related, to a greater or lesser degree, to the story of Noah's flood as found in Genesis.

An important point, however, is rarely noticed in connection with all of these stories. In each case it is a local group of people, not a faraway group, who have survived the flood. If all (or even a few) of the stories are true, that would mean that local survivors all over the world started the local traditions, and that in turn would mean that the biblical story, which speaks of only one surviving family, is mistaken.[9] But since we always start with the presupposition that the biblical account is true, then the other stories are either fictional, or based on local floods in the areas of their origin, or corruptions of the biblical story. If they are the latter, then their ultimate origin is the Near East. Whether Noah's flood was local or universal, such stories were eventually brought to their present locations by survivors of that flood. Their widespread distribution, therefore, says nothing about whether the flood was universal or local.

10. *Noah's ark can still be seen on Mount Ararat, and since Ararat is 17,000 feet high the flood was universal.* Ancient reports from such diverse authors as Berossus and Josephus combine with modern reports of ark sightings to authenticate the continued existence of Noah's ark. Fragments of wood from the

9. Custance, *The Flood*, 33.

ark brought down from Ararat by Fernand Navarra, an intrepid explorer, were shown to be 5,000 years old when first subjected to scientific analysis.[10]

As we have seen, however, the designation of Mount Ararat as the landing site for Noah's ark is highly suspicious. In the flood story itself we are told only that "the ark came to rest on the mountains of Ararat" (Gen. **8:4**)—that is, ancient Urartu, an extensive region (see chapter nine). Furthermore, we have good reason to believe that the mountain today called Ararat did not receive that name until just a few hundred years ago.[11] Recent radiocarbon tests performed on Navarra's fragments indicate that they are only 1200 to 1500 years old, which means that the structure on Ararat claimed to be "Noah's ark" is probably a replica built by Byzantine monks.[12] An American expedition of eleven men hoping to get a closer look in July of 1970 was turned back by the Turkish government because the mountain is so close to Turkey's border with Russia.

In any event, the "freshly plucked olive leaf" brought to Noah by the dove (**8:11**) virtually rules out Ararat as the ark's landfall since olive trees do not grow within thousands of feet of that high elevation. In fact, that one olive leaf may turn out to be the Achilles' heel of the universal-flood theory, because it implies that somewhere an olive tree had survived the flood (probably atop a relatively low mountain).

The Local-Flood Theory

I have tried to show that the above ten major arguments, far from proving that the flood was universal, actually tend to support the local-flood theory. While most Christian geologists affirm that the earth's strata bear no traces of a universal flood, archaeologists and other scientists have unearthed abundant evidence that there were many widespread and extensive local floods in antiquity. In fact, we have an embarrassment of riches in this regard. Various reports, to give just a few examples, would date the flood (Noah's, or one similar to it) at about 10,000 B.C.[13]

10. E. Yamauchi, *Eternity*, February 1978, 29.
11. W. F. Albright, quoted in *St. Paul Pioneer Press*, February 22, 1970, 17.
12. *Newsweek*, January 31, 1977, 56.
13. W. F. Albright, *Yahweh and the Gods of Canaan* (Garden City, N.Y.: Doubleday, 1968), 99.

or 8500 B.C.[14] or 6500 B.C.,[15] each time caused primarily by the melting of polar ice caps.

A much more likely candidate for the biblical deluge, however, is the devastating flood that swept through the city of Ur in about 3500 B.C. It left an eight-foot-thick deposit of clean, uniform clay in its wake.[16] According to archaeological evidence, later floods that inundated the same general area appear not to have been quite so destructive. When we remember that Ur was Abraham's home town (11:28, 31; 15:7), the identification becomes even more attractive. Abraham may have brought the flood account with him to Canaan, where it became a part of the inspired biblical tradition as mediated to God's people through Moses.

Although in my judgment the evidence in Genesis favors the local-flood theory over the universal-flood theory, and although in my judgment other evidence tends to do the same, I do not wish to be dogmatic about these findings. Nor do I wish to reduce in any way the strong element of miracle that permeates the biblical account. But I believe that the sovereign God of the universe used the principle of the economy of miracle by choosing to employ a devastating, widespread, and extensive but geographically restricted flood in destroying the sinful human race.

When all is said and done, I find myself in agreement with this assessment:

> In conclusion, the predominance of qualified Christian scholarship appears to favor a local flood interpretation because of the lack of evidence for and the problems attendant on a universal flood. . . . In the final analysis the true interpretation of the Biblical flood account will fully accord with true science. At this time we may favor one viewpoint over another but must seek continually to integrate all the pertinent data which seem well established.[17]

14. *Christianity Today*, November 7, 1975, 74.

15. *Christianity Today*, September 10, 1976, 74.

16. J. Finegan, *Light from the Ancient Past*, 2d ed. (Princeton: Princeton University Press, 1959), 27–28.

17. W. U. Ault, "Flood (Genesis)," in *The Zondervan Pictorial Encyclopedia of the Bible*, ed. M. C. Tenney (Grand Rapids: Zondervan, 1975), 2:563.

11

The Aftermath of the Flood (8:20–9:29)

A New Promise (8:20–22)

New Commands (9:1–7)

A New Relationship (9:8–17)

A New Temptation (9:18–23)

A Final Word (9:24–29)

As I noted in chapter nine, the receding of the floodwaters gave mankind the opportunity for a brand-new start. Even one of the dates in Noah's logbook signaled the beginning of a new era: "By the first day of the first month of Noah's six hundred and first year, the water had dried up from the earth" (Gen. **8:13**). More than any other event since creation itself, the aftermath of the great flood inaugurated a time of beginning again.

A New Promise (8:20–22)

The first recorded acts of righteous Noah after he left the ark were building an altar and offering sacrifices on it. Abel, one of

Noah's spiritual ancestors, had also offered an animal sacrifice to the Lord many centuries earlier (4:4). As in the case of Noah, Abel's offerings pleased the Lord; like Noah, Abel was a "righteous man" (Heb. 11:4). We are reminded again that the motivation of the worshiper is always more important than the method he uses in his worship. For example, Jesus condemned the prayers of hypocrites (Matt. 6:5), but "the prayer of a righteous man is powerful and effective" (James 5:16).

Worship properly offered is a very personal matter. For that reason, Noah brought his sacrifice to God as "the LORD", and "the LORD" responded to Noah's act of worship (Gen. **8:20–21**). "LORD" is the intimate, redemptive name of God in the OT (see chapter two), and as such it regularly appears in contexts of worship and sacrifice (see also 4:4).

In a vivid word picture that is painted often in the Bible (see, e.g., Exod. 29:18, 25), the Lord is portrayed as smelling the "pleasing aroma" of Noah's offering (Gen. **8:21**). This is a beautiful way of expressing the delight that God takes in his children when they worship him "in spirit and truth" (John 4:23). The image of an aroma has many practical applications, as when Paul said that "Christ loved us and gave himself up for us as a fragrant offering and sacrifice to God" (Eph. 5:2) or that gifts sent to him by the Christians at Philippi "are a fragrant offering, an acceptable sacrifice, pleasing to God" (Phil. 4:18). Of course, it can be a double-edged image as well, since believers, who are "the aroma of Christ," are at one and the same time "the fragrance of life" to those who are being saved and "the smell of death" to those who are perishing (2 Cor. 2:15–16).

The new promise solemnized by Noah's offering and symbolized by the Lord's response is that God will never again curse the ground or destroy all living creatures because of man (Gen. **8:21**). He had sent the great flood because of the evil inclinations of the thoughts of men's hearts (6:5), but he will never do so again, "even though every inclination of (man's) heart is evil from childhood" (**8:21**). In an unforgettable way God had taught his people the lesson that sin inevitably brings judgment. No useful purpose would have been served by a divine decision to destroy mankind every few generations.

Therefore God promised that the normal cycles and processes of nature would continue unhindered "as long as the earth endures" (**8:22**). The functions of time and season, mandated by

God from the very beginning (1:14), would not be interrupted again until the end of history. The Lord's "covenant with day and night and the fixed laws of heaven and earth" (Jer. 33:25) would never cease. Like God's other universal promises, this one is also to us and to our children.

New Commands (9:1–7)

The divine judgment represented by the flood resulted in death for all mankind—except for the eight people in the ark. After the flood, however, "God blessed Noah and his sons" (**9:1**) by giving them three commands, either direct or implied, and all three had to do with life.[1]

1. *Life will be propagated* (**9:1, 7**). The command to fill the earth that was given to man at the time of creation (1:28) is now repeated twice, word for word: "Be fruitful and increase in number." It begins and ends the series of commands, as if to emphasize the importance of multiplying the members of the human race in the shortest possible time.

Although the main purpose of the divine command was doubtless to populate the earth and give mankind the power to rule over it (see **9:2**), large families in ancient times were not only a sign of God's favor but were also an economic necessity. In this largely agrarian culture, parents enlisted their children at an early age to assist them in the numerous daily chores. The same situation obtains today in much of the Middle East.

The words of the psalmist, then, reflect practical reality as well as spiritual blessing: "Sons are a heritage from the LORD, children a reward from him. Like arrows in the hands of a warrior are sons born in one's youth. Blessed is the man whose quiver is full of them" (Ps. 127:3–5).

2. *Life will be sustained* (**9:2–4**). Man would rule over the entire animal kingdom, which would be given into his hands. One of the uses to which various animals would be put would be to serve as food for mankind. It would seem that until the time of the flood both men and animals were vegetarians (1:29–30). Now, however, animal meat would supplement man's diet (**9:3**).

Later in Israel's history a distinction would be made between

1. G. Vos, *Biblical Theology* (Grand Rapids: Eerdmans, 1948), 64.

clean and unclean animals, the former alone being considered ritually acceptable for human consumption (Lev. 11). During this earlier period, however, Noah and his sons were given only one restriction: "You must not eat meat that has its lifeblood still in it" (Gen. **9:4**). Since "the life of every creature is its blood" (Lev. 17:14 stresses this principle by stating it twice), severe penalties are inflicted on all who eat meat that still has its blood in it (Lev. 17:10, 14).

Blood is supremely important for another reason as well: "It is the blood that makes atonement for one's life" (Lev. 17:11). Although "it is impossible for the blood of bulls and goats to take away sins" (Heb. 10:4) in the ultimate sense, it is equally true that "without the shedding of blood there is no forgiveness" (Heb. 9:22). When Jesus died on the cross for us, he shed his lifeblood so that we might have life. In God's perfect plan, Christ's blood poured out in death was the only possible price that could be paid for our salvation, because "it is the blood that makes atonement for one's life."

3. *Life will be protected* (**9:5–6**). Man and beast alike would be held accountable for the lives of any human beings they killed. This principle would later be formalized in the law of Moses (see Exod. 20:13; 21:12, 28–29).

God's command in Genesis **9:6** gives man not only the right but also the responsibility to put murderers to death.[2] The reason is clear: God has made man in his own image, and therefore the murderer, in taking the life of a man, displays contempt for God as well. This principle has important implications for the function of the state in the area of capital punishment. Civil government, as instituted by God, involves the power of life and death. It is not the mindless blood revenge of a murdered man's relatives but the orderly processes of civil law that should be the deciding factor in capital cases (Num. 35:6–30). In this respect, government is God's gracious provision for the preservation of human life in a fallen world (Rom. 13:1–5; 1 Tim. 2:1–3; 1 Pet. 2:13–17).

---

2. Genesis 9:6 is not universally hailed as sanctioning capital punishment, however. For arguments pro and con with respect to this issue, see the treatments by C. F. H. Henry and M. A. Reid in *The Genesis Debate*, ed. R. Youngblood (Grand Rapids: Baker, 1991), 230–50.

A New Relationship (9:8–17)

Life and the promise of its continued preservation is also the theme of Genesis **9:8–17**. The covenant that God had earlier said he would establish with Noah (6:18) is now described in detail. As is the case with every other covenant in the Bible, God's covenant after the flood is "with" his creatures (6:18; **9:9, 10, 11**), "between" himself and his creatures (**9:12, 13, 15, 16, 17**). A covenant is an agreement that stresses relationship, and "with" and "between" are the prepositions of relationship in the Noahic covenant, the first leading logically and inevitably to the second. God establishes his covenant "with" his creatures, and it is then defined as a covenant "between" him and them—a covenant that he binds himself to honor.

He establishes it, and it is his from the outset. He initiates it and places no limitations on it; it is both unilateral and unconditional. Its provisions can be summed up in a single sentence: "Never again will all life be cut off by the waters of a flood" (**9:11**).

The "never again" (see also **9:15**) means that the covenant is in force in perpetuity, "for all generations to come" (**9:12**). It is, in short, "everlasting" (**9:16**). God, "who does not change like shifting shadows" (James 1:17), pledges himself never again to destroy all life by means of a flood. Though we may be faithless, he remains faithful (2 Tim. 2:13).

As a visible sign and seal of the provisions of his covenant with Noah, God invested the rainbow with new significance. From that time on, whenever it appeared in the clouds it would serve as a reminder of God's covenant with all his creatures (Gen. **9:12–17**). Just as circumcision would later become the sign of the Abrahamic covenant (17:11), and just as the Sabbath would become the sign of the Sinaitic covenant (Exod. 31:16–17), so also the rainbow is the sign of the Noahic covenant for all time. And just as circumcision and the Sabbath were in existence long before the institution of the covenants they came to signify, so also the rainbow almost certainly did not make its first appearance in the days of Noah. Scientists tell us that there is clear evidence of rainfall long before the time of Noah's flood (no matter how early we date it). But the rainbow was invested with new meaning in Genesis 9, and the believer who understands this fact should never be able to look at rainbows in quite the same way again. For others it may simply be a beautiful natural phenomenon, but for us it is also a perpetual reminder of God's covenant promise to Noah and his family and all the animals: Floodwaters will never again destroy all life. The Lord's bow, hung in the clouds and pointing away from earth, will never again be used as a weapon against his creatures.

A New Temptation (9:18–23)

After a brief transitional paragraph we read the sordid account of how even a righteous man like Noah could fall into sin. Like his father Lamech (5:19), Noah was a farmer, a "man of the soil" (**9:20**). Whether he "proceeded to plant a vineyard" or "was the first to plant a vineyard" (either translation is possible), the result was the same: He drank some of its wine and "became drunk" (**9:21**).

No serious student of Scripture can fail to be impressed by the fact that this first mention of wine in the Bible immediately points out its potentially devastating effects. Christians may differ as to whether the Scriptures teach temperance in the sense of abstinence or of moderation, but all must ultimately agree with the warning voiced by Solomon: "Wine is a mocker and beer a brawler; whoever is led astray by them is not wise" (Prov. 20:1). Since drunkenness often induces people to lower their defenses, they can readily succumb to the basest forms of immorality, including incest (Gen. 19:30–35).

In Noah's case the situation initially seems innocent enough—he was simply lying "uncovered inside his tent" (**9:21**). Although nakedness was not a cause for shame prior to the fall (2:25), afterward it was looked at quite differently (3:7, 10–11, 21). Ham, Noah's youngest and perhaps brash and immature son (**9:24**), "saw his father's nakedness and told his two brothers outside" (**9:22**). We have no way of knowing what Ham said to his brothers, but we are left with the impression that it involved mocking of some sort. Shem and Japheth, being older and more mature, were determined not to bring further disgrace on their father. So they covered his nakedness with a garment and did not look at him.

A Final Word (9:24–29)

Noah eventually awoke from his drunken stupor and discovered what Ham had done. He then uttered a prophecy that was to have far-reaching consequences for centuries to come.

The prophecy focused on Canaan, who was Ham's son (**9:18, 22**). Children are often punished for the sins of their fathers (Exod. 20:5), and Canaan was no exception. His special curse was that he would be the lowest of slaves to his brothers, and that fact is stated no less than three times in three verses (Gen. **9:25–27**).

We observe immediately that Noah's prophecy cannot be used to justify the enslavement of blacks by whites[3] (such an interpretation was quite common in the nineteenth century, and it is still found here and there even today). As far as we know, Noah's three sons were all Caucasian. Even though some have argued that Ham was the progenitor (ultimately) of the black race, Noah did not curse Ham but Canaan—and the Canaanites were definitely Caucasian. Historically, the Canaanites were conquered and subdued by various peoples, including the Israelites under Joshua (see, e.g., Josh. 9:22–23). This is doubtless the main intent of Noah's prophecy.

Genesis 9 ends with a reminder that Noah was an outstanding member of the Genesis 5 genealogy. Like his forebears in that chapter, he lived to a very advanced age. Like Enoch, he had "walked with God" (5:21, 23; 6:9) earlier in his life. If Noah had not fallen into sin after the flood, perhaps God would have taken him away as he did Enoch (5:24). But in Noah's case that was not to be. Like his other ancestors in Genesis 5, Noah died (**9:29**).

3. C. T. Francisco, "The Curse on Canaan," in *Christianity Today*, April 24, 1964, 8–10.

12

The Spread of the Nations (10:1–11:26)

THE CONFUSION OF TONGUES (11:1–9)

THE DIFFUSION OF NATIONS (10:1–32)

THE FIRST SEMITIC GENEALOGY (11:10–26)

As Genesis 10 begins, Noah is dead but his sons are very much alive. The story of their role in fulfilling the divine command to "be fruitful and increase in number" (9:1, 7) concludes the primeval history of 1:1–11:26. It is divided into two main sections: "the account of Shem, Ham and Japheth, Noah's sons" (10:1–11:9), and "the account of Shem" (11:10–26). The first section includes the story of the tower of Babel, a flashback narrative that gives us the main reason for the spread of the nations described in Genesis 10. Since 11:1–9 (the Babel account) is chronologically prior to 10:1–32, I will treat it first.

The Confusion of Tongues (11:1–9)

The story of the tower of Babel displays one of the finest examples of inverted or hourglass structure to be found anywhere in literature.[1] **11:1–2** parallels **11:8–9**; both are narrative passages, and both emphasize the fact that at one time the whole world had only one language. **11:3–4** matches **11:6–7**; both consist totally of direct discourse, both highlight the phrase "Come, let us," and when taken together as a single unit they begin and end with the phrase "each other." **11:1–4** deals totally with what men did, and **11:6–9** deals totally with what God did in response. **11:5** is the narrow aperture of the hourglass that joins the upper and lower compartments. To change the image, just as 8:1 is the hinge of the flood story (see chapter nine), so **11:5** is the hinge of the Babel account: "But the LORD came down to see the city and the tower that the men were building." Before that verse there was only human activity, and after it there was only divine activity. As always, God had the final word.

As might be expected, the survivors of the great flood spoke only one language.[2] Their descendants eventually moved to Shinar (an ancient name for Babylonia) and settled there **(11:2)**. They decided to build a city and a tower in order to make a name for themselves as well as to demonstrate their sense of unity. If they had been living in Canaan they would have used stone and mortar as building materials, but since they were in Babylonia they used brick and tar **(11:3)**. There was very little stone available for use in building in ancient Mesopotamia, as the brick structures routinely excavated by archaeologists in that part of the world so vividly illustrate.

The tower built on the site was doubtless of a particular type known technically as a *ziggurat*. Square at the base, its sloping, stepped sides culminated in a small shrine at the top. The builders of the ziggurats often painted such shrines with blue enamel in order to make them blend in with the celestial home of one or more of their gods. They believed that a deity would live temporarily in the shrine when he came down to meet with his people. The worshiper would climb the outside staircase of the ziggurat all the way to the top in the hope that his god would condescend to meet with him in the little chapel there.

1. I. M. Kikawada, "The Shape of Genesis 11:1–9," in *Rhetorical Criticism: Essays In Honor of James Muilenburg*, ed. J. J. Jackson and M. Kessler (Pittsburgh: The Pickwick Press, 1974), 18–32.

2. Although this idea is often ridiculed, the theory of one original language for the entire world at a much earlier time is gaining respectability in the scientific community; see, e.g., W. F. Allman in *U.S. News & World Report*, November 5, 1990, 60–70.

The story of Jacob's dream in 28:12 refers to "a stairway resting on the earth, with its top reaching to heaven." Similarly, Genesis 11 speaks of "a tower that reaches to the heavens" (**11:4**). Other Mesopotamian temple towers had comparable names, indicating that they were intended as staircases from earth to heaven. The one at Asshur was called "The House of the Mountain of the Universe," Borsippa's tower was called "The House of the Seven Guides of Heaven and Earth," and Larsa's people knew theirs as "The House of the Link Between Heaven and Earth." The tower at Babel was referred to by the Babylonians themselves as "The House of the Foundation-Platform of Heaven and Earth." Partial restoration of the city of Babylon and the reconstruction of the tower there were topics discussed some time ago by the Iraqi government and Japan's Kyoto University.[3] Although work on the project is in progress, completion (especially of the tower) remains many years in the future.

The original tower of Babel was a monument not to the one true God but to egotistical mankind: "Let *us* build *ourselves* a city, . . . so that *we* may make a name for *ourselves*" (**11:4**). Hardly the "cathedral of antiquity," as one author describes it,[4] the tower represented a prideful human attempt to storm the bastions of heaven and force the gods to bend to the will of men. And so the Lord himself came down and effectively halted the construction project by confusing the language of the builders, making it impossible for them to communicate with each other.

The Akkadian word transcribed as "Babel" in **11:9** means literally "gateway to a god"—an apt description of a ziggurat intended to connect heaven and earth. (Jacob's ziggurat was similarly called "the gate of heaven"; see 28:17.) But the word "Babel" sounds enough like the Hebrew word *bālal* (pronounced bah-LAHL), "confused," to provide an opportunity for an appropriate pun by the writer. To this day, a "babel of voices" means a confusion of cries or other vocal sounds. Though originally built to bring God and man into joyful communion with each other (a feat successfully accomplished in Jacob's dream; see 28:15–16), the tower of Babel ended in confusion and scattering. Such is the inevitable fate of all such man-made schemes.

---

3. *Christianity Today*, February 22, 1980, 53.
4. A. Parrot, *The Tower of Babel* (New York: Philosophical Library, 1955), 68.

At the Constitutional Convention of 1787, Benjamin Franklin quoted the King James version of Psalm 127:1: "Except the LORD build the house, they labor in vain that build it." He then continued: "I firmly believe this, and I also believe that without his concurring aid we shall succeed in this political building no better than the builders of Babel."[5]

Babel was reversed on the day of Pentecost, when the coming of the Holy Spirit restored linguistic harmony. Galileans were suddenly heard speaking in a dozen different languages, "declaring the wonders of God" (Acts 2:11). Bewilderment always gives way to understanding when we genuinely submit ourselves to the perfect will of a loving God.

The Diffusion of Nations (10:1–32)

Genesis 10 is often called the Table of Nations, but it could just as easily and correctly be called a map of the ancient Near East. In form it is a modified genealogy, and it uses the words "son" and "father" even more flexibly than do the genealogies of Genesis 4, 5, and 11. "Son" in Genesis 10 may mean "descendant," "successor," or "nation," and "father" may mean "ancestor," "predecessor," or "founder." In content Genesis 10 describes the end results of the scattering of mankind caused by the debacle at the tower of Babel (11:1–9).

The nations of the then-known world are divided into three broad categories, corresponding to the three sons of Noah. The Japhethites are listed first, possibly because Japheth was the oldest of the sons (**10:21**). The Shemites (later called Semites) are listed last because they were to be the progenitors of the chosen people. A separate genealogy is devoted to them in 11:10–26. The Hamites are listed second even though Ham was the youngest of Noah's three sons (9:24).

When we add up the nations that came from Shem, Ham, and Japheth, we discover an intriguing fact: the total number is seventy (fourteen from Japheth, thirty from Ham, and twenty-six from Shem). This is a further example of the sevens and tens and seventies that we have observed so often up to this point in the text of Genesis. But it is more. It seems to anticipate the number of the members of Jacob's family in Egypt, who were "seventy in all" (46:27; Exod. 1:5). The seventy nations of Genesis 10 are con-

---

5. *Decision*, June 1976, 9.

veniently summarized in 1 Chronicles 1:5–23, which lists them in exactly the same order.

By and large, the Japhethites lived far to the north and east of Canaan and spoke Indo-European languages. The people of Gomer and the associated nations of Ashkenaz, Riphath and Togarmah (Gen. **10:3**) lived around the Black Sea. The name Gomer is reflected in the later Cimmerians, while Ashkenaz became the Scythians of later times. Magog was located north of the Caspian Sea, and the southern shores of the Black Sea provided a home for Tubal and Meshech (not related to modern Tobolsk and Moscow in the Soviet Union, as is sometimes claimed). These three nations are all mentioned in Assyrian inscriptions of a later period as well as in Ezekiel 38:2. Tiras is probably Thrace, located west of the Black Sea. Madai, the Medes, lived south of the Caspian Sea in the later history of the area.

Associated with Javan (Ionia, the southern part of Greece) were "Elishah, Tarshish, the Kittim and the Rodanim" (Gen. **10:4**). Elishah may refer to Sicily and southern Italy, or perhaps to Alashia, an ancient name for Crete. Tarshish is probably southern Spain, while the Kittim lived on the island of Cyprus. The word Rodanim is perhaps reflected in Rhodes, one of the Greek isles.

Genesis **10:5** (see also **10:20, 31**) indicates that the criteria for distinguishing the various groups from each other were rather complex. "Territories" is a geographic term, "clans" an ethnic term, "nations" a political term, and "language" a linguistic term. This may explain why Canaan, for example, is listed under Ham (which often exerted strong political influence over Canaan in ancient times; see also 9:18, 22, 24–27) instead of under Shem (to whom Canaan is more closely related linguistically). It may also explain why some nations are listed twice: Sheba appears under both Ham (**10:7**) and Shem (**10:28**), as does Havilah (**10:7, 29**). Of course, it is also possible that there was more than one Sheba and more than one Havilah.

The Hamites migrated primarily to northeast Africa, the eastern Mediterranean region, and southern Arabia. Cush in **10:6–7** is the territory of the upper Nile south of Egypt. Related nations in southern Arabia were Seba, Havilah, Sabtah, Raamah, Sabteca, Sheba, and Dedan. Raamah, Sheba, and Dedan (**10:7**) reappear in Ezekiel 27:20–22, while Sheba and Dedan (or their namesakes) occur as the names of two of Abraham's grandsons in Genesis 25:3. Sabtah and Sabteca are perhaps reflected in the names of two later Egyptian pharaohs.

A second Cush (**10:8**) was located in central and southern Mesopotamia. Its name may be related to that of the later Kassite kingdom. Nimrod is perhaps the Hebrew name of Sargon the Great of the city of Akkad. A mighty warrior and hunter, he is obviously intended as an individual historical figure in this passage. Among other cities under his rule were Babylon, Erech (called Uruk by the ancient Babylonians), Nineveh, and Calah.

"Mizraim" is the Hebrew word for Egypt. It literally means "two Egypts" and referred historically to Upper Egypt (i.e., southern Egypt) and Lower Egypt (i.e., northern Egypt). Middle Egypt was inhabited by the Pathrusites (**10:14**). Other nations frequently under the control of Egypt were the Ludites (possibly the Lydians in Asia Minor, although this is not certain), the Lehabites (possibly the inhabitants of the Lybian desert), the Casluhites (ancestors of certain Philistine groups), and the Caphtorites (Caphtor, another name for Crete, was the original homeland of other Philistine groups; see Jer. 47:4; Amos 9:7).

Canaan (later called "Palestine" after the Philistines) included a number of well-known tribes and nations. Among them were the people of Sidon, the port city on the northern coast. The Hittites eventually became one of the most powerful nations in the entire region, mainly because of their monopoly in the smelting of iron (see chapter six). The Jebusites were the original inhabitants of Jerusalem, while the Amorites (the name comes from a Babylonian word meaning "westerner") lived in other parts of the hill country. Most of the lesser-known groups (Gen. **10:16–18**) lived in small city-states. Especially interesting is the almost incidental mention of Sodom, Gomorrah, Admah, and Zeboiim (**10:19**), four of the five cities of the plain referred to in 14:2, 8.

Although Eber occurs as a name far down the list among the Shemites (Semites), his importance is called to our attention early in the passage: "Shem was the ancestor of all the sons of Eber" (**10:21**). Since "Eber" is related to the word "Hebrew," scholars generally agree that he was the ancestor of the Hebrew people. Amazingly enough, his name has also turned up in the Ebla tablets (recently excavated in northern Syria and dating to about 2400 B.C.) in the form "Ebrium," a king who ruled over Ebla for 28 years.[6] One can only speculate, however, as to whether King Ebrium and the biblical Eber are one and the same person.

Most of the nations associated with Shem are well known indeed. The Elamites lived between the Medes to the north and the Persian Gulf to the south. Asshur (Assyria) was northern Mesopotamia, while Arphaxad (perhaps Chaldea) was probably southern Mesopotamia. Lud is almost surely the Lydians of Asia Minor, and the Arameans lived in the land known today as Syria.

One of Eber's sons was named Peleg (a Hebrew word meaning "division"), "because in his time the earth was divided" (**10:25**). Various geological phenomena of a catastrophic nature have been read into this verse, but the language is so general that we cannot be sure what kind of division (physical? geographical? spiritual? social?) is intended.

Joktan lived in southern Arabia, and three of the thirteen nations associated with him are of special interest. "Hazarmaveth" survives in the term Hadhramautic, one of the most important dialects of the South Arabic language. Sheba is famous as the homeland of the queen who visited Solomon in the tenth century B.C. (1 Kings 10:1–13). Ophir was the source of much of the gold in which Solomon traded (9:28; 10:11).

Genesis 10 is a remarkable chapter indeed. Scholars continue to be fascinated by the wealth of geographic knowledge it contains, and Bible students of all ages long to visit its faraway places and thrill to its strange-sounding names. A true map of oriental lands, it is without peer for its time. It reminds us that mankind, however fragmented and alienated today, has a common origin in the ancient past.

The First Semitic Genealogy (11:10–26)

"The account of Shem," however brief, is the fifth main section of the primeval history in Genesis (see the introduction). Like the Genesis 5 genealogy, Genesis 11:10–26 consists of exactly ten names. As the Genesis 5 genealogy begins and ends with a famous name (Adam, Noah), so the Genesis 11 genealogy does the same (Shem, Abram). As the ten names of the Genesis 5

6. *National Geographic*, December 1978, 755.

genealogy are conveniently summarized in 1 Chronicles 1:1–3, so the ten names in the Genesis 11 list are summarized in 1 Chronicles 1:24–27. Half of the names in the Genesis 11 genealogy appear in the same order in 10:21–25, where additional details are also given.

Two major differences between the genealogies in Genesis 5 and 11 are that the former gives total figures for the ages of the men at death and concludes nearly every paragraph with the phrase "and then he died." The main purpose of the Genesis 11 genealogy seems to be to provide the briefest possible transition between Shem and Abram. Thus the author omitted all but the most important facts.

The first Semitic genealogy ends by telling us that Terah "became the father of Abram, Nahor and Haran" (**11:26**), the latter dying while his father was still alive (**11:28**). In commenting on Abraham's pagan background, Joshua 24:2 states that Israel's forefathers, "including Terah the father of Abraham and Nahor, . . . worshiped other gods." From this idolatrous environment God called Abraham (Gen. 12:1)—a call that Abraham obeyed without hesitation (12:4).

But that story, a story of yet another new and exciting venture of faith, a story known as the patriarchal history, begins where the primeval history ends.

Part 3

Abraham

13

The Beginning of God's Covenant People

THE BIBLICAL SOURCE MATERIAL

THE HISTORICAL SETTING

THE DATES

THE PATRIARCHS THEMSELVES

ARCHAEOLOGICAL INSIGHTS

Permit me to start the second half of this commentary by asking a basic, fundamental question: Who was the founder of "the faith that was once for all entrusted to the saints" (Jude 3)?

Some might answer, "The apostle Paul, of course. After all, he took the teachings of Jesus and combined them into a comprehensive theology that tells us how we can be reconciled to God and properly related to each other."

But another might say, "No, actually we have to go back to Jesus himself as the founder of our faith. In fact, Hebrews 12:2 calls him the pioneer, the 'author,' of our faith, so that would seem to settle the matter."

Still another might argue, "Wait a minute. Jesus himself would have been the first to admit that much of what he said was not new. Many of the things Jesus taught are found in the OT, the only Bible he knew. One of his favorite books was Deuteronomy, and he quoted often from its pages (e.g., Matt. 4:4–10). He placed Moses' writings on a par with his own words (John 5:46–47), so we should probably trace the origins of our faith all the way back to Moses."

Now each of these three answers is a good one, and each contains a certain measure of truth in it. But when all is said and done, we would do well to observe that the Bible itself traces our faith back to a period earlier than that of Paul or of Jesus or even of Moses: It traces our faith to the period of the patriarchs, the period of Abraham, Isaac and Jacob. When the Hebrew people were at their spiritual best, they placed their complete faith and trust in "the LORD, the God of their fathers—the God of Abraham, the God of Isaac and the God of Jacob" (Exod. 4:5). "The LORD" was a favorite name of the God of the patriarchs, who often enjoyed intimate spiritual fellowship with him.

The unexcelled leader of the patriarchs was Abraham, who became the prototype of the man of faith, "the father of all who believe" (Rom. 4:11). We who are Christians "are of the faith of Abraham" (4:16); in effect, we share his faith (Gal. 3:29).

Needless to say, people worshiped the one true God long before Abraham's time (Gen. 4:26). Nevertheless, it is true that the basic covenant promises of God were first given to Abraham, the spiritual father of the Hebrew people. It was through Abraham's Hebrew descendants that God's promises were transmitted to the nation of Jacob (later renamed Israel), the tribe of Judah, and the family of David, from which eventually came our Lord Jesus Christ, the supreme object of our faith. Significantly, the NT takes us back to Abraham in its very first verse: "A record of the genealogy of Jesus Christ the son of David, the son of Abraham" (Matt. 1:1).

The Biblical Source Material

As we observed earlier (see the introduction), the Book of Genesis is divided into two unequal halves: 1:1–11:26 and 11:27–50:26. Each half has five sections, and each section is introduced by the phrase "This is the account of . . ." or its equivalent. The second half of Genesis, sometimes called the "patriarchal history," exhibits the characteristic phrase at the beginning of the stories dealing mainly with Abraham (11:27–25:11), Ishmael (25:12–18), Jacob (25:19–35:29), Esau (36:1–37:1), and Joseph (37:2–50:26). Terah (Abraham's father), Ishmael, Esau, and even Isaac do not receive much attention in the narrative. The writer is concerned primarily with the careers of Abraham, Jacob, and Joseph, and so he gives each of them ten or more chapters. In other words, more than sixty percent of the Book of Genesis deals with the lives of these three men. I therefore wish to concentrate most of our attention on their careers in order to observe the law of proportion, usually a helpful approach when studying Scripture.

The Historical Setting

Were the patriarchs merely wandering shepherds, primitive nomads in a world of very little culture and sophistication? That is what people used to think. But research carried on over the past 150 years or so has led many historians to conclude that the patriarchs lived at some time during what archaeologists call the Middle Bronze Age (ca. 2100–ca. 1550 B.C.), a period of high cultural achievement.

Mesopotamia

During the later years of the patriarchal age, the First Dynasty of Babylon (ca. 1894–ca. 1595 B.C.)[1] held sway in Mesopotamia. Roughly Syria and Iraq today, "Mesopotamia" was the name given to the territory by ancient Greek writers because it was the land "between the (Euphrates and Tigris) rivers."

In many respects, the First Dynasty of Babylon represented a kind of "golden age" in the history of Mesopotamia. It was a time that later generations looked back to fondly as the "good old days" when they thought about their past history. It included the reign of the famous King Hammurapi (ca. 1792–ca. 1750 B.C.), whose code of laws is justly the most enduring monument to his greatness. So powerful and so cultured was Mesopotamia during this period that its language, Akkadian, became the lingua franca, the language of diplomacy, throughout the then-known civilized world.

---

1. For the most part, the dates given in this chapter are those used by W. W. Hallo and W. K. Simpson in their brief history of ancient Mesopotamia and Egypt entitled *The Ancient Near East: A History* (New York: Harcourt Brace Jovanovich, Inc., 1971).

Mesopotamian society became unified and stabilized; science and literature assumed characteristic forms that would last for centuries; religion became canonized and took on new prominence.

Such was the milieu in which the later patriarchs found themselves.

Egypt

Genesis 37–50 portrays the migration of Jacob and Joseph to Egypt and their settlement in that land. There people were also enjoying a kind of "golden age" during part of the patriarchal period. The Egyptian Middle Kingdom era (Dynasty XII), which lasted from 1991 to 1786 B.C., represents in many respects the highwater mark of ancient Egypt's art and literature, of her commercial and political power. People looked back fondly to the Middle Kingdom period as the "good old days" in their past history. Egypt instituted and exploited a flourishing copper and turquoise mining industry deep in the interior of the Sinai peninsula, and the Egyptians were able to exert control over much of Syria and Canaan. They erected magnificent buildings, fashioned exquisite jewelry, and wrote literary epics of lasting impact. Among the greatest of these was the *Tale of Sinuhe*, a story describing the voluntary exile of an Egyptian nobleman and incidentally demonstrating the ease of travel and communication between Egypt and Canaan at the time of the Middle Kingdom.

During this period Egyptian science also reached its highwater mark. So careful were the observations made by Egypt's astronomers and so exact was their record-keeping that 1991 B.C., the first year of Dynasty XII, is also the earliest precise year-date in human history. And Egypt's best-known and most enduring monuments, the pyramids in the Gizeh group near modern Cairo, had already been built 500 years before the Twelfth Dynasty began.

Such was the storied civilization that may have struck awe in the hearts and minds of the patriarchs who visited Egypt when famine ravaged their own lands.

The Hittites

Sprinkled throughout Genesis 11:27–50:26 are numerous references to the Hittites, the sons of Heth (10:15). Now recognized as the third great Near Eastern empire of ancient times, the Hittites flourished in Asia Minor (modern Turkey) from about 1800 to about 1200 B.C. While the word "Hittite" in the OT refers to several different cultures (see Gen. 23 and 2 Sam. 11 for two of them), the early Hittites were instrumental in importing the horse into Asia Minor on a large scale. They also used chariots from the beginning of their history, and until the onset of the Iron Age (ca. 1200 B.C.) they had a virtual monopoly on iron-smelting techniques, which made them fearsome warriors.

Ancestors or predecessors of the Hittites of historical fame doubtless made their own impact on the patriarchs, as Genesis 23 illustrates.

The Dates

A promising start in attempting to date the patriarchs might be to tabulate the figures representing the ages of the patriarchs at various key occasions in their lives:

Birth of Isaac = 100 years Abraham (21:5)
Birth of Jacob = 60 years Isaac (25:26)
Jacob's migration to Egypt = 130 years Jacob (47:9)
Israel's sojourn in Egypt = 430 years (Exod. 12:40)

Adding the four figures together yields 720 years as the period between Abraham's birth and the time of the exodus. This schema assumes that Israel's sojourn is to be calculated from the date of Jacob's migration to Egypt. If, however, we assume Joseph's descent into Egypt instead, the figure would be reduced by twenty years or so (see Gen. 37:2; 41:46, 53; 42:1–2; 46:5–6; 47:9). In any case, the biblical figures indicate a period of approximately 700 years between Abraham's birth and the exodus. If the date of the exodus is ca. 1445 B.C., the patriarchal period would then have begun with the birth of Abraham in 2150 B.C. or so—just about at the end of the Akkadian period at Ur of the Chaldeans. Abraham would have lived for many of his adult years during the glorious Ur III period of his hometown's history.

The above paragraph assumes a literal understanding of the numerical data in Genesis 12–50. As I have suggested throughout this commentary, however, we should sometimes understand numbers figuratively in the Book of Genesis. The following table, which represents one way of interpreting the ages at death of

Abraham (25:7), Isaac (35:28), Jacob (47:28), and Joseph (50:26) respectively, demonstrates that we should keep such an interpretive option available:

$$175 = 7 \times 5^2$$
$$180 = 5 \times 6^2$$
$$147 = 3 \times 7^2$$
$$110 = 1 \times 5^2 + 6^2 + 7^2$$

To assume that the symmetry and beauty of the above calculations, which begin and end with the symbolic number seven, are merely coincidental is difficult at best.[2] We observe also that 110 years—Joseph's age at the time of his death—was considered by the Egyptians to be the ideal life span and was regularly used by Egyptian scribes to record the age at death of many pharaohs and other high officials (even when we know from other reports that the person in question actually died at a much younger age).[3] It is quite possible, then, that Joseph's recorded death age in Genesis 50:26 should be understood qualitatively rather than quantitatively.

Even if the ages of the patriarchs in Genesis 12–50 are in fact figurative, it is not necessary to conclude that they have no chronological value. The author obviously intends to describe the passage of long periods of time, even if only in a general way. The 700 years or so between Abram's birth and the exodus, although approximate in the nature of the case, are doubtless still to be understood as placing the beginning of the patriarchal period near the end of the third millennium B.C. Despite recent attempts by a few scholars to lower the patriarchal dates by several centuries—even into the first millennium[4]—the archaeological data currently at our disposal continue to favor the traditional earlier dating.[5]

2. For additional details and supporting bibliography, see D. L. Christensen, "Josephus and the Twenty-Two Book Canon of Sacred Scripture," *Journal of the Evangelical Theological Society* 29 (1986): 45–46.

3. See N. M. Sarna, *Understanding Genesis* (New York: Schocken, 1970), 226.

4. T. L. Thompson, *The Historicity of the Patriarchal Narratives: The Quest for the Historical Abraham* (Berlin: de Gruyter, 1974), 315–26; J. Van Seters, *Abraham in History and Tradition* (New Haven: Yale University, 1975), 309–12.

5. A. R. Millard and D. J. Wiseman, eds., *Essays on the Patriarchal Narratives* (Leicester: Inter-Varsity, 1980); K. L. Barker, "The Antiquity and Historicity of the

The Patriarchs Themselves

Of course, there were more than three patriarchs. When we think of the patriarchs, however, we normally think only of Abraham, Isaac, and Jacob (as, e.g., in Exod. 4:5 or Matt. 8:11). In a passage like Acts 7:9, however, the term "patriarchs" is used in a wider sense, referring to the brothers of Joseph. Zion National Park in the state of Utah boasts three impressively high rock formations known as "The Three Patriarchs," named individually after Abraham, Isaac, and Jacob, again demonstrating the narrower use of the term. The names of some of the biblical patriarchs have been found in non-biblical documents contemporary with the patriarchal period. But more about this later.

What "Patriarch" Means

The word "patriarch" means "father who rules." It refers to the fact that in the culture of those times the father was the undisputed head of the family and the clan. At the risk of being called a male chauvinist, I would like to strongly affirm my support of that arrangement, which I believe to be thoroughly biblical (see esp. Eph. 5:21–6:4). Generally speaking, societies in which the father is the head of the home experience very little juvenile delinquency. This has been traditionally the case in countries as diverse as China and Italy.

This understanding of family relationships does not relieve the mother of her obligation to share in the difficult task of raising the children in the nurture and admonition of the Lord. It simply emphasizes the fact that the ultimate responsibility and burden for that task rest squarely on the shoulders of the father.

Their Original Homeland

One of my students proposed several years ago, only half seriously, that the story of Abraham's life could be entitled "From Ur to Eternity." Actually that is not a bad title, since the patriarchs originally came from the city of Ur of the Chaldeans in Mesopotamia.

We know that their forefathers worshiped other gods (Josh. 24:2) and were no doubt idolaters, since the patron deity of Ur was a moon god. Even though Abraham's father Terah had appar-

Patriarchal Narratives," in *A Tribute to Gleason Archer*, ed. W. C. Kaiser, Jr., and R. F. Youngblood (Chicago: Moody, 1986), 131–39.

ently intended to go directly to Canaan from Ur, he and his family stopped for a while in Haran (also a center of moon-god worship), where he died (Gen. 11:31–32). It has even been suggested that the name Terah is derived from a Semitic word meaning "moon."

God told Abraham to move on to Canaan, and that call of God, together with Abraham's obedient response of believing faith, are basic to biblical religion.

Their Occupations

How did Terah and his sons earn their living?

The late W. F. Albright developed the tantalizing idea that the patriarchs were basically donkey caravanners, that they owned herds of donkeys utilized to transport goods from one place to another.[6] They would have served the same purpose in ancient times that our modern trucking industry does now. If Albright's thesis is correct, the patriarchs would have been seminomads who confined their travels to the settled land and its fringes, the territory that James Breasted called the "Fertile Crescent," which stretched in an enormous arc from the Persian Gulf northwestward up the Tigris-Euphrates river valley to the Haran region and then southwestward into the heartland of Canaan. This would have made it easy for them to pull up stakes and leave Ur at almost any time. Also, the theory fits in well with the biblical narrative of the patriarchs.

The fact that the Book of Genesis represents them as herdsmen would then simply indicate what their occupation was between business trips. When they were not on the road with their donkey caravans, they were home on the range tending their flocks.

Their Customs

When we read the Genesis narrative, many of the patriarchal customs seem rather strange to us, and a few of them actually shock us. But we need to remember two basic facts in this connection. First, the customs that seem strange to us do so because they were eastern customs and did not develop from the thought patterns that are characteristic of us westerners. We must continually remind ourselves that the patriarchs lived thousands of years ago and thousands of miles from our western culture.

6. See conveniently W. F. Albright, *Yahweh and the Gods of Canaan* (Garden City, N.Y.: Doubleday, 1968), 64–73.

Second, the customs that shock us, although they were prevalent in the ancient Near East generally, are customs that were not condoned by God. When they were indulged in by the Hebrew people they invariably brought untold grief to them, as we shall see.

Archaeological Insights

Ancient artifacts, both inscriptional and noninscriptional, have cast such a flood of light on the ancient Near East that in some respects we know more about patriarchal Babylonian villages in Mesopotamia than we do about eighteenth-century American colonial villages. Inscriptional remains include hoards of ancient documents, written in Akkadian and other languages, giving us detailed descriptions of life in those early days.

The Mari Letters

Thousands of clay letters (or tablets) excavated by the French beginning in 1933 at the ancient Amorite city of Mari on the Euphrates River illustrate the freedom of travel that existed between various parts of the Amorite world in the eighteenth century B.C. From them we learn also that the personal names of the patriarchs were typical of those and earlier days. Names similar to those of Abraham, Jacob, Job, and others are found frequently in the letters.

Ur of the Chaldeans

Today Ur (modern Tell el-Muqayyar) is little more than a camel stop in the desert. A number of years ago, a visitor stayed overnight in the small hotel there and wrote these words in the guest register: "No wonder Abraham left Ur!" Under that phrase a later traveler wrote: "Even Job would have!"

But those negative evaluations of Ur do not take into account the British excavations conducted at the site of Ur from 1922 to 1934. Sir Leonard Woolley's expedition discovered, among other things, the royal death pit at Ur, gold jewelry, a gold helmet, a gold crown worn by the queen of the ancient city, and many other items reflecting the fabulous wealth of ancient Ur. In fact, Ur was at the height of its prosperity approximately when Abraham was living there. God did not call him to leave a dirty little town; he called him to leave a cultured and sophisticated city.

Soon after Ur's destruction by the Elamites in about 1950 B.C., a Sumerian lament was composed that reminds us somewhat of the biblical Lamentations that were written to mourn the destruction of Jerusalem at the hands of Nebuchadnezzar in 586 B.C.

Haran and Nahor

Haran was a flourishing city in the nineteenth and eighteenth centuries B.C. Ancient cuneiform sources mention it frequently. During the days of Hammurapi, an Amorite prince ruled over it. The word *har(r)āns* "crossroads" or "caravan" in Akkadian, giving some support to Albright's theory that the patriarchs were donkey caravanners.

As for the city of Nahor (mentioned in Gen. 24:10 as the home of Rebekah), the Mari letters (as well as later Assyrian records of the seventh century B.C.) refer to it as being located in the Haran district. Like Mari, Nahor was ruled by an Amorite prince in the eighteenth century B.C. It may well be that Abraham himself was an Amorite.

The Nuzi Tablets

These documents were discovered beginning in 1925 near Kirkuk on a branch of the Tigris River. Although dated in the 15th century B.C., they throw a great deal of light on patriarchal customs because customs generally linger on for generations in that part of the world. The people of Nuzi were basically non-Semitic Hurrians (the Horites of the Bible). Contract documents found at Nuzi illustrate, among other matters, the following: (1) the obligation of a wife to furnish her husband with sons, even through his cohabitation with a servant girl if necessary (see Gen. 16:2–4); (2) the importance and salability of the birthright (see 25:29–34); (3) the inheritance rights of an adopted slave when there are no sons in the family (see 15:1–4); (4) strictures against expelling a servant girl and her child (see 21:10–11); (5) the validity of the death-bed bequest (see 49:28–33).[7]

These are a few of the strange and shocking customs we mentioned earlier. As we proceed through the Genesis stories of the patriarchs, we will make further comments about their significance.

7. See the useful summary by C. H. Gordon in *The Biblical Archaeologist Reader, 2*, ed. D. N. Freedman and E. F. Campbell, Jr. (Garden City, N.Y.: Doubleday Anchor, 1964), 21–33.

Beni Hasan

Moving now from Mesopotamia to Egypt, we observe that a scene painted on the wall of a tomb at Beni Hasan there (the tomb is dated ca. 1890 B.C.) pictures thirty-seven Asiatics bringing gifts to an Egyptian nobleman. The painting is important because it shows what Asiatics (and thus Abraham and Sarah) looked like during the patriarchal period. The men wore knee-length skirts and sandals, while the women wore long dresses and shoes that covered the entire foot. Some of the travelers are portrayed as smiths and musicians, reminding us of Genesis 4:21–22. The gifts and other items are being carried on the backs of donkeys. We recall that Abraham made a trip down into Egypt during a time of famine in Canaan.

The 'Apirū

Ever since the discovery in 1887 at Tell el-Amarna in Middle Egypt of the now-famous Amarna letters, which mention bands of soldiers of fortune called ḥapirū (or, more precisely, 'apirū), attempts have been made to connect the term 'apiru (plural 'apirū) with the term "Hebrew" and to equate the invasion of Canaan under Joshua with the intermittent raids of the 'apirū during the fourteenth century B.C. While certain similarities between the two groups do exist, such attempts have met with limited success since certain basic differences are likewise apparent.

'Apirū are mentioned from the nineteenth to the twelfth centuries B.C. all the way from Egypt in the west to Mesopotamia in the east and in Egyptian, Canaanite, and Akkadian historical sources. The term is always applied to a population composed of diverse ethnic elements, having in common only an inferior social status. On the other hand, "Hebrew" is a clearly ethnic term denoting descent from Eber (Gen. 10:21, 24–25; 11:14–17; see chapter twelve). An earlier and broader term than "Israelite," "Hebrew" is generally used to distinguish Israelites from other peoples (see, e.g., 39:14, 17; 40:15; Exod. 2:6–7, 11, 13; 9:1; 1 Sam. 4:6, 9). As the father of the Hebrew people, Abram was the first person in the OT to be called a "Hebrew" (Gen. 14:13).

14

The Land of Abram
(11:27–14:24)

ABRAM'S CALL (11:27–12:3)

FROM HARAN TO CANAAN TO EGYPT TO CANAAN (12:4–20)

SETTLING DOWN (13:1–18)

THE BATTLE OF THE KINGS (14:1–24)

The real hero of the Book of Genesis is, of course, God himself, the God who acts in vigorous and marvelous ways on behalf of his people.

Humanly speaking, however, the hero of our story is Abram. (We must get used to calling him "Abram" until we reach Gen. 17:5, where he is renamed "Abraham.") He was the forefather of the other patriarchs, and the patriarchs were wanderers, whether donkey caravanners or shepherds or both.

The patriarchs as wanderers is a common biblical theme. Deuteronomy 26:5 begins a beautiful creedal statement that calls one of the patriarchs "a wandering Aramean." Psalm 105:12–15 is part of a poem that refers to the patriarchs as "strangers" who "wandered from nation to nation."

Because the patriarchs were wanderers in a foreign land, it is understandable that they would long for a land of their own. And because God is a loving God, it is understandable that he would promise to give it to them.

These early chapters of the patriarchal story in Genesis focus their attention on God's promise of a land to Abram and his descendants.

Abram's Call (11:27–12:3)

First of all, we receive a formal introduction to Abram's family. His father's name was Terah, he had two brothers named Nahor and Haran, and he had a nephew named Lot (**11:27**). His wife's name was Sarai, and we are served notice at the beginning of the story that Sarai was sterile, unable to bear children (**11:29–30**).

Terah decided to make a trip to Canaan and to take along Abram, Sarai, and Lot (**11:31**). Was it a business trip? Were the patriarchs fleeing from marauders, or from attackers who were planning to conquer Ur? We do not know why Terah made his decision, but whatever the reasons, God used that decision for his own redemptive purposes.

Halfway to Canaan they stopped at Haran (spelled differently, in Hebrew, from the name of Abraham's brother). Like Ur, Haran was another place where the moon god was worshiped. Since Terah was doubtless an idolater (Josh. 24:2), he probably felt comfortable living in Haran and apparently had neither the strength nor the will to continue the journey to Canaan. So there the family stayed until Terah died (Gen. **11:32**). And there also God confirmed his choice of Abram as a man who was to do his bidding.

Sometimes God issues a call to an individual more than once, as he did to Jeremiah (see Jer. 1:4–19; 15:19–21). This seems to have been the case also with Abram. According to Stephen's speech in Acts 7:2 God had already appeared to him "in Mesopotamia, before he lived in Haran." Now God was calling him once again (Gen. **12:1**). He was saying to him, in effect, "I want you to leave Ur, to leave Haran, to leave everything behind, and to follow me." And so, "By faith," that is exactly what Abram did: He "went, even though he did not know where he was going" (Heb. 11:8).

Genesis 20:7 tells us that Abram was a prophet. The word

"prophet" literally means a "called one," a person who has been called by God to do God's bidding. Working for God, doing God's will, is a "calling," a vocation, not a profession. We do not choose to work for him; rather, he chooses us to do his work—and it is always because of his grace, not because of any merit or ability of our own. Whenever we do his work in accord with his will, whether part-time or full-time, it is his idea and his choice, not ours.

The Lord granted to Abram the two gifts of land and people (three gifts, if blessing is counted as a separate category). Those twin (or triple) aspects of the Abrahamic call are divisible into seven promises: (1) land ("the land I will show you"); (2) descendants ("a great nation"); (3) blessedness ("I will bless you"); (4) fame ("I will make your name great"); (5) opportunity for service ("you will be a blessing"); (6) protection ("I will bless those who bless you, and whoever curses you I will curse"); and (7) universal influence ("all peoples on earth will be blessed through you").

A proper understanding of Abram's call is basic for a proper understanding of biblical religion generally. One or more elements of the call were repeated and reaffirmed to Abram in Genesis **12:7**; 15:5–21; 17:4–8; 18:18–19; 22:17–18; to Isaac in 26:2–4; to Jacob in 28:13–15; 35:11–12; 46:3; to Moses in Exodus 3:6–8; 6:2–8.

As Christians, we should be most interested in the seventh promise in Abram's call. (The final item in a biblical list is often the most memorable; see, e.g., 2 Sam. 23:29.) Abram's descendants are understood in both a physical and a spiritual sense in the NT. In Acts 3:25 Peter referred to the seventh promise in his great temple sermon and related it to his Jewish listeners— Abram's physical descendants (see Acts 3:12). In Galatians 3:8, however, Paul quoted the seventh promise and related it to his Gentile listeners, to Abram's spiritual descendants. If we are Gentile Christians, Paul said, then we are Abram's spiritual brothers and sisters; we share Abram's faith and heritage.

From Haran to Canaan to Egypt to Canaan (12:4–20)

The title of this brief section underscores for us the fact that the patriarchs were wanderers. Abram traveled a great distance in the space of just seventeen verses.

His response to God's call was both noteworthy and praise-worthy. Characterized by prompt obedience, Abram wasted no time. He didn't hesitate, he didn't beat around the bush; when God asked Abram to do something, he did it right away. This characteristic of obedient promptness followed him throughout his life (see Gen. 17:23; 21:14; and, supremely, 22:3).

So when the Lord told Abram to "go" (**12:1**), he simply packed his bags and "left" (**12:4**). At seventy-five years old he was starting out on a new venture ten years beyond modern retirement age. According to Genesis 25:7, however, he would live for yet another century. Since he would live to be 175 years old, at seventy-five he was still relatively young—and maybe that is the way he felt. His father Terah, after all, had died at the age of 205 (**11:32**).

How are we to understand these references to the longevity of the post-flood patriarchs? Did they really live to such advanced ages? Many different answers have been given to this question, but we will confine ourselves to those that seem most probable.

1. *The numbers are to be understood literally.* Perhaps people in those days lived at a slower pace; they did a hard day's work each day, got a good night's rest each night, escaped the high-powered tensions of modern life, and ate natural (unprocessed and therefore unpolluted) foods. Tribespeople in our own time who follow such a regimen often live unusually long lives. For example, people live well over 100 among the Hunzukuts of north central Pakistan[1] and in certain sections of the Soviet Union.

    Shirali Muslimov of the village of Barzavu in the Soviet Caucasus is said to have died on September 2, 1973, at the age of 168.[2] Many researchers doubt this and similar reports, however, since they are based on hearsay rather than any kind of documentary evidence: "No man or woman with a verifiable birth record is known to have lived longer than 113 years."[3] But such doubts should not necessarily cause us to deny the possibility of genuinely unusual longevity among the patriarchs, since unknown

---

1. C. Percy in *Parade*, February 17, 1974, 11.
2. *Newsweek*, September 17, 1973, 51.
3. *Time*, August 12, 1974, 78.

factors may have been working to help them live to greatly advanced ages.

2. *Some of the numbers, at least, are to be understood figuratively.* Joseph, for example, is said to have died in Egypt at the age of 110 (Gen. 50:26). We know from ancient Egyptian records that 110 years was considered to be the ideal lifespan and that the number 110 in such cases is therefore usually to be understood qualitatively rather than quantitatively. The lifespans of other patriarchs and their wives—127 years (23:1), 137 (25:17), 147 (47:28), 180 (35:28)—could also be similarly evaluated and interpreted.[4]

3. *The patriarchs were special people whom God preserved in special ways for special purposes, and their lifespans should not be judged by normal ancient or modern standards.* If other ordinary people, then or now, have not lived to such advanced ages, that should not bother us, because the biblical patriarchs were not ordinary people. God's protecting hand was over their lives, and he had promised Abram, for example, that he would be buried "at a good old age" (15:15).

Each of these three widely held answers has merit, and they are not necessarily mutually exclusive. Perhaps some of the figures are quantitative and others qualitative. But whatever the ultimate answer to the question of patriarchal longevity, the OT wants us to understand that life itself is a gift of God and that long life, in the case of the patriarchs, was a mark of God's blessing and gracious love.

And now back to our story. Abram, Sarai and Lot set out from Haran in the northern Mesopotamian river valley. They headed southward and probably passed through Damascus, where Abram acquired the services of Eliezer (see 15:2). They also stopped at the sanctuary at Shechem in central Canaan. There the Lord appeared to Abram and confirmed to him the promise of land that he would eventually receive (**12:7**). Abram expressed his gratitude by worshiping the Lord and building an altar to him

---

4. See chapter thirteen for details.

(see also **12:8**). He often built altars in places where he had unusually intense spiritual experiences (**13:18; 22:9**). When God does great things for us today, we too should thank him in similarly sacrificial and worshipful ways.

Abram and his party then continued on past Bethel and Ai toward the Negev (**12:9**), the wasteland area south of Beersheba. At some time during their trip famine struck, so when they ran out of provisions they went down to Egypt to stay until the famine was over.

Abram did not want to die of hunger, but neither did he want to lose his life because of Sarai's beauty. He knew that when they arrived in Egypt the pharaoh's men would see how beautiful Sarai was. Thinking Abram was her husband, the men would kill him and make Sarai just another concubine in the pharaoh's harem.

Sarai's beauty is described only briefly in Genesis **12:11** and **12:14**, but it is described in great detail in the so-called *Genesis Apocryphon*, one of the Dead Sea Scrolls. Ancient Jewish tradition obviously remembered Sarai as being an unusually beautiful woman, and rightly so. We can therefore understand Abram's concern to save his own life as he, Sarai, and Lot approached the borders of Egypt.

Suddenly he had an idea. He told Sarai to claim she was his sister. Intended to deceive the pharaoh, this strategy was only a half-truth at best, since she actually was Abram's half-sister (20:12). In effect, Abram shaved the truth a bit to get out of his predicament.

Whatever one might think about the morality of the ancient Egyptians, a major principle of their ethics was what they called *maat*, which included a strong emphasis on truth as opposed to falsehood.[5] In other words, the Egyptians had no patience with liars. An incongruous scene, then, unfolds before us: a man of God telling a "white" lie to a pagan ruler. When the pharaoh later confronted Abram with that lie and its implications, Abram must have felt very small indeed.

But before that happened, the Lord afflicted the pharaoh's household with dreadful diseases to preserve the fidelity of Sarai's marriage to Abram. The pharaoh rightly interpreted the

5. K. Kitchen, "Egyptian Ethics," in *Dictionary of Christian Ethics*, ed. C. F. H. Henry (Washington, D. C.: Canon Press, 1973), 202.

affliction as God's way of punishing him for something evil that he had done, and he eventually figured out that Sarai was Abram's wife. As soon as the lie was discovered, the pharaoh reprimanded Abram and then deported him and the other members of his party. It must have been an embarrassing scene, but unfortunately Abram did not learn the lesson from it that he should have, as we shall see in Genesis 20.

Settling Down (13:1–18)

After being chased out of Egypt by the pharaoh, Abram, Sarai, and Lot retraced their steps back through the Negev, back to Bethel and Ai. There Abram again called on the Lord's name (**13:4**), as he had done earlier (12:8). When we are caught in a lie, or when some other moral or spiritual problem plagues us, we should go back to the place where we met God. There we can beg forgiveness and reaffirm our faith, just as Abram did.

Lot tagged along behind Abram (**13:1, 5**), as he had done before (**12:4**). But now he begins to assume a more important role in the story. He and Abram had both become wealthy, and their wealth was measured primarily in terms of cattle (**12:16; 13:2, 5**). Camels are mentioned among their animals (12:16), and many scholars consider such references in the partiarchal narrative anachronistic, claiming that camels were not domesticated until a much later period. Careful research has shown, however, that some domestication of the camel did in fact take place during the period of the patriarchs.[6]

Lot's and Abram's herds continued to grow, and pastureland for them became more and more scarce. As often happens in such cases (see 36:7), the land could not support the herds of both men. Soon their herdsmen began to quarrel with each other, trying to gain the best pastureland and the best water holes for their flocks (see also 26:20). To make matters worse, we are told that Canaanites and Perizzites were living in the same area (**13:7**), and presumably they would also need grazing land for their own animals.

6. K. Kitchen, *Ancient Orient and Old Testament* (Chicago: Inter-Varsity Press, 1966), 79–80; "Camel," in *The Illustrated Bible Dictionary*, ed. J. D. Douglas et al. (Wheaton: Tyndale, 1980), 1:228–30; J. J. Davis, "The Camel in Biblical Narratives," in *A Tribute to Gleason Archer*, ed. W. C. Kaiser, Jr., and R. F. Youngblood (Chicago: Moody, 1986), 143–46.

Abram realized that something had to be done quickly. One of the characteristics that made him a great man was his generosity, which is revealed nowhere more clearly than here. He gave his nephew Lot the choice of the available land.

Lot, a young man with his whole life still before him, perhaps decided that it was only logical for him to choose the best land. After all, his uncle Abram was getting along in years and would not need good grazing land much longer. Whatever his reasons, however, Lot chose the well-watered Jordan valley. In so doing, he took the *first* of seven downward steps (**13:11, 12; 14:12**; 19:1, 8, 14, 33)—steps that would lead to his spiritual destruction. He chose that valley "for himself" (**13:11**); he made a selfish choice. Selfishness is often the first downward step in a person's spiritual decline (cf. Cain's attitude in 4:3–5). In Lot's case, it formed quite a contrast to Abram's generosity.

Lot's *second* downward step was that he moved his tents in the direction of Sodom (**13:12**). By doing that, he was putting himself in a precarious spiritual position because Sodom had already gained a reputation for its wickedness (**13:13**).

We noted that Lot's selfishness was in contrast to Abram's generosity. I now want to suggest two other contrasts between Lot and Abram in Genesis 13.

Lot "looked up" (**13:10**; lit. "lifted up his eyes") and coveted the well-watered Jordan valley. The Lord said to Abram, "Lift up your eyes" (**13:14**), and then he showed him the land that would eventually belong to him and his descendants. (Hundreds of years later, the Lord would show Moses the same land on the eve of its conquest; see Deut. 34:1–4.) Lot lifted up his eyes and collapsed under the pressures of his own desire; Abram lifted up his eyes at God's command and was blessed because of his submissive obedience.

Lot "pitched [lit. "moved"] his tents" (**13:12**) in the direction of a wicked city. Abram "moved his tents" (**13:18**) in the direction of Hebron, and there he built an altar to worship the Lord. Lot moved for his own convenience and comfort; Abram moved for spiritual reasons.

Lifting up one's eyes and moving one's tents are intrinsically neither good nor bad. Both are neutral activities. However, Lot stubbornly followed his own will, while Abram tried only to do the will of God, and their actions produced distinctly different results.

The Battle of the Kings (14:1–24)

If we could identify any of the four northern kings (or any of the five southern kings) mentioned in Genesis 14 with any degree of certainty, we could then date the patriarchs more precisely than we were able to do in the last chapter (see chapter thirteen). But all we can say about these kings is that the two parts of Kedorlaomer's name (Elamite *kutir-* and the divine name *Lagamar*) are authentically Elamite, that the name Arioch is either Amorite or Hurrian, that the name Tidal is clearly Hittite, that the name Amraphel (not to be equated with the famous Babylonian king Hammurapi, as was formerly thought) is probably Amorite, and that all of the elements in all four names are attested in documents of the first half of the second millennium B.C.—which of course implies that one or more of them could have originated somewhat earlier.

Some of the place names and peoples mentioned in Genesis 14 are relatively unknown, while others are more familiar. Elam (**14:1**) was the nation located some distance east of Ur. Sodom and Gomorrah (**14:2**) were the infamous towns situated somewhere near the southern end of the Dead Sea, here called the "Salt Sea" (**14:3**) because of its high chemical content. The Horites (**14:6**), formerly thought of as cave dwellers because the Hebrew word *hōr* means "cave," are now known to have been the non-Semitic Hurrians, a people who lived at Nuzi and elsewhere. The Amalekites (**14:7**) lived in the Negev and in the Sinai peninsula, while the Amorites (**14:7**) lived in Canaan and northern Mesopotamia.

The Dead Sea region became the scene of a battle in which four powerful northern kings emerged victorious over five rebellious southern kings who had been their vassals. Genesis 14 records the story of the battle because when the northern kings took plunder from Sodom and Gomorrah they also seized captives, among whom was Abram's nephew Lot (**14:12**). By now Lot was "living in Sodom," and this was his *third* downward step. He had moved right into town and was living among the wicked people of Sodom. Interestingly enough, although Lot lived in Sodom, its citizens apparently never really considered him to be one of them, because in 19:9 they call him an "alien." Maybe 2 Peter 2:6–8 provides a clue to Lot's status; the passage states three times that Lot was "righteous," in contrast to the men of Sodom, who were "ungodly," "filthy," and "lawless."

At any rate, a fugitive from the defeated side in the battle came and told Abram that Lot had been captured. So, together with his allies and 318 "trained men," Abram pursued the enemy as far as "Dan" (**14:14**). Genesis **14:14** is a fascinating verse for the historian, because it contains a unique and very old Hebrew word ("trained men," perhaps better translated "armed retainers")[7] as well as a late editorial touch ("Dan," the well-known city in northern Canaan, was not so named until the time of Israel's judges; see Judg. 18:29).

Abram's wealth and power are well illustrated in this story. He had 318 men capable of bearing arms at his beck and call. And that was a formidable enough force to rout the enemy and retrieve the plunder and captives—including, of course, the unfortunate Lot.

Genesis **14:18–20** is a brief but very important interlude in the story. It gives us a few tantalizing details about a man named Melchizedek. He was a Canaanite priest of "God Most High, Creator of heaven and earth" (**14:19**); titles such as "most high" and "creator of earth" were commonly applied in ancient times to the chief deity in the Canaanite pantheon. Melchizedek was also the king of Salem (a shortened form of "Jerusalem"; see Ps. 76:2). In ancient times, priestly and kingly duties were often performed by a single individual. Melchizedek blessed Abram, who responded by giving him a tenth (tithe) of the plunder. The patriarchs recognized the importance of the tithe; we will observe this fact again in Genesis 28:22, where Jacob promised to pay God a tithe of all he possessed.

As a Canaanite priest, Melchizedek was evidently a pagan. But Abram, recognizing in him the potential of becoming a believer in the one true God, identified Melchizedek's "God Most High" with "the Lord" (**14:22**). Since only the Lord deserves the title "God Most High," Abram in effect was acknowledging that Melchizedek was genuinely seeking God's will. And since giving a tithe is a spiritual act, Abram probably would not have given one to Melchizedek if he had not considered him a man spiritually worthy of receiving it.

Melchizedek figures prominently in the NT in Hebrews

---

7. See W. F. Albright, *Yahweh and the Gods of Canaan* (Garden City, N.Y.: Doubleday, 1968), 69–70.

4:14–7:28 (esp. 7:1–28). In that passage, Genesis **14:18–20** is alluded to several times and Psalm 110:4 (the only other biblical passage referring to Melchizedek) is directly quoted several times. The point of the argument in Hebrews is that Melchizedek is a prefiguration or type of Christ, our great high priest. The priesthood of Jesus is, therefore, "in the order of Melchizedek" rather than "in the order of Aaron." Since Melchizedek lived centuries earlier than Aaron, his priesthood must be greater than that of Aaron.[8] And since the Jewish priests of Jesus' time were priests in Aaron's order, Jesus was greater than any of them because only he was a priest in Melchizedek's order.

After his meeting with Melchizedek, Abram returned to the king of Sodom to restore the plunder and captives to him. The king said to him, "Give me the people and keep the goods for yourself." He apparently felt that Abram deserved a sizable payment for having routed the northern kings and having retrieved the plunder.

But Abram responded that he had made an oath to the Lord not to keep anything belonging to the king or people of Sodom. Genesis **14:22** reminds us that the means of taking an oath in ancient times was raising one's hand (see also Deut. 32:40; Rev. 10:5–6), a practice still followed in modern courtroom procedure. In effect Abram said, "I have raised my right hand on solemn oath to the Lord that I would keep absolutely nothing belonging to you. I do have some allies, so give them their expenses, but don't pay me anything. I don't want you to be able to claim that you made me rich."

We should not understand this to mean that the laborer is unworthy of his hire. It is important to remember that Abram was already a wealthy man, as we have noted before. Also, we might compare Abram's situation with that of Elisha in 2 Kings 5. Just as Elisha refused to accept gifts from the commander-in-chief of the army of Aram (2 Kings 5:16), so Abram refused to accept favors from Sodom's king. Both men ultimately trusted in God alone—and so should we.

---

8. Another proof that Melchizedek was greater than Aaron, according to Heb. 7, is that Abram, Aaron's ancestor, paid a tithe to Melchizedek. Aaron, therefore, also in effect paid a tithe to Melchizedek, since Aaron's ancestor Levi was still in the body of Abram at the time. If all of this sounds a bit complicated, it would well repay anyone's effort to study Heb. 7 carefully. The author's arguments are easy to follow, and other comparisons between Melchizedek and Jesus as well as contrasts between the priesthoods of Melchizedek and Aaron are clearly set forth.

These three chapters of Genesis describe Abram's travels through much of Canaan. But although the promise of inheriting the land was given to him and to his descendants, he himself received not one square foot of it (Acts 7:5). He simply had to accept God's statements on faith. He had to trust that the God who had promised was also a God who would keep his word.

15

The Covenant of Abram (15:1–17:27)

THE COVENANT ESTABLISHED (15:1–21)
THE COVENANT IGNORED (16:1–16)
THE COVENANT SEALED (17:1–27)

Genesis 14 ends with Abram's forfeit of all claim to the plunder that he had retrieved from the four northern kings (Gen. 14:22–24). He did not want the king of Sodom to be able to boast about having made him rich.

Genesis 15 begins with the Lord's reassurance to Abram that he was rich beyond measure. This was not because of the gold and silver and animals and servants that Abram possessed, but because God himself was Abram's treasure (**15:1**). When the Lord promises to be our treasure, financial reverses or other similar problems are easier to bear. The Levites would learn this fact centuries later (Deut. 10:9), and God wanted Abram to learn it now.

The Covenant Established (15:1–21)

For the fourth time in four chapters of Genesis (see 12:1–3; 12:7; 13:14–17; and now **15:1**) God spoke to Abram. We cannot be certain that it was in an audible voice, but it might well have been; we know that audible conversations between God and his choicest servants did in fact take place (see 1 Sam. 3:4–14). In any event, the patriarchs enjoyed an intimate relationship with God. The atmosphere was often conversational; they talked together about matters that were mutually important to them.

Yet Abram was not satisfied with God's comments in Genesis **15:1**. Abram had other concerns: He was getting old, he had no sons of his own, and Eliezer of Damascus, one of his household slaves whose services he may have acquired on the way south-ward from Haran (see 12:5), would inherit Abram's entire estate. Why so?

The Nuzi documents (discussed briefly in chapter thirteen) —as well as earlier texts from the Old Babylonian period—illustrate the fact that if a man did not have a son of his own, he could legally adopt a young man and pass his inheritance on to his newly adopted son. Often the adopted son would be one of the man's servants, a servant he had come to know and trust, a servant who had perhaps already demonstrated his dependability around the household in a variety of ways.[1]

Apparently that is what had happened here. Since Sarai his wife was barren (11:30), Abram had adopted Eliezer as his son and was now unhappy that he would be his heir. But God spoke again and assured Abram that Eliezer would not be his heir. On the contrary, a son coming from Abram's own body would be his heir (**15:4**).

Once again, the Nuzi documents supply a helpful explanation of patriarchal custom. They illustrate the fact that if the man of the house eventually had a son of his own, the rights of that son would supersede the rights of the adopted son. In other words, Eliezer's rights to Abram's property were not absolute or inviolable; if Abram should have a son of his own, Eliezer's claim would be invalidated.

So God promised Abram that he would have his own son. That promise would be fulfilled in Abram's old age when Isaac was born (21:2). Isaac would thus be the son "of promise" (Gal. 4:28), and we who belong to Jesus Christ are children of promise, Isaac's spiritual descendants, as Paul declares in Galatians 4:21–31.

1. M. J. Selman, "The Social Environment of the Patriarchs," *Tyndale Bulletin* 27 (1976): 127.

God further promised Abram that his offspring would be as numerous as the stars in the sky (Gen. **15:5**). In the pitch blackness of the Near Eastern night, unillumined by any artificial light, Abram could look up and see thousands of stars. He would become weary indeed if he tried to count them all. But that was how many descendants he, already an old man with no children, was going to have!

The promise was repeated to Abram in 22:17 after he had demonstrated his obedience to God by his willingness to offer up Isaac as a sacrifice. And the promise was fulfilled at the time of the people of Israel's entrance into Canaan (Deut. 1:10). The NT writers marveled at the promise, which is mentioned in Romans 4:18 and which Hebrews 11:12 confirms as having been fulfilled.

We must constantly remind ourselves, however, that Abram's descendants are often a spiritual rather than a physical entity in NT references. Galatians 3:29 states that people who belong to Christ are Abram's offspring. Using language reminiscent of Genesis **15:5**, Revelation 7:9 refers to a huge ingathering of God's people at the end of time, "a great multitude that no one could count, from every nation, tribe, people, and language."

Abram's response to God's promise was one of faith. We are told that he "believed the LORD" (Gen. **15:6**). This is the first use of the verb "believe" in the Bible, and Genesis **15:6** gives us a concise definition of what faith is all about. "Faith" means "believing God," "believing what God tells us." And Abram was "the father of all who believe" (Rom. 4:11), the spiritual father of everyone who has ever had saving faith. Perhaps the wording of Genesis 15:6 describes Abram's conversion to faith in the one true God.

Genesis **15:6** is so important that the NT writers quoted it several times. It appears in whole or in part three times in Romans 4 (4:3, 22, 23), as well as in Galatians 3:6 and James 2:23. In Romans 4:23–25, Abram's faith is compared with our faith in the death and resurrection of Christ. In other words, his faith in what God had told him up to that point is placed on the same level as our faith in what God has told us and revealed to us through Christ. In Galatians 3:6–7 we learn that believers in general are children of Abraham. Also, James 2:23 quotes Genesis **15:6** as proof that faith apart from works is dead. If we do not prove our faith by working for Christ and living as he wants us to live, our faith is not worth much. It is as good as dead.

James 2:23 also calls Abram "God's friend," a name also applied to him in 2 Chronicles 20:7 and Isaiah 41:8. Believers in God are God's special friends. Abram lived in or near Hebron for much of his life, and the modern Arabic name for Hebron is *El-Khalil*, "the friend"—an honorific reference to Abram.

When Abram believed in the Lord, his faith was credited to him as righteousness (Gen. **15:6**). Like Abram, we have no genuine righteousness of our own. All of our righteousness has to be credited or imputed to us, and that can happen only as a result of our faith (Heb. 10:38; 11:7), our believing in God and his word.

Now a covenant scene unfolds before our eyes. Exodus 20:1–17, the Ten Commandments, exhibits a literary outline similar to that of Hittite treaties dating from ca. 1450–1200 B.C. These treaties contained several elements, including (1) the self-identification of the king, in this case "I am the LORD your God" (Exod. 20:2); (2) the historical prologue, in this case "who brought you out of Egypt, out of the land of slavery" (20:2); and (3) the stipulations of the covenant, in this case the Ten Commandments themselves (20:3–17).[2]

Genesis **15:7** exhibits the first two elements in a strikingly similar way: (1) "I am the LORD," and (2) "who brought you out of Ur of the Chaldeans to give you this land to take possession of it." These elements tend to mark out the scene before us as a covenant scene, a fact that would be confirmed later in Genesis 15.

Abram's response to God's promise this time was one of doubt rather than faith (**15:8**). How characteristic this is! Even people of great faith experience their moments of doubt. Living the life of faith is not like starting at the bottom of an escalator that always and continually moves upward to heaven. It is more like riding a roller coaster with its hills and valleys. In Genesis **15:6** Abram was on the mountaintop; in **15:8** he was down in the valley, doubting: "How can I know that I will gain possession of it?" Centuries after Abram's time, Zechariah, soon to be the father of John the Baptist, would ask a similar question (Luke 1:18).

So God, in his great condescension, told Abram to go and get certain animals three years of age, and two birds as well. Three years was the prime age for most animals used in sacrifices (see 1 Sam. 1:24). Abram was then told to cut the animals in half and

---

2. See conveniently G. E. Mendenhall in E. F. Campbell, Jr., and D. N. Freedman, *The Biblical Archaeologist Reader, 3* (Garden City, N.Y.: Doubleday Anchor, 1970), 32–42.

line them up in two rows (Gen. **15:10**). He did not cut the birds in half, however, apparently because they were too small (see also Lev. 1:17). At Mari on the Euphrates, the donkey was used as the main sacrificial animal to solemnize covenants during the patriarchal period.[3] The animals used by Abram at God's command were a heifer, a female goat, and a ram.

At sunset Abram fell into a deep sleep, during which the Lord told him his descendants would live for 400 years in a foreign land, where they would be enslaved and exploited. That land (Egypt, as later events demonstrated) would in turn be judged, however, and then Abram's descendants would return to Canaan (see Gen. 46:4). Stephen's historical summary in Acts mentioned these important events (Acts 7:6, 7, 17).

Abram was told that his descendants would come back "in the fourth generation" (Gen. **15:16**). Apparently a "generation," usually referring to the age of a man when his first son is born, was considered to be a hundred years in length during the patriarchal period. This tallies well with the statement that Abraham was a hundred years old when Isaac, his firstborn son from the legal standpoint, was born (21:5). In turn, the 400 years of **15:13** is perhaps a round number for the 430 years of Exodus 12:40, "the length of time the Israelite people lived in Egypt."

Abram's descendants would be able to return to Canaan only when the sin of the Amorite inhabitants of the land had "reached its full measure" (Gen. **15:16**). God would not destroy the Amorites until they were ripe for judgment and destruction. From their own epic literature, discovered at the site of ancient Ugarit on the Syrian coast beginning in 1929, we have learned that the worshipers of many of the Canaanite deities involved themselves in such degraded practices as violent atrocity in warfare and promiscuity in sexual matters—all in the name of religion.[4] God is merciful, but his long-suffering and forbearance are not granted to people indefinitely. When stubborn disobedience passes the point of no return, God punishes the sinner.

In the meantime, God promised Abram that he would not die until he had reached a good old age (**15:15**), a promise that he kept, as always (25:7–8). The Canaanites would be punished, but

3. See W. F. Albright in J. B. Pritchard, ed., *Ancient Near Eastern Texts*, 2d ed. (Princeton: Princeton University Press, 1955), 482 n. 4.

4. See, e.g., the analysis of W. F. Albright in *Archaeology and the Religion of Israel*, 4th ed. (Baltimore: John Hopkins, 1956), 71–84.

Abram would be rewarded. This is just as true now as it was then: God judges sin, but he honors righteousness.

Genesis 15 concludes with an eerie but highly significant scene. Darkness came across the land while Abram was still apparently sound asleep. Suddenly, "a smoking firepot with a blazing torch" (**15:17**) passed between the halves of the animals that Abram had earlier slaughtered and arranged in two rows (**15:10**). The firepot and torch marched, as it were, down the aisle formed by the animal parts. This was a solemn ceremony confirming and solemnizing the covenant about to be established (see esp. Jer. 34:18–19). In such ancient ceremonies, a participant in a covenant would vow something like this: "If I violate the terms of this covenant, may what happened to these animals happen to me!" Obviously, covenants were not entered into lightly or unadvisedly in ancient times.

The firepot and torch undoubtedly symbolized the presence of God, as fire often does in the Bible (see Exod. 3:2; 14:24; 19:18; 1 Kings 18:38; Acts 2:3–4). There were two main types of covenant in ancient times: suzerainty and parity. Covenants between equals were parity covenants, while those between a superior and an inferior were suzerainty covenants.[5] Needless to say, all covenants between God and man in the Bible are suzerainty rather than parity covenants. In Abram's case, God, the suzerain, established the covenant and was the active participant; Abram, the vassal, received the covenant and was the passive participant. His passive role is stressed by the fact that he apparently remained asleep during the entire transaction.

Once again we observe the condescension of our God. As he symbolically passed between the pieces of the slaughtered animals, he in effect was laying his own reputation on the line. He was expressing his willingness to accept the fate of those animals if he should break his covenant promise.

The Lord, as the suzerain, "made" (**15:18**) the covenant with Abram. The verb "made" literally means "cut" ("made" and "cut" translate the same Hebrew verb in Jer. 34:18) and refers to the sacrifice that accompanied formal covenants in the OT period (see Ps. 50:5). To "cut" a covenant meant to establish or make a covenant.

The covenant terms that God made with Abram included the

5. *The Biblical Archaeologist Reader*, 3, 28–32.

promise that he would give his descendants the territory that began at the eastern border of Egypt and stretched all the way to the Euphrates River. Abram's descendants did, in fact, receive that land during the OT period. God commanded the Israelites to go in and take it (Deut. 1:7–8), which they did under Joshua's leadership (Josh. 21:43). During the days of the judges they lost huge sections of it. Later under David they regained it and lived in it during the reign of Solomon (1 Kings 4:20–21). So God's promise of land was fulfilled already more than once in ancient times.

This does not mean that it cannot be fulfilled yet again, of course. For example, whether the modern state of Israel is a further fulfillment of the patriarchal promise is a question that is being hotly debated in our day. Modern Israel may well be such a fulfillment, but it is clearly not the only fulfillment, as some would claim.

The ceremony solemnizing the covenant with Abram was intended to confirm to Abram that what God had promised he would surely fulfill. It was the sign Abram had asked for (Gen. **15:8**). Significantly, covenants in the Bible were always solemnized by blood. There is no such thing as a biblical covenant without a blood sacrifice. This fact has supremely important implications for us as well, since our covenant relationship to Christ was sealed with his own precious blood. We are reminded of his words of institution at the Last Supper: "This cup is the new covenant in my blood" (Luke 22:20; 1 Cor. 11:25).

The Covenant Ignored (16:1–16)

Land and people—that was the twofold promise implied in God's covenant with Abram. They cannot be separated, because without the land the people are homeless and without the people the land is unfulfilled. Holy land and holy people go together.

Now Abram and Sarai knew that God had promised Abram a son (Gen. **15:4**). But Sarai, as before (11:30), was still barren (**16:1**). So she made a proposal to Abram that, by our standards, was shocking: "Go, sleep with my maidservant; perhaps I can build a family through her" (**16:2**). It was a proposal that the wives of her grandson, Jacob, would later repeat to him (30:3, 4, 9).

How could the wives of the patriarchs suggest such a thing? Once again, it was the legally authorized custom of that time for a man who had no son to take measures that would insure the orderly disposition of his inheritance when he died. He could adopt a son, as Abram had apparently already done (see **15:2–3**). Or, according to section 146 of the Old Babylonian Code of Hammurapi and one of the Nuzi documents, in certain circumstances he could produce a son by cohabiting with one of the servant girls in his household. If a son were born as a result of such cohabitation, the inheritance rights of that son would supersede the rights of any previously adopted son.[6] In a polygamous society, where men commonly had a wife and one or more concubines (as Abram did; see 25:6), sleeping with a servant girl was not nearly so strange or shocking as it might seem to us.

But just because it was commonly done does not mean that God condoned it. In fact, Abram and Sarai were ignoring God's promise that Abram would have a son of his own. By trying to assist God they demonstrated their own impatience. They assumed that Sarai's old age formed a barrier to God's power.

So when Sarai spoke, Abram listened (**16:2**)—just as Adam had to Eve (3:17). In both cases the result was tragic. Rivalry arose between the two wives, Sarai and Hagar (the Egyptian servant girl, **16:4**). Sarai became angry with Abram because of Hagar's impertinence (**16:5**). Finally, Sarai mistreated Hagar so severely that she was forced to run away while still pregnant (**16:6**). All of these unfortunate circumstances took place because Abram and Sarai were impatient and disobedient.

Hagar naturally headed west toward Egypt. She stopped at a spring of water on the way to Shur, a site located east of Egypt (25:18; 1 Sam. 15:7). There the angel of the Lord found her and talked to her (Gen. **16:7–12**).

Who was the angel of the Lord? Many answers have been given to this question. In Genesis **16:13** he seems to be equated with the Lord himself. Thus some students of Scripture have taught that the angel of the Lord was really Jesus Christ in a preincarnation form. I would observe, however, that in Hebrews 1 the author goes to great lengths to point out that Jesus is far superior to all of God's angels. Also, if the angel of the Lord were Jesus, the uniqueness of the incarnation would be severely weakened.[7]

6. M. J. Selman, "Nuzi," in *The Illustrated Bible Dictionary*, ed. J. D. Douglas et al. (Wheaton, Ill.: Tyndale, 1980), 2:1104.

7. For a convenient summary, see G. F. Oehler, *Theology of the Old Testament* (New York: Funk and Wagnalls, 1883), 129–34. See also, however, J. Borland, *Christ in the Old Testament* (Chicago: Moody, 1978).

Since the Hebrew word for "angel" also means "messenger," it is perhaps best to explain the angel of the Lord as a special messenger from the court of heaven who bears the credentials of the King of heaven and can therefore speak on his behalf. This was the case with other messengers in ancient times. They had the right and the authority to speak on behalf of the one who had sent them. On some occasions such a messenger would use the first-person pronoun, as though he were in fact the sender himself. At other times he used the third-person pronoun in reference to the sender (cf. Judg. 6:12 with 6:16). In either case he symbolized the presence of the king who had given him his mission.

In this regard Judges 13 is instructive. There the angel is called "the angel of the LORD" (Judg. 13:3, 13, 15–17, 20, 21), a "man of God" (13:6, 8), an "angel of God" (13:6, 9), a "man" (13:10, 11), "God" (13:22), and "the LORD" (13:23). Perhaps he could bear all of these titles at once because he looked like a man but at the same time was a messenger representing someone else. When the "angel" or "messenger" of the Lord appeared, then, the Lord himself was symbolically present.

Since Hagar believed that seeing the angel of the Lord was tantamount to seeing the Lord himself, she reacted with surprise (Gen. **16:13**). Like Jacob many years later (32:30), she wondered how it was possible for her actually to see God without being severely judged for it. In memory of the event, the well where the meeting took place was named Beer Lahai Roi. If it was named from God's standpoint, it means "The well of the one who sees me and lives"; if named from Hagar's standpoint, it means "The well of the Living One who sees me." Although either translation is possible, the first would seem to be the most likely in context. But why did the angel intercept Hagar in the first place? He wanted to tell her to go back to Sarai, to tell her that she would have many descendants, that God had "heard" her cry of affliction (**16:11**), and that she would bear a son named Ishmael (lit. "God hears"; see Gen. **17:20** for a similar pun on Ishmael's name.) We may sometimes feel that God is unconcerned about us, but he is faithful and always hears and "sees" (Exod. 3:7) the misery of his people.

So it was that Abram, at 86 years of age (Gen. **16:16**), became the father of Ishmael. As there was antagonism between Hagar and Sarai (**16:4–6**), so there would be (**16:12**) between Ishmael (and his descendants) and Sarai's own firstborn son Isaac (and his descendants). But that still lay in the future. For now we can be sure that Abram rejoiced in the birth of Ishmael, believing that he was the fulfillment of God's promise stated in **15:4**.

The Covenant Sealed (17:1–27)

Thirteen years later (**17:1**) the Lord again appeared to Abram in a covenant context, just as he had to Abram in **15:7**, and just as he would to Moses and the people of Israel centuries later (Exod. 20:2). He revealed himself to Abram by a new name, *El Shaddai* (Gen. **17:1**), which is usually translated as "God Almighty." It was the special name that God used to reveal himself to the patriarchs, as Exodus 6:3 points out. The name is found many times throughout the rest of Genesis, and *Shaddai* alone occurs most commonly in the Book of Job (who was himself a patriarchal figure). *El Shaddai* may have originally meant "God, the Mountain One," as many recent scholars have asserted.[8] Later it came to mean "God Almighty" because it describes the God who makes things happen by means of his majestic power and might.

God came to Abram and wanted him, like Noah before him (Gen. 6:9) and believers in Thessalonica after him (1 Thess. 5:23), to walk before him and be blameless (Gen. **17:1**). The Lord can best use people who are willing to live godly lives.

Now God confirmed his covenant with Abram (**17:2**). Unlike the earlier covenant with Noah (9:8–17), this covenant was conditional on the obedience of Abram and his descendants (**17:1, 9**; 18:19; 22:18; 26:4–5; Deut. 30:15–20).[9] From God's standpoint all covenants are eternal (Gen. **17:7, 13**), but from man's standpoint they can be broken (Isa. 24:5; Jer. 31:32). When we break God's covenants we also break his heart, since then he must punish us, which is something he does not enjoy doing (2 Pet. 3:9). The covenant at Mount Sinai was also conditional (Exod. 19:5), but unfortunately the people of Israel broke it innumerable times throughout their long history, and God therefore had to judge them for their sin over and over again.

8. See W. F. Albright, *Yahweh and the Gods of Canaan* (Garden City, N.Y.: Doubleday, 1968), 188–89.

9. See R. Youngblood, "The Abrahamic Covenant: Conditional or Unconditional?", in *The Living and Active Word of God: Studies in Honor of Samuel J. Schultz*, ed. M. Inch and R. Youngblood (Winona Lake, Ind.: Eisenbrauns, 1983), 31–46.

We observe once more the twin poles of the covenant promises to Abram: land (Gen. **17:8**) and descendants (**17:2, 4–6, 16, 20**). As the land received the major emphasis in Genesis 15, so the descendants receive it in Genesis 17.

God changed Abram's name to Abraham (**17:5**), a fact noted by Nehemiah in his summary of Israel's history (Neh. 9:7). "Abram" means "exalted father," a reference not to Abram himself but to God. Many names in ancient times contained the name of a deity, and "father" was a commonly used divine element in such names. For example, "*Ab*ijah" means "my *Father* is the LORD," and "Eli*ab*" means "my God is *Father*." The *ab*-element in such Hebrew names meant "father" in reference to God, so that "exalted *Father*," the meaning of "*Ab*ram," refers to God himself rather than to Abram, the man who bore the name.

When Abram's name was changed to "Abraham," a significant twist took place. The *ab*-element now referred to Abram himself, who received the new name "*Ab*raham," which means "*father* of a multitude" (Gen. **17:5**). The new name reflected his new status as promised him by God: He would become "a father of many nations."

Having Abraham as one's ancestor could become an unfortunate source of pride in later generations (see Matt. 3:9). But the ultimate intention of God's covenant promise to Abraham was sensed by Paul, who emphasized the spiritual aspect of Abraham's fatherhood to both Jew and Gentile (Rom. 4:17; Gal. 3:29).

From the physical standpoint the covenant also had meaning, of course. Kings would descend from Abraham (Gen. **17:6**), a prediction to be fulfilled during the days of the Israelite monarchies (see also Deut. 17:14–20, a description of what those kings would be like if they were diligent in following God's will).

Most important of all, however, was the fact that the Lord promised to be the God of Abraham and his descendants (Gen. **17:7–8**). The statement, "I will be their God, and they will be my people," became a prominent and characteristic phrase in covenant contexts (Jer. 31:33; 24:7; Ezek. 34:30; Hos. 2:23; Zech. 8:8). This is only as it should be, since a covenant is an agreement that stands or falls on the basis of personal relationship. If the signatories are not trustworthy, if they fail to love and respect each other, the covenant is not worth the material it is written on.

As the rainbow is the sign of the Noahic covenant (Gen. 9:13), and as the Sabbath is the sign of the Sinaitic covenant (Exod. 31:16–17), so circumcision became the sign of the Abrahamic covenant (Gen. **17:11**). The rainbow and the Sabbath already existed prior to the institution of the covenants they came to signify. So also circumcision did not originate with Abraham. It was practiced in Egypt and elsewhere centuries before his time,[10] but it received new meaning in Genesis 17. Similarly, thousands of people were crucified before the time of Jesus, but the cross took on a vastly new and different meaning when our Lord was crucified.

Circumcision symbolized the removal of uncleanness, and so the word was sometimes used in the figurative sense for the removal of ethical or spiritual uncleanness, as in Deuteronomy 10:16 (of the heart) or in Jeremiah 6:10 (which mentions uncircumcised ears; see also Lev. 26:41; Deut. 30:6; Jer. 4:4; 9:25–26). Although literal and physical, the circumcision of Genesis 17 would become more meaningful to Israel through her long history because of its added ethical and spiritual significance.

In the letters of Paul, physical circumcision loses its importance entirely. Spiritual circumcision, which involves faith in Christ coupled with moral purity, becomes predominant (see Rom. 2:28–29; 1 Cor. 7:19; Gal. 5:6; 6:15; Col. 2:11; 3:11; esp. Phil. 3:3).

Physical circumcision, however, became the badge of Abraham's male descendants. Abraham at the age of ninety-nine and Ishmael at the age of thirteen were circumcised along with all the other males in the household (Gen. **17:23, 26**; note again the promptness with which Abraham obeyed God's command). From that time on, every male child in Abraham's line through Isaac was circumcised when eight days old (**17:12**; thus Isaac, 21:4; John the Baptist, Luke 1:59; Jesus, 2:21; Paul, Phil. 3:5). Even today Jewish baby boys submit to the same operation at the same age.

The operation is performed on the organ of reproduction because the covenant emphasized the procreation of descendants. The implication is clear: If the foreskin was not cut off, then the individual himself would be cut off from the people of God because the covenant would have been broken (Gen. **17:14**).

---

10. See, e.g., H. O. Forshey, *Restoration Quarterly* 16 (1973): 151–53.

The image was vivid indeed. Perhaps not so incidentally, the operation itself reminds us that covenants are solemnized only through the shedding of blood.

In addition to Abraham, two others played a role in the covenant drama. Sarai his wife also had her name changed—to "Sarah," a name that, like "Sarai," means "princess." In her case the change of name was not so significant as was that of Abraham, although it did reflect the fact that she would become a "mother of nations" (**17:16**). For the first time, Abraham was now told that Sarah would bear a son and so share in the blessing of Abraham's descendants. Incredible! A 100-year-old man, and a ninety-year-old woman, to have a child of their own? It was too much for Abraham—so he "laughed" (**17:17**). But the boy would be born in spite of Abraham's doubt, and "Isaac" (which means "he laughs") would be his name (**17:19**). (Further puns on Isaac's name appear in 18:12–15; 21:6.)

The other actor in the drama was Ishmael. Despite Abraham's initial lack of faith, he requested that God bless Ishmael. But God had other plans. Ishmael would be blessed (**17:20**) and would become the ancestor of twelve chieftains (a prediction fulfilled in 25:12–16). He was not the son of promise, however. That honor went to Isaac.

As we have read Genesis 15–17, we have observed that Abraham wavered between faith and unbelief. If he, the spiritual father of believers, could do so and still be called "God's friend," there is yet hope for us.

16

The Family of Abraham
(18:1–21:34)

THE DESTRUCTION OF SODOM AND GOMORRAH (18:1–19:38)
ABIMELECH AND SARAH (20:1–18)
THE BIRTH OF ISAAC (21:1–34)

Genesis 15–17, the section on the Abrahamic covenant, forms a bridge between Genesis 12–14 (which is concerned mainly with the promise of land) and Genesis 18–21 (which is concerned mainly with Abraham's family). The Abrahamic covenant itself focuses on the twin concerns of land and family. Our purpose in studying Genesis 18–21, then, will be to observe what happened in subsequent history to several members of Abraham's family and clan.

The Destruction of Sodom and Gomorrah (18:1–19:38)

One hot afternoon, the Lord again "appeared" to Abraham (Gen. **18:1**). He did not appear personally since, as Jesus reminded us, "no one has ever seen God" (John 1:18). Abraham was visited by the Lord through the agency of "three men" (Gen. **18:2**), later identified as divine messengers whose number was reduced to two ("angels," **19:1**) after the departure of one of them (whose presence was apparently a theophany, an appearance of the Lord; see **18:10, 13, 17–33**).

The keynote of Genesis **18:1–8** and **19:1–3** is hospitality. Hebrews 13:2 is probably a reflection of these incidents: "Do not forget to entertain strangers, for by so doing some people have entertained angels without knowing it." Genuine hospitality is almost a lost art in many circles today. In the ancient Near East, however, it was a quality that characterized every host and was expected by every guest. That same quality can also be observed in many areas of the Middle East today.

In Abraham's case, he bowed down to greet his visitors, welcomed them courteously, brought water to wash the dust from their feet, and presented them with a sumptuous meal. And he took care of all their needs quickly: He "hurried" (Gen. **18:2, 6**) and "ran" (**18:7**). He did everything he could to make them feel right at home, to give them the personal attention they deserved. There are lessons in abundance for us here, because to the extent that our activities and actions become more impersonal, we ourselves become less hospitable.

From inside the tent where she could not be seen, Sarah overheard the word of the Lord to Abraham as mediated through the three men: "Sarah your wife will have a son" (**18:10**). This was the first inkling Sarah had of God's incredible promise. When Abraham had heard it initially, he had laughed (17:16–17). Now it was Sarah's turn to laugh, and for the same reason. After all, she had already passed menopause and was much too old to have children.

But the Lord was displeased, not only with Sarah's laughter but also with her subsequent denial that she had laughed. He asked Abraham, "Is anything too hard for the LORD?" (**18:14**). We sometimes forget how powerful our God is. An angel had to remind the virgin Mary of the same truth concerning her own pregnancy and that of her aged kinswoman Elizabeth: "Nothing is impossible with God" (Luke 1:37). Can Mary, a virgin, conceive? Of course! Can an elderly woman become pregnant? Absolutely!

But how about in the spiritual realm? Can sinners be saved? We can indeed—because here, too, "with God all things are possible" (Matt. 19:25–26)! Salvation is the greatest miracle of all, a miracle that every true believer in Christ has experienced. The miracle of Sarah's forthcoming pregnancy pales by comparison.

When Abraham's guests prepared to leave for Sodom, he walked along with them for a short distance (Gen. **18:16**). The Lord decided to tell Abraham of his plans to destroy Sodom and Gomorrah because he did not want to hide those plans from him. After all, Abraham was God's "friend" (2 Chron. 20:7; Isa. 41:8; James 2:23), and good friends often share intimate secrets with each other. Abraham was also a "prophet" (Gen. **20:7**), and God does nothing without disclosing his plans to his servants the prophets (Amos 3:7).

The wickedness of Sodom and Gomorrah was already well known (Gen. 13:13). It would become proverbial in later generations (see, e.g., Deut. 29:23; Isa. 1:9–10; Ezek. 16:49–50; Amos 4:11; Matt. 10:15; Luke 17:28–30; 2 Pet. 2:6–8; Rev. 11:8). The Lord would therefore go down and look over the situation (Gen. **18:21**), just as he had done in the days of the building of the tower of Babel (11:5). He would entrust that mission to his faithful messengers, Abraham's guests (**18:16, 22; 19:1**).

By now Abraham had come to realize that the destruction of Sodom was a live possibility. So he was determined to intercede for its people, particularly Lot. The result is one of the boldest and most famous intercessory prayers in all of Scripture (**18:23–32**). His eloquent plea demonstrates the fact that the prayer of a righteous man does, in fact, reach the waiting ear of God and make its impact on people and events (James 5:16).

In his prayer Abraham was not bargaining with God, as it is often thought. He knew that God, Ruler over all, is a just and honest Judge (Gen. **18:25**), as Moses would later learn to know him (Deut. 32:4). He also knew that, by comparison, he himself was nothing but dust and ashes (Gen. **18:27**). In other words, he clearly understood how important it is to be humble in the presence of a sovereign God (see Job 40:3–5; Isa. 2:11, 17; 5:15–16; Mic. 6:8).

Nevertheless, Abraham persevered in his plea, asking God to spare Sodom for the sake of fifty righteous people in it (if that many could be found there), then forty-five, then forty, then thirty, then twenty, and finally ten. In the end God promised that if only ten righteous people could be found in Sodom, he would indeed spare the city.

It may be that Abraham stopped at the number ten because he had been doing a bit of mental arithmetic on the scratchpad of his mind. Perhaps he had counted Lot, his wife, at least two sons (Gen. **19:12**), at least two married daughters and their husbands (**19:14**), and two unmarried daughters (**19:8**)—exactly ten. Even if the daughters of **19:14** had not yet married their fiancés and were the same as the daughters of **19:8**, it was plausible to assume that two other righteous people could be found somewhere else in Sodom. The city was obviously safe.

When two of the three angel-messengers who had visited Abraham arrived in Sodom, it soon became apparent that Lot himself had become deeply involved in the life of the city. He was sitting in the gateway of Sodom, which probably meant that he was a member of the ruling council there (see Ruth 4:1, 2, 11 for an example of the prosecution of legal matters in a city gateway, often used as a courtroom in ancient times). If Lot was indeed one of Sodom's ruling elders, that fact would constitute his *fourth* step downward, spiritually speaking. (For the first three, see Gen. 13:11, 13:12, and 14:12.)

As Abraham had done earlier, Lot extended hospitality toward his guests. He invited them into his house for a hearty meal and a good night's sleep (**19:2–3**). Now the wickedness of Sodom's male citizens was revealed in all its horror: They demanded that Lot bring his two guests outside to them so that they could have sex with them (see Jude 7). This immoral practice was so characteristic of Sodom's men that homosexuality is often called "sodomy" even today. The Bible always and everywhere states that homosexuality is sin, and no amount of propaganda to the contrary by so-called "gay liberation" movements here and abroad can change that basic fact.

Lot refused to release his guests to the lust of his neighbors, but he did agree to allow the Sodomites to abuse his two virgin daughters if they so desired (Gen. **19:8**). This incredible offer constituted Lot's *fifth* step downward. The Sodomites, however, wanted only Lot's male guests. The whole sordid incident has its counterpart later on in the period of the judges (see Judg. 19:22–26), during a time when "everyone did as he saw fit" (Judg. 21:25). "Do what you like with [my daughters]," Lot said

(Gen. **19:8**). So it goes: When God's sovereignty is denied and his laws are ignored, anarchy reigns and sinful people take over.

Apparently the men of Sodom never did consider the unfortunate Lot to be one of them (despite his own spiritual problems, he did not sink to the Sodomites' lowest level; see 2 Pet. 2:7–8). He was recognized as a foreigner and accused of setting himself up as a judge (Gen. **19:9**), as Moses was centuries later (Exod. 2:14). When the Sodomites decided to break down the door of Lot's house in order to get at his guests, the guests struck them blind so that they could not even find the door.

Sodom's wickedness made it ripe for judgment and annihilation. The Lord's messengers told Lot to take all his relatives out of the city to escape the coming destruction. When Lot relayed the message to his sons-in-law they thought he was joking (Gen. **19:14**), so low had his witness and credibility slipped by that time. The loss of the power of moral persuasion constituted Lot's *sixth* step downward.

Seemingly only four righteous people were left in Sodom instead of the ten required to save it: Lot, his wife, and their two unmarried daughters. The destruction of the city was now inevitable, so the angels urged the four to run for their lives. When Lot hesitated (would he have to leave some of his prized possessions in Sodom?), the men took the four by the hand and led them out of town. In so doing, they demonstrated God's mercy to them (Gen. **19:16**). People who are blind, whether spiritually or physically, need the gentle hand of the Lord to lead them out of their difficulties (see esp. Mark 8:23).

But Lot still balked. He did not want to go into the hills outside of town, because he was sure he could not get there in time. So he requested permission to flee to a nearby village to find shelter from the destruction. Because Lot stressed the smallness of the village (and therefore the smallness of his request) more than once (Gen. **19:20**), its name became "Zoar" (which means "small"). The Lord agreed to Lot's request, and once again we catch a glimpse of God's grace and love. He allows himself to be limited by his people's foibles: "I cannot do anything until you reach it" (**19:22**).

As soon as Lot arrived at Zoar, the Lord destroyed Sodom, Gomorrah, and the other towns of the plain (except Zoar) in a fiery holocaust. The catastrophe was remembered by later generations as a clear example of divine judgment (Isa. 13:19; Lam.

4:6; Jude 7). It was often compared in severity and scope to the judgment on mankind by the great flood in the days of Noah (Luke 17:26–30; 2 Pet. 2:5–8). Current archaeological evidence points to five sites at Bab edh-Dhra (on the tongue of land that juts into the Dead Sea on its eastern side) and nearby as the most likely locations for ancient Sodom, Gomorrah, and the other three cities of the plain (Gen. 14:8). Each "tell" (mound of ruins) was destroyed late in the third or early in the second millennium B.C., never to be inhabited again.

When Lot's wife looked back to watch the awful scene (was she, too, concerned about leaving her prized possessions behind?), she became a pillar of salt, perhaps soon indistinguishable from the innumerable grotesque salt formations found to this day near the southern end of the Dead Sea (often called the "Salt Sea"; see, e.g., 14:3). Her fate also became proverbial in its own right. The memory of Lot's wife serves as a reminder to us not to turn back, no matter how temptingly the things of this world may beckon (Luke 17:32). Her hesitation cost her everything she had, including her very life.

So Sodom was destroyed. In spite of that, however, the prayer of Abraham was answered. Lot had been spared, and that was the basic motive behind Abraham's prayer in the first place. God had "remembered Noah" (Gen. 8:1) when the great flood was at its worst; at a time of similar peril, he "remembered Abraham" (**19:29**). Our prayers of faith are not always answered in the way we might expect or prefer. Nevertheless, they are always answered, but always in God's way, which is always the best way.

Genesis **19:30–38** details the *seventh* and last downward step that Lot took: an incestuous relationship with his two daughters. To be sure, his role was passive. They gave him wine to drink, and then they slept with him while he was in a drunken stupor. But he had obviously not brought them up in the nurture and admonition of the Lord, and so he was ultimately responsible for what they did.

In response the two daughters tried to justify their actions by claiming that their father was the only man left alive and that they simply wanted to preserve the family name by producing offspring. But their motive, however worthy, did not remove their guilt. The result was the birth of two boys, one through each daughter: (1) a son named "Moab" (traditionally thought to mean "from [my] father"), who became the ancestor of the

Moabites; and (2) a son named "Ben-Ammi" (which means "son of my kinsman"), who became the ancestor of the Ammonites (see Deut. 2:9, 19).

How tragic that Lot's seven downward steps eventually led to the founding of two nations who were to become bitter enemies of the descendants of his uncle Abraham (see, e.g., 2 Chron. 20:1; Ps. 83:5–8)!

Abimelech and Sarah (20:1–18)

Genesis **20:1–18** and 26:6–11 are often simply considered to be duplicates or alternates of the story told in 12:10–20.[1] But we should observe the differences between the accounts as well as their similarities. There is no reason why Abraham should not try again (**20:1–18**) what had gained him so much wealth the first time (12:10–20). Also, there is no reason why his son Isaac should not do (26:6–11) what had worked twice for his father.

Abraham and Sarah left the Dead Sea region and took a trip westward into the Negev. They eventually stopped for a while in Gerar, a town located about halfway between Gaza and Beersheba. Once again, in order to save his own life, Abraham pretended that Sarah was his sister. She was therefore taken to the palace of Abimelech, the king of Gerar.

In a dream, God told Abimelech that he was as good as dead because he had taken another man's wife to become one of the women in his harem. The Lord was determined not only to preserve the sanctity of marriage but also to guard the purity of the covenant line (Isaac had not yet been born to Sarah).

At the same time, God also respected Abimelech's protestations of innocence. After all, he had not yet so much as touched Sarah. In any event, he did not know she was Abraham's wife. So the Lord told Abimelech to release Sarah to Abraham, who, as a prophet (Gen. **20:7**; see also Ps. 105:15), would intercede for Abimelech's life. How intricate are the ways of God, and how marvelous is his grace: He instructed the deceiver to pray for the deceived!

Like the pharaoh before him (Gen. 12:18–19), Abimelech summoned Abraham, confronted him with the lie he had told, and asked him why he did it. We must not miss the irony of

---

1. See, e.g., H. H. Rowley, *The Growth of the Old Testament* (New York: Harper & Row, 1963), 17–18.

Abraham's reply: "I said to myself, 'There is surely no fear of God in this place' " (**20:11**). Obviously, Abimelech feared God more than Abraham did at this point. The Spirit of the Lord moves where he will, and often God's people are too hasty in making judgments about where he can and cannot work.

Abraham then explained (or, rather, gave the excuse) that Sarah was indeed his sister—or at least his half-sister. Abraham and Sarah had been born of the same father, but not of the same mother (**20:12**). They may have been offspring resulting from Terah's polygamy. If so, we have before us yet another demonstration of the evils of marrying more than one wife.

After Abimelech had given Abraham a substantial gift of animals and servants, he restored Sarah to him and invited him to stay in his territory if he so desired. He also gave Sarah a thousand shekels of silver as proof of her innocence in the whole matter. Then Abraham, perhaps somewhat sheepishly in the light of the circumstances, prayed for the removal of the affliction that had overcome Abimelech and his household because he had taken Sarah into his palace (**20:17–18**; see also 12:17).

The Birth of Isaac (21:1–34)

Even men of God like Abraham may sometimes disappoint us, but God himself never fails. Always true to his word, he gave Sarah her promised son Isaac (Gal. 4:28), just as he had said he would (Gen. **21:1–2**; see 17:16, 21; 18:10, 14). Soon after Isaac's birth and in accord with God's command (17:12), a 100-year-old man circumcised his eight-day-old baby boy. Joy reigned in that home (**21:6**), reflecting the meaning of Isaac's name ("he laughs"; see also 17:17; 18:12–15).

Since mothers in the ancient Near East nursed their babies for a much longer period of time than modern western mothers do, Isaac may have been two or even three years old[2] when Abraham prepared a sumptuous feast to celebrate his weaning (**21:8**). On that occasion Sarah saw Ishmael "mocking" (**21:9**; "mocking" here is another nuance of the Hebrew root underlying the name Isaac, "he laughs"). He was now in his late teens (see 16:16), and she suddenly realized that he was a potential threat to Isaac's inheritance.

2. E. A. Speiser, *Genesis* (Garden City, N.Y.: Doubleday, 1964), 155.

According to the legal practices of that time, she had no genuine cause for worry. The Nuzi documents, to which I have already referred on more than one occasion, imply that just as the inheritance rights of a son born to a man and his servant girl take precedence over the rights of an adopted son, so also do the inheritance rights of a son born to a man and his wife take precedence over those of a servant girl's son.[3] To summarize the matter in the context of Abraham's family, just as Ishmael's rights superseded those of Eliezer, so also Isaac's rights would now supersede those of Ishmael.

In another sense, however, we can understand Sarah's fears. Ishmael was much older than Isaac, and that fact may have played a part in her anxiety. In any event, she asked Abraham to drive Hagar and Ishmael out of the house. Such an act would have had the effect of disinheriting Ishmael.

Abraham was displeased at this request (**21:11**), and perhaps for more than one reason. He had doubtless come to love Ishmael very much by now. Also, there was the legal question, once again illuminated by documents from Nuzi. Because of the relatively weak legal status of a servant girl's son, the law protected him by forbidding that he be driven out of the household. Sarah, then, was not within her legal rights by requesting the expulsion of Ishmael.

Nevertheless, God overruled and told Abraham to do as Sarah had asked, because it was Isaac who would carry on Abraham's line and receive his inheritance (**21:12**). Paul quoted part of this verse to show that only children of "promise," not "natural" children, are Abraham's true descendants (Rom. 9:6–8). In other words, being a physical descendant of Abraham is not a guarantee of also being his spiritual heir, a genuine believer.

The writer of Hebrews continued to stress the importance of Genesis **21:12** by relating it to God's command to sacrifice Isaac in Genesis 22 (Heb. 11:17–19). In so doing, he demonstrated the close connection between Genesis 21 and 22 by showing that it was Isaac, the son of promise, the one through whom Abraham's descendants would be named, that God was telling Abraham to slaughter on an altar of sacrifice.

As we have seen, the NT recognized the significance of Isaac as the son of promise (Gal. 4:28). But God assured Abraham that

3. C. F. Pfeiffer, ed., *The Biblical World* (Grand Rapids: Baker, 1966), 423.

Ishmael would also be the ancestor of a powerful nation (Gen. **21:13**), just as he had promised Hagar earlier (16:10) and would promise her again (**21:18**). Because our faith is often weak, God gives us repeated assurances of his loving concern.

And so, for the second time, Hagar was driven out of Abraham's household through Sarah's instigation. This time her teenage son Ishmael accompanied her into the desert. When their water supply ran out, the Lord directed her to a well so the boy would not die of thirst (**21:19**). Ishmael grew up in the desert of Paran in the Sinai peninsula, and eventually he married an Egyptian girl at his Egyptian mother's request (**21:21**). As often happens in the Near East today, marriages in ancient times were arranged by the parents of the young people involved and not by the young people themselves.

Meanwhile Abraham and his family had stayed in Abimelech's territory, the land of Philistia, for some time (**21:34**). So important did the Philistines become in that part of the world that the entire area was eventually named "Palestine" after them. They did not arrive there in large numbers until after 1200 B.C. during a time of general political and social ferment in the Near East; however, it is not unlikely that smaller settlements of "Philistines" had lived there intermittently in previous centuries.[4] The description in Genesis 21 indicates that their presence in Canaan tended to be peaceful during those early years. Abimelech was impressed by Abraham's obviously close relationship to God, and so he decided he wanted Abraham as an ally rather than as an enemy. Abraham readily accepted Abimelech's offer of friendship (**21:22–24**).

Genesis 21 closes with an account of Abraham's complaint to Abimelech concerning a well that was owned by Abraham but that had been taken over by Abimelech's servants. The dispute was settled when the two men agreed to "make" (lit. "cut"; see 15:18) a covenant, taking an oath to resolve their differences in a mutually beneficial way. Abimelech accepted seven of Abraham's lambs as a witness to Abraham's ownership of the well. In memory of the event, the place was named "Beersheba," which means both "well of seven" and "well of the oath." To this very day an

---

4. K. A. Kitchen, *Ancient Orient and Old Testament* (Chicago: InterVarsity Press, 1966), 80–81; for discussion and additional bibliography, see T. C. Mitchell, "Philistines, Philistia," in *The Illustrated Bible Dictionary*, ed. J. D. Douglas et al. (Wheaton, Ill.: Tyndale, 1980), 3:1222.

ancient well in modern Beersheba is pointed out as "Abraham's well," but it is not authentic.

Abraham planted a tree in Beersheba in honor of the Lord, who is called here, and here only, *El Olam*, "the Eternal God" (**21:33**). This name stresses his everlasting nature. God's promises and covenants are everlasting because God himself is eternal.

17

The Trial of Abraham
(22:1–23:20)

AT MORIAH (22:1–24)

AT MACHPELAH (23:1–20)

The twin covenant promises of descendants and land, given by God to his friend Abraham, seemed to be well on their way to fulfillment.

Isaac had now been born and weaned. He had therefore successfully weathered the most critical period of his early life. All other things being equal, he should have had very little trouble growing up to be a strong young man, spiritually and physically, in the environment of a loving home.

Abraham had now settled down in the land of Canaan. He had come to know the land intimately and had been living there with his family for a long time. But suddenly each of the two promises—the promise of descendants, and the promise of land—met an obstacle designed to test Abraham's faith. And the first obstacle tested it almost to the breaking point.

At Moriah (22:1–24)

If I were asked to choose the three most important chapters in the story of Abraham's life, I would select Genesis 12, telling us of his call; Genesis 15, describing his conversion and the covenant God made with him; and Genesis 22, detailing the most severe test that God ever put him through.

If I were then asked to choose the most important chapter among these three, I would find it very difficult to do so. But on balance I think I would have to select Genesis 22, because in it Abraham faced the most profound spiritual crisis of his entire life.

A long time had elapsed (21:34), and Isaac was no longer a small child. Ties of mutual love and respect had had a chance to grow and develop between Abraham and his son. So, from God's standpoint, the time was now ripe to "test" Abraham (**22:1**).

That crucial verb is capable of more than one translation, as the various English versions demonstrate. But in this context it is better to render it "prove" (ASV) or "test" (NASB, RSV, NIV) than "tempt" (KJV), since God never tempts anyone (James 1:13). We can be tempted by Satan (1 Cor. 7:5) or by our own desires and lusts (James 1:14), but we can never be tempted by God.

In commenting on the fall of mankind in Genesis 3, I suggested that there are two important differences between tempting and testing that we need to keep in mind. One has to do with their subject and the other with their object. It is Satan who tempts us, but it is God who tests us. Satan tempts us to destroy us (1 Pet. 5:8; James 1:15; Rom. 6:23), but God tests us to strengthen us (Exod. 20:20; Deut. 8:2). When God tests you, it is so that "in the end it might go well with you" (Deut. 8:16).

God knows his people intimately, so when he came to test Abraham he called him by name. Abraham answered with the response of the servant: "Here I am" (Gen. **22:1**). His response would be echoed by Joseph (to his father Jacob, in this case; 37:13), Samuel (1 Sam. 3:4, 6, 8), Isaiah (Isa. 6:8), and many others, right down to our own time. Sensitive and devout people are still hearing and responding to God's call today.

God said to Abraham (Gen. **22:2**), "Take your son."

"But which one, Lord?" Abraham may have thought. "After all, I have two sons, Ishmael and Isaac."

"Your only son."

"That's still ambiguous, Lord. I need more specific directions than that."

"Whom you love."

"But Lord, I love both of my sons."

"Isaac."

"Thank you, Lord. Now I know exactly who you mean. And what shall I do after I go and get Isaac? Is it something that will further your will and purpose for his life?"

"Go to the region of Moriah."

"A little vacation for us! Fine! And then what?"

"Sacrifice him there as a burnt offering on one of the mountains I will tell you about."

At that point Abraham must have nearly fainted, overcome by disbelief. Had he heard God correctly? Was Isaac, the son of promise, finally born, finally grown into vigorous young manhood, now going to die? Was the glorious promise of God (15:4) now going to be nullified?

In telling Abraham to go and get one of his sons, our loving God broke the news to him gently, withholding Isaac's name till the very end (as the Hebrew text indicates). At the same time, God used terms that were calculated to make Abraham fully aware of the high price he was asking him to pay: "Take . . . your *only* son, *whom you love*" (**22:2** [italics added]).

But God never asks us to do something he himself is unwilling to do. We need to remember that God, also, gave his one and only Son (John 3:16; 1 John 4:9; Acts 2:23) as a once-for-all sacrifice (Heb. 9:28) for the sins of the world (1 John 4:14).

Abraham surely did not yet know that God was going to do that, however. So his response of prompt obedience was all the more remarkable: Not understanding and yet believing, he got up "early the next morning" (Gen. **22:3**) to begin the journey. If ever a man was tempted to procrastinate, Abraham could easily have been such a man that day. But prompt and unquestioning eagerness to do the will of God was one of Abraham's admirable characteristics, as we have already seen (12:4; 17:23; 21:14).

His destination was Moriah (**22:2**), a place mentioned elsewhere only in 2 Chronicles 3:1. There it is called "Mount Moriah," the site on which Solomon's temple in Jerusalem was eventually built, "the mountain of the LORD" (**22:14**; see Ps. 24:3; Isa. 2:3; 30:29; Zech. 8:3). The temple was destroyed in 586 B.C.

by the Babylonians, and Zerubbabel's temple was built and dedicated on or near the same location seventy years later. In turn, that temple was strengthened and refurbished by Herod the Great. It stood proudly until its destruction by the Romans in A.D. 70. Today the site is occupied by the Dome of the Rock (reputedly the "rock" where Isaac was laid on a sacrificial altar), an impressive Muslim shrine constructed there in A.D. 691. During the centuries that the Israelites controlled the area, untold thousands of animal sacrifices were offered to God there—but none so fraught with peril or charged with destiny as the one demanded of Abraham.

Accompanied by two of his men, a donkey, and of course his son Isaac, Abraham set out for Moriah. When they were almost to their destination, Abraham told the men to wait while he and Isaac went on ahead. He said to them, "We will worship and then we will come back to you" (Gen. **22:5**).

The text clearly states that Abraham told his men that both he and Isaac would return to them after he and his son had concluded their ceremony of worship. Was Abraham just trying to prop up his own courage? Was he engaging in wishful thinking? Was he trying to lead Isaac and the men off the track, to keep them from learning of his true intentions? Or did he already know that God was somehow going to save Isaac's life?

Hebrews 11:17–19 provides us with some helpful comments at this point. Abraham, after all, was a man of faith. He had never seen a resurrection before, but he believed that God was able to perform one if he wanted to do so. And, in a figurative sense, that is exactly what God did.

So Abraham's faith was faith in the ultimate, faith in resurrection from the dead, faith in the greatest miracle of all. This is why Paul could affirm that Abraham's faith in God was of the same quality and caliber as the believer's faith in the resurrection of Christ (Rom. 4:16–25). The outcome of Isaac's near sacrifice was a figurative resurrection (Heb. 11:17–19); the outcome of Jesus' finished sacrifice for our sakes was a literal, historical resurrection (Acts 2:24; 10:42; 17:31).

But we are getting a bit ahead of our story. Abraham took wood for the burnt offering and laid it on his son (Gen. **22:6**). Are we justified in seeing in that wood a symbol of our sin (Isa. 53:6)? Or are we justified in seeing in it a symbol of the cross of

Christ (John 19:17; see also Gen. **22:9**)? Perhaps so. At any rate, the burden was placed on Isaac by someone else. It was not of his own doing, even though he voluntarily accepted it.

Abraham escorted Isaac, as it were, up the hill of Moriah to the place of sacrifice. We are told twice that "the two of them went on together" (Gen. **22:6, 8**). In a similar way, God the Father and God the Son walked the long road together up the hill of Calvary to the place of sacrifice. The seven last statements of Jesus on the cross allow us to catch a glimpse of the depth of that relationship. In the first statement, Jesus addressed God as "Father" (Luke 23:34). By the time of the fourth and central statement, the unspeakable suffering of Jesus had strained his relationship to his heavenly Father, and he cried out with a loud voice, "My God, my God" (Matt. 27:46). But the seventh and final statement reflects the close and intimate fellowship they normally enjoyed, for Jesus addressed God once again as "Father" (Luke 23:46). In the human realm as well, when father and son are at their God-ordained best, their mutual relationship of love and respect can only be strained; it can never be broken.

With the natural curiosity of a boy, Isaac asked Abraham, "Where is the lamb for the burnt offering?" (Gen. **22:7**). Abraham, not knowing but believing, answered that God himself would provide the lamb at the proper time (**22:8**). At a deeper spiritual level, Isaac was asking his question for all humanity in every age. Every man and woman, every boy and girl in the world today needs to hear John the Baptist's ultimate answer to that question as he introduced Jesus Christ to the people of his time: "Look, the Lamb of God, who takes away the sin of the world!" (John 1:29, 36).

After Abraham had built an altar of sacrifice, Isaac submitted to his father as he "bound" him and laid him on the altar on top of the wood (Gen. **22:9**). During the Middle Ages, Judaism developed from its perspective the implications of the "binding" (Heb. *'ăqēdâ*) of Isaac, asserting that Isaac's submission is the submission of every Jew and that Isaac's sacrifice guarantees the eventual resurrection of every child of the Abrahamic covenant. For their part, Christians have stressed the fact that, like Isaac, Jesus submitted to his role of being the Son under obedience to his Father (Heb. 5:8).

At this point our story reaches its climax. When Abraham

picked up a knife to kill his son, the angel of the Lord shouted from heaven, "Abraham! Abraham!" (Gen. **22:11**). God had already spoken Abraham's name earlier, but not in this duplicated form (**22:1**). When God repeats the name of a person as he calls him, a situation of urgency is indicated, as with Jacob (46:2), Samuel (1 Sam. 3:10), Saul of Tarsus (Acts 9:4), and others. In Abraham's case, hearing his name shouted twice stopped the downward plunge of the knife.

The angel told Abraham not to harm the boy. Abraham had proved that he feared God because he had not withheld from God his only son, Isaac. His willingness to sacrifice Isaac was clear proof of his deep and abiding faith in God. James saw in it a sterling example of how true faith must be activated and completed by works (James 2:21–22).

Perhaps a comment is in order about Abraham's "fear" of God (Gen. **22:12**). To "fear" God in contexts like this is not so much to "be afraid of" him or to "dread" him as it is to "respect" or "revere" him. In this latter sense the "fear" of the Lord is the beginning of wisdom and knowledge (Prov. 1:7; 9:10). The stock phrase "fear of God" (Heb. *yir'at 'ĕlōhîm*) in the OT is practically a synonym for "true religion," as it was elsewhere in the world of those days (e.g., Akk. *puluḥti ili*, "fear of God"). In the mind of the ancient Israelite, fearing the Lord included loving him and trusting him (see esp. Deut. 10:12).

True to his promise as Abraham had perceived it by faith (Gen. **22:8**), God provided a sacrificial animal by calling Abraham's attention to a ram caught by its horns in a nearby thicket. In gratitude for God's goodness, Abraham named the place "The LORD Will Provide" (**22:14**; traditionally, "Jehovah Jireh").

When Abraham sacrificed the ram, he offered it up "instead of" his son (**22:13**). This is the first clear example of the important biblical doctrine known as substitutionary sacrifice. People of other nations in those early days sometimes offered up human beings as sacrifices to their various gods. But human sacrifice was absolutely forbidden by God to the Israelite (see, e.g., Jer. 7:31; 19:4–5), and for obvious reasons. This meant that the sacrificial system God instituted for Israel depended exclusively on substitute sacrifices, usually animals but in some cases plants or plant products. In fact, the whole sacrificial system of the OT is thoroughly infused with the dual principles of (1) a gift of unblemished life to God and (2) a substitute for the sinful life who offers it.[1]

Jesus Christ died for our sins to reconcile us to God (2 Cor. 5:17–21). He atoned for our sins, because we could not atone for them ourselves. Theologians often refer to this process as "vicarious atonement" or "substitutionary atonement." The phrase means that Christ, the perfect sacrifice (see 1 Pet. 1:18–19), died in our place so that our sins could be forgiven. Why did Jesus Christ come to this earth? Mark 10:45 tells us: He came to give his life as a ransom "for" (lit. "instead of") many.

After Abraham had sacrificed the ram as a burnt offering, the angel of the Lord called to him a second time from heaven. He told him that the Lord would indeed bless him and multiply his descendants, promises that were familiar to Abraham by now (see, e.g., Gen. 12:2; 13:16; 17:6). The Lord took an oath to that effect in his own name (**22:16**), because there is no greater name by which he can swear (Heb. 6:13–15).

Abraham's descendants would not only be as numerous as the stars visible in the sky with the naked eye and numbering in the thousands, as promised earlier (Gen. 15:5). More than that, they would be as numerous as the grains of sand along the seashore, a number so huge it staggers the mind (**22:17**; see also Heb. 11:12).

His descendants would also occupy the city gates of their enemies (Gen. **22:17**), which was tantamount to occupying the cities themselves since controlling the gate was the key to controlling the city. (The gateway of a city was also its most important area in the judicial sphere as well, because that is where legal matters were ordinarily debated and decided; see 19:1.) This promise was later renewed to Rebekah (24:60), who was to become Isaac's wife (24:67).

All of these blessings would take place because Abraham had been obedient to God (**22:18**). He had not withheld his son, his only son Isaac, his most precious possession, from the Lord (**22:12, 16**). The parallel between Abraham's devotion and God's love is unmistakable: As Abraham gave to God everything he had, so also God himself "did not spare his own son, but gave him up for us all" (Rom. 8:32). Amazing grace indeed!

After his mountaintop experience at Moriah, Abraham and his

---

1. For further details, see R. Youngblood, *The Heart of the Old Testament* (Grand Rapids: Baker, 1971), 77–86.

companions returned to Beersheba (Gen. **22:19**) where he had lived for a while some time earlier (21:33–34). His spiritual pilgrimage to the place of sacrifice was a memory that he would treasure forever, but for now he found it necessary to return to his former home and occupation.

Genesis 22 closes with the happy news that Abraham's brother Nahor had become the father of twelve sons. They would later become the ancestors of twelve Aramean tribes (**22:21**) in their own right.

This brief section describing Nahor's family and including a list of strange names is similar to what Bernard Ramm in another connection has delightfully dubbed "connective tissue."[2] Of only modest interest in itself, it nevertheless serves at least one useful purpose for every reader by giving him an opportunity to catch his breath before plunging into the next chapter of our fast-moving Genesis story.

At Machpelah (23:1–20)

In due course, Abraham's wife Sarah died at the age of 127 years (**23:1**). Her death occurred in Hebron, where the family was living at the time. Hebron was known as "Kiriath Arba" (lit. "the town of Arba") in those days. Arba was the most prominent member of one of the tribes living in the Hebron area (Josh. 14:15). Hebron was also known as Mamre (see Gen. 13:18; **23:19**; and esp. 35:27), perhaps in memory of one of Abraham's old Amorite friends and allies (14:13, 24).

Abraham had always been a dutiful and loving husband. So we can expect that he would mourn the loss of his wife, who had shared so much anxiety and grief with him (**23:2**).

At the time of Sarah's death the Hittites were apparently in control of the Hebron area. Abraham therefore found it necessary to negotiate with them for a gravesite in which to bury his deceased wife.

The burial plot would be used first for Sarah and later for Abraham himself as well as for other patriarchs and their wives (**23:9**; 25:8–9; 35:29; 40:28–33). It was known as the cave of Machpelah. The traditional tombs of Abraham and Sarah, Isaac and Rebekah, and Jacob and Leah are located to this very day deep beneath the Mosque of Abraham, a Muslim shrine in

2. B. L. Ramm, *His Way Out* (Glendale, Calif.: Regal Books, 1974), 52–53.

Hebron, and are revered both by Jews and Muslims. Because the mosque is considered a holy place, modern visitors cannot go beneath it to see the tomb area itself but must content themselves with seeing the memorial sarcophagi located on an upper level.

When Abraham began his discussion with the Hittites preparatory to negotiating with them for the purchase of the cave, he openly admitted that he was "an alien and a stranger" among them (23:4). These were titles that the patriarchs and their descendants were fond of using when referring to themselves (see, e.g., David's prayer in 1 Chron. 29:15; see also Ps. 39:12). Hebrews 11:9, 13 characterize the patriarchs as aliens, as strangers, as exiles. While on this earth they pitched their tents in various places, usually living in the most temporary of dwellings. Nevertheless, they looked forward to living in a city with real foundations, whose architect and builder would be God himself (Heb. 11:10).

In a sense, we, too, are strangers and pilgrims on this planet. While in no way neglecting our duties as good citizens and good neighbors, we nevertheless need to remember that our real and ultimate citizenship is in heaven (Phil. 3:20). Like the patriarchs, we have no lasting city here; we must look forward to the city yet to come (Heb. 13:14).

Owning "not even a foot of ground" in Canaan (Acts 7:5), Abraham was forced to buy a gravesite for Sarah. Genesis 23:3–16 is a classic account of the way in which bargaining was and often still is practiced in the Near East. The verb "give" also meant "sell" in ancient Hebrew, so it occupies a prominent place in the story (Gen. 23:4, 9, 11).

Abraham, the would-be purchaser, bowed down to the Hittites more than once (23:7, 12). He needed some land, and so he wanted to be in their good graces. For their part the Hittites politely offered him the choicest land they had, and apparently at no cost, or at least without mentioning any cost (23:6, 11). It is quite clear, however, that they had an eventual selling price in mind (23:15). The story is told graphically and tersely. It may even be that not all of the details of the bargaining process are given to us here. But finally Abraham and the Hittites arrived at the mutually agreeable price of 400 shekels of silver at the current market value (23:16). (During the patriarchal period the shekel was a weight, not a coin. Coinage was not invented until hundreds of years later.)

The price of that piece of property was probably just as exorbi-
tant for Abraham's time as the seventeen-shekel price for a plot
of ground in Anathoth was cheap in Jeremiah's time (Jer. 32:9).
But Abraham was in no position to bargain. His need was desperate and he was a stranger, so the Hittites exploited him. The
transaction took place at the city gate in the presence of witnesses (23:18). As we noted earlier (see 22:17), the gateway of a
city was often the locale for legal transactions of various kinds in
ancient times (see esp. Ruth 4:11).

What we would call the legal sections of Genesis 23 are written with unusual care. They contain many intentional repetitions
and duplications because they describe an important transaction.
Like modern legal documents, they want to avoid misunder-
standing if at all possible.

Recent studies of ancient Hittite law have made it likely that
Abraham was not interested in buying the entire field in which
the cave of Machpelah was located but only the immediate area
around the cave itself. To have bought the whole field would
have made Abraham responsible for certain feudal obligations in
the society of that time. He therefore may have been requesting
only "the end" of the field where the cave was situated (23:9).
The Hittites, however, wanting to be completely free of the obligations mentioned, held out for the sale of the whole field,
including "all the trees within the borders of the field" (23:17).[3]

At any rate the Hittites proved to be very shrewd bargainers,
and they took advantage of Abraham's desperate situation.
Modern parallels are evident everywhere. Consumer advocacy
and other similar groups continually warn us to buy burial plots
and learn the various costs involved in funeral arrangements
before death occurs in the family. Only by being prepared in
advance can we avoid the possibility of being swindled during a
time of grief and bereavement.

Having purchased the field, Abraham finally owned a small
part of the promised land. But he had had to pay for it with hard-
earned silver, and the occasion for its purchase was the death of
his dearly loved wife Sarah.

Abraham's faith in God's promises was being sternly tested
once again.

3. See M. R. Lehmann in *Bulletin of the American Schools of Oriental Research* 129
(1953): 15–18. G. M. Tucker, however, denied that Hittite law is relevant to the narrative
of the Machpelah transaction ("The Legal Background of Genesis 23," *Journal of Biblical
Literature* 85 [1966]: 77–84).

18

The Last Days of Abraham (24:1–25:18)

ABRAHAM SEEKS A WIFE FOR ISAAC (24:1–67)
ABRAHAM MARRIES KETURAH (25:1–6)
ABRAHAM DIES AND IS BURIED (25:7–11)
THE ISHMAELITE GENEALOGY (25:12–18)

By now, Abraham had become an old man. He decided to make good use of his "golden years" by getting his house in order.

For one thing, he wanted to be sure that his son Isaac married the right girl. In accord with God's promise, Isaac would perpetuate Abraham's name and continue his line, so Abraham was determined to find the perfect mate for his son.

As we observed earlier (see 21:21), it was the parents who chose spouses for their sons and daughters in those days, a practice still followed today in many parts of the Middle East. Because of the importance of cementing clan and family relationships, the best marriages of all were considered to be those contracted within one's own tribe rather than with members of another tribe.

Abraham Seeks a Wife for Isaac (24:1–67)

The Lord's blessing had followed Abraham throughout his entire life (**24:1**), and he now wanted that blessing to fall on his son Isaac as well.

After Sarah's death (23:1–2; **24:67**) Abraham put his chief servant (perhaps Eliezer of Damascus; see 15:2) in charge of finding a suitable bride for Isaac. To impress the servant with the importance of his mission, Abraham made him take a solemn oath while placing his hand under Abraham's thigh (**24:2–3**). The servant was required to put his hand near Abraham's organ of reproduction because the oath was related to the continuation of Abraham's line through Isaac. Years later, Jacob would make Joseph take an oath in a similar way (see 47:29).

Abraham asked his servant to take the oath in the name of "the LORD, the God of heaven and the God of earth" (**24:3**). That name, majestic indeed, is reminiscent of the one invoked in Abraham's memorable meeting with Melchizedek so many years before (14:19, 22).

The servant was told to find a bride for Isaac, but not from among the girls of Canaan. He was to get her from Abraham's homeland, Mesopotamia, because that is where Abraham's relatives were living. If the chosen bride should refuse to leave Mesopotamia and return to Canaan with the servant, he was not to take Isaac to where she was. In such a case, the servant would be free of the oath he had taken. Abraham's descendants were to live in the promised land of Canaan, not in Mesopotamia, and Abraham had the faith to believe that the girl of God's choice would readily agree to return to Canaan with the servant.

After he had loaded "all kinds of good things" (**24:10**) on ten of Abraham's camels (of which Abraham had a large number; see 12:16; **24:35**), the servant started out from Canaan, taking a few men along with him as companions and aides (see **24:32**). Their destination was the city of Nahor (**24:10**, perhaps named for Abraham's brother; see **24:15**) near Haran (see 11:32; for additional information on these two towns, see chapter thirteen). Like Haran, Nahor was located in Aram Naharaim, which means "Aram [modern Syria] of the Two Rivers" (referring to the Tigris and Euphrates rivers). It was the Hebrew name for the northwestern portion of what the Greeks would later call "Mesopotamia" (lit. "between the [Tigris and Euphrates] rivers"). The men arrived outside Nahor one evening at the coolest time of the day, the time when women normally came out to the town well to get water for their household needs (**24:11**). Such a scene forms a stark contrast to the otherwise similar picture drawn for us in John 4. There a Samaritan woman, much married and living in sin (and therefore ostracized; John 4:17–18), found it necessary to go to the well outside her town at "about the sixth hour" (4:6–7). Since the ancient Near Eastern day was thought of as beginning at about what would correspond to our six A.M., the woman of Samaria was forced by community pressure to get her water supply at around high noon—the hottest time of the day.

Abraham's servant had apparently learned many lessons from his master. Like Abraham (Gen. 15:8), he too looked for a sign from God to validate his mission. He prayed that God would help him identify the girl he had chosen for Isaac. He prayed that it would be the first girl who would not only offer him a drink of water but also offer to provide water for his camels.

Prayer in such situations is commendable. When we are in need of divine guidance, prayer should be our first activity rather than our last resort. Our faithful God is always ready to open the storehouse of his blessing, and prayer is often the key that unlocks the storehouse door.

In the case of Abraham's servant, his simple faith in God's providence was not ill-founded. He appealed to the intimate, covenant relationship that existed between Abraham and God (**24:14**). The Lord had bound himself in a pact of "kindness" to his master Abraham. The servant rightly felt that such a covenant was reason enough for the Lord to give him success on his important mission.

And our gracious God was quick to answer that earnest request. Before the servant had even finished praying, a beautiful virgin girl came to the well and began to fulfill the conditions of his prayer. God is not slow in responding to our pleas. Even before we conclude our prayers, his answer is already on the way.

But the servant wanted to be absolutely sure that what he had just seen would not turn out to be a false alarm. So, in silence, he watched the girl finish the task of watering his camels (**24:21**).

He then gave her a gold nose ring (**24:22**; see **24:47**) and two gold bracelets as gifts. He asked her whose daughter she was, and also whether her father's estate had room for him, his companions, and his animals for the night.

When she told him that she was Nahor's granddaughter and that there was indeed plenty of room, the servant bowed his head in worship and prayer. He now knew that God had made his journey successful by leading him to the right place (**24:26–27**).

The girl, whose name was Rebekah (**24:15, 29**), ran to her house to break the news that a camel caravan had been sent to Nahor by their relative Abraham. In turn, her brother Laban ran out to the well to invite the servant into the house and to give him a royal welcome. But the servant refused to eat the food that was set before him until he had given a full account of his errand (**24:33**).

Genesis 24 is the longest chapter in the Book of Genesis. This is partly because the servant, at this point in the chapter, now repeated the whole story of his mission (**24:34–49**), a story that we have already read. But the repetition is not monotonous or slavish. It contains a few elegant variations, as well as a few additional details.

Also, Genesis 24 as a whole is an excellent example of the ancient storyteller's art. In those days people enjoyed repetition—in fact, they preferred it—as they listened to tales or read them. Repetition served several purposes. It was used (1) to linger over sites and scenes that were especially enthralling or otherwise important; (2) to lend additional emphasis wherever necessary; and (3) to serve as a memory aid to the hearer (or reader). Far from being signs of inept editing or dual authorship, repetition and duplication were often deliberately employed as effective literary devices.

In one sense Genesis 24, in spite of its length, comes to a rather abrupt conclusion. After hearing the servant's story, Rebekah's brother Laban and her father Bethuel agreed to allow Rebekah to leave with him. They believed that it was the Lord's will (**24:50**) for her to do so, and they could easily have echoed a later psalmist's shout of wonder: "It is marvelous in our eyes" (Ps. 118:23). They also realized, as did Gamaliel the Pharisee two thousand years later (Acts 5:38–39), that if a matter originates with God and is therefore God's will, we had better do nothing to oppose it or him.

Bethuel's and Laban's consent to allow Rebekah to leave caused Abraham's servant again to worship the Lord in gratitude (Gen. **24:52**). He must have been an unusually godly man to display so frequently his dependence on the Lord in all matters. Abraham had doubtless taught him well and had been a worthy example to him.

After a good night's rest, however, Rebekah's relatives had second thoughts about allowing her to leave home so quickly. So they requested that she be permitted to remain in Mesopotamia for ten days or so. It is understandable that they would want to keep her with them as long as possible, since Canaan was a long distance away and therefore they might never see her again.

But the servant wanted to be on his way, because God had made his journey successful up to this point and he now wanted to see it through to its conclusion. So Rebekah was asked her opinion on the matter, and she immediately agreed to leave right away (**24:58**). Her relatives then gave her a blessing of their own (**24:60**; for a similar blessing, see 22:17) and sent her off together with her nurse (**24:59**), whose name was Deborah (see 35:8), and her servant girls (**24:61**). And so they started out on their long journey to Canaan.

On the evening of their arrival in the Negev in the southern part of the Promised Land, Isaac happened to be out walking in the fields. He had recently come from Beer Lahai Roi, the well where the angel of the Lord had met Hagar (16:14) and where Isaac himself would settle down after his father's death (**25:11**).

When Rebekah saw Isaac approaching and found out who he was, she covered herself with her veil, an act of modesty as well as a sign of her forthcoming marriage. After the servant had told Isaac the whole story, Isaac brought Rebekah into his deceased mother's tent and she became his wife. For Isaac, married life began at forty (25:20).

In summary, from Genesis 24 we can learn a great deal about how marriages were contracted in ancient times in that part of the world. By and large, the parents decided who their sons and daughters would marry. Sometimes the arrangements were made through an intermediary, such as a trusted servant. The best marriages were considered those contracted within one's own tribe rather than with a member of another tribe. To marry one's cousin was especially desirable, although such inbreeding often had unfortunate consequences when sickly or even deformed children were born as a result of such unions. A modern example of the fact that this practice is unwise can be found among the present-day Samaritan community in Israel who, until quite recently, have seen their numbers gradually depleted by such marriages. Inbreeding through the course of the centuries has reduced their population to just a few hundred.

Substantial gifts were customarily given by a young man (or his parents) to the bride, as well as to members of her immediate family (24:53). The girl herself remained veiled until after the marriage. Interestingly, these two customs have remained in force in a modified form in Western marriages even today.

But details about ancient marriages, however interesting in themselves, are merely incidental to the main point of Genesis 24: An all-loving and all-powerful God was working in and through the lives of all the people involved in the story. An oath was taken in his name; he led Abraham's servant to the right town and the right girl; Rebekah's relatives recognized him as the one whose will had to be obeyed in the matter; and Rebekah was so impressed by the servant's obviously sincere and honest account of how God had guided him step by step that she accompanied him back to Canaan without hesitation.

As for Isaac himself, it is entirely possible that he, too, had sensed the Lord's guidance in preparing his own heart to welcome Rebekah when she arrived. The traditional interpretation of Genesis **24:63** indicates that he had gone out into the fields to "meditate" that very evening. Unfortunately, we cannot be certain about the meaning of the verb in question, and other translations have been proposed (see, e.g., NASB marg.). But meditation is the kind of spiritual exercise that would have been entirely in character for Isaac, because many years later he would pray that the Lord would be gracious to Rebekah and allow her to bear children (25:21), and his prayer would be answered. So he may well have been praying and meditating on his wedding night.

If ever a marriage was made in heaven, this one was.

Abraham Marries Keturah (25:1–6)

These six verses describe another marriage and its results, but in a much briefer way. The section is perhaps a flashback, since Abraham would have been 140 years old by now if chronological order were demanded.

Strictly speaking, Keturah was Abraham's concubine (1 Chron. 1:32) rather than his wife. The Hebrew word for "wife" in Genesis **25:1** can also just as legitimately be translated "woman."

In fact, Abraham had more than one concubine (**25:6**), a matter that we must take into consideration in attempting to understand the sexual morality of that early period of history. The OT nowhere condones concubinage, but at the same time it does not try to gloss over it, even when its principal characters, many of whom were godly men, indulged in it.

There were six Keturite tribes in all, and Medan and Midian were ancestors of two of them (**25:2**). They in turn were related to Ishmael, Abraham's son through the Egyptian servant girl Hagar. When we take the time to observe these complex relationships, we are then able to explain how the caravanners who later sold Joseph into Egypt can be called "Ishmaelites" (37:25, 27, 28, 39), "Midianites" (37:28), and "Medanites" (37:36 NIV footnote) all at the same time (see also Judg. 8:22, 24, 26).

After he had given gifts to the sons of his concubines, Abraham sent them all away to their future homes east of the Jordan River (Gen. **25:6**). The lion's share of his estate, however, went to Isaac, his firstborn under the law (**25:5**).

Nuzi contract documents clearly illustrate the so-called law of primogeniture in effect in ancient times. That law provided for the transmission of at least a double share of the father's property to the firstborn son upon the father's death (see, e.g., Deut. 21:15–17). In other words, the firstborn was to receive at least twice as large a share of the estate as any other son received. (The wording of Gen. **25:5** indicates that Isaac received far more than the double share to which he was entitled by law.)

The law of primogeniture was universally followed, except in unusual circumstances. A case in point was that of the daughters of Zelophehad. Their father had died without leaving any sons, so they understandably requested title to his estate. When Moses brought their case before the Lord, he was told that the women were indeed entitled to their father's property. In fact, the case became the basis of expanding the laws of inheritance to take care of other contingent situations as well (Num. 27:1–11).

An interesting spiritual application of the terms of the law of primogeniture took place just before Elijah was taken by the Lord. When Elijah gave Elisha the opportunity of making a request of him, Elisha said, "Let me inherit a double portion of your spirit" (2 Kings 2:9). In the light of the law of primogeniture, Elisha was clearly not asking for twice the spiritual power that Elijah had possessed. He merely wanted Elijah to designate him as his main spiritual heir.

Abraham Dies and Is Buried (25:7–11)

"Precious in the sight of the LORD is the death of his saints" (Ps. 116:15).

When he was 175 years old, a full century after his departure from Haran (if we interpret the numbers literally), Abraham died at "a good old age" (Gen. **25:8**), as God had promised he would (15:15). Dying at "a good old age" was as much a reference to quality of life as it was to length of life. The phrase is not used, for example, of Ishmael at the time of his death (**25:17**). Like the patriarch Job, Abraham left this life as "an old man and full of years" (**25:8**; see Job 42:17). He was buried in the cave of Machpelah near the grave of his beloved wife Sarah. It was "his sons Isaac and Ishmael" who buried him (Gen. **25:9**). The order in which the names of the sons is mentioned is significant, since Ishmael was the older of the two. It underscores the fact that Isaac was recognized as Abraham's firstborn in the eyes of the law and in the eyes of God. Isaac, not Ishmael, was the chief heir of their father's estate and the sole recipient of the original divine promises given to Abraham in 12:1–3.

If the sheer number of chapters devoted to his life is any indication, the most important man in the Book of Genesis had now passed from the scene. But although gone, he was not forgotten. He would be recalled by future generations of believers as a man of faith and obedience, eventually to be honored by Jew, Christian, and Muslim alike. His towering figure would cast a long and beneficial shadow over the history of his descendants.

As God had promised, Abraham would indeed become the "father of many" (17:5). He would be the revered ancestor of the people of Israel, the chosen people, the people who would make the most lasting impact on the religious history of mankind.

Most significant of all, to both Jew and Gentile, Abraham would be remembered as the spiritual "father of all who believe" (Rom. 4:11).

The Ishmaelite Genealogy (25:12–18)

Although a literary unit in its own right, bearing the catchphrase introduction "This is the account of . . ." (see the introduction), this paragraph also serves as an appendix to the story of Abraham's life. It is somewhat anticlimactic, bridging the gap between Abraham's story and Jacob's story. It is essentially a genealogy, another example of "connective tissue" (see 22:20–24). Not particularly noteworthy in itself, it nevertheless performs the useful function of attaching one major part of Genesis to another.

Like Nahor, one of Abraham's brothers (22:20–24), Ishmael became the ancestor of twelve tribes. Many of their names indicate that Arabs were included among their descendants. This fact gives credence to the Arab tradition that Abraham was the ancestor of the Arabs through Ishmael.

Although **25:18** is rather difficult to translate and interpret, it at least states that Ishmael's descendants settled down in an extensive area east of Egypt and that they tended to be antagonistic toward other tribes (see also 16:12) including, of course, the tribes of Israel. So the Arab-Jewish rivalry that has exploded into open hostility now and then through the centuries had its beginnings among the early descendants of Ishmael and Isaac.

Ishmael's ancestry of twelve tribes was in direct fulfillment of the Lord's promise to Abraham (17:20). Our God, who never changes, can always be trusted to keep his word to us, just as he did to Ishmael through Abraham, who was his father, our spiritual ancestor, and God's friend.

> The God of Abraham praise,
>   Who reigns enthroned above;
> Ancient of everlasting days,
>   And God of love.
>
> Jehovah, great I AM,
>   By earth and heaven confessed;
> I bow and bless the sacred Name,
>   Forever blest.
>
> —Daniel ben Judah

Part 4

Jacob and Joseph

19

Jacob's Early Years at Home (25:19–27:46)

BIRTH AND BIRTHRIGHT (25:19–34)

MISCELLANEOUS EPISODES (26:1–35)

BLESSING FOR JACOB AND ESAU (27:1–46)

We have now come to a major break in the Book of Genesis. It is signalized by the telltale phrase, "This is the account of . . ." (**25:19**; see the introduction). To all intents and purposes we have left the story of Abraham behind us, although his memory will continue to exercise a strong and beneficial influence over the people and events discussed in the rest of Genesis.

But the life of Abraham's grandson Jacob will now occupy our attention for the most part. In many respects the personalities and activities of Jacob and Abraham provide quite a series of contrasts, as we shall see.

Birth and Birthright (25:19–34)

After Isaac's marriage to Rebekah (24:67) many years passed, and Rebekah did not become pregnant (for another example of the theme of the barren wife, see 11:30). In similar situations today, most couples tend to go to the doctor's office to find out what is physically or psychologically wrong with the husband or wife. Or they simply wring their hands in despair.

But Isaac knew what to do: He prayed to the Lord on his wife's behalf (25:21). His example reminds us that we should pray for things that we desire and that we believe to be in the will of God. Isaac believed that God wanted him to have a son—perhaps because his father had told him about God's promise of many descendants. Since the covenant with Abraham was eternal and unbreakable from God's standpoint (17:7), Isaac decided to take the matter of Rebekah's sterility directly to God himself. If God could not make Rebekah fertile, he reasoned, no one could.

Specializing (as he does) in the art of answering difficult prayers, the Lord answered Isaac's prayer in a lavish way: Rebekah conceived twin boys (25:24).

The new surge of life inside her must have made Rebekah very happy. But before long the babies began to jostle each other in her womb to the point where she was in such physical distress that she wondered whether pregnancy was really such a desirable experience after all (25:22). Many years later she would have similar doubts and ask similar questions when one of her boys had married two Hittite girls and she was afraid the other boy would do the same (27:46). Raising children has never been a simple matter, and the boys in Rebekah's womb would doubtless give their parents more than the usual number of problems as they grew up in their home.

At some point during her difficult pregnancy, however, the vitality of Rebekah's prayer life evidently matched that of her husband Isaac. She went to ask the Lord for an explanation of what was happening inside her (25:22). The Lord told her that the boys in her womb would become the ancestors of two nations and that the older would serve the younger (25:23).

In Romans 9:10–12 Paul referred to this incident during a discussion of God's sovereign right to make choices according to his own good pleasure. Paul's description of the scene and his theological understanding of it are worth quoting in full and without comment: "Not only that, but Rebekah's children had one and the same father, our father Isaac. Yet, before the twins were born or had done anything good or bad—in order that God's purpose in election might stand: not by works but by him who calls—she was told, 'The older will serve the younger.' "

And so the younger of Rebekah's twins was chosen by God in preference to the older, and this meant that God's covenant promises to Abraham would be fulfilled through the younger boy.

How often have we seen this to be true throughout biblical history! It seems that God almost always chose a younger son in preference to the oldest. Perhaps this was partially so in order to break the hammerlock hold that the sacrosanct law of primogeniture had over society in ancient times, the law that provided for a double share of the father's estate to become the inheritance of the firstborn son (see the discussion at Gen. 25:5). But most supremely it was so in order that God would be able to demonstrate his sovereign will in defiance of man-made laws and institutions. We observe that most of the great men of the OT—Jacob, Joseph, Judah, Moses, and David, for example—were not the firstborn sons in their respective families.

In Rebekah's case, her firstborn son emerged from the womb all red and covered with hair, so he was named Esau (which apparently meant "hairy"). His twin brother was born immediately afterward with his hand firmly holding Esau's heel, so he was named Jacob ("heel-grasper," "supplanter," or "deceiver"; the same word is used, e.g., in Jer. 9:4 with the meaning "deceiver"). A similarly unusual birth of twin boys is described in Genesis 38:27–30.

Isaac was sixty years old when Esau and Jacob were born (**25:26**), and Abraham had been 100 years old at the time of Isaac's birth (21:5). Since Abraham lived to be 175 (25:7), he was still living when Isaac's twin boys were born. He probably saw and played with Esau and Jacob in their formative years and recognized in them the continuing fulfillment of God's promise of many descendants.

Esau would eventually become the ancestor of the Edomites and Jacob of the Israelites. Although the mutual relationships of those tribes should have been brotherly, such was unfortunately not always the case (see Num. 20:14–21; Obad. 9–10).

As the two boys grew up, striking differences between them soon became evident. Esau was an outdoorsman who loved to hunt, while Jacob tended to be a quiet homebody (Gen. **25:27**). Unfortunately, Isaac favored Esau because he thoroughly enjoyed the meat that Esau brought in from the hunt, while Rebekah preferred Jacob's company, probably because he provided companionship for her and maybe even assisted with the household chores.

Parental favoritism is never a good thing. Yet all of us know of homes in which one child is favored over the others. Such partiality can easily destroy not only the children who are comparatively neglected but also the pampered one as well. The Christian home has no place for the rivalry and bitterness that inevitably result from parental favoritism toward one or more of the children. While it is true that some children are naturally more lovable than others, the beauty of the less lovable child will never be nurtured by neglecting him. The temptation to be partial may sternly test the character of any parent. But unless we resist that temptation, we will make it very difficult for some of our children to develop their abilities and capacities to the fullest. Parental favoritism turned out to be bad in the case of Esau and Jacob, as we will see in our study of Genesis 27.

Since he spent a lot of time at home, Jacob became a good cook. One day when Jacob had made a pot of lentil stew, Esau came in from the hunt. He was famished, so he asked Jacob for a helping of the reddish-colored stew. (The memorable incident gave him the nickname "Edom," which means "red" [**25:30**]; we recall also that he had been red when he emerged from his mother's womb [**25:25**].)

Jacob readily agreed to give Esau some stew if he was willing to trade his birthright for it. That was hardly a bargain offer for Esau, since by definition the birthright belonged only to the first-born son and guaranteed him at least twice as much inheritance from his father's estate as any of his brothers could expect to receive (Deut. 21:17). But Esau thought he was starving to death (Gen. **25:32**). Feeling that his birthright was of no use to him in such circumstances, he agreed on oath to sell it to Jacob in exchange for the stew.

The legality of such a sale is now known to have been a part of ancient life, as contract documents from Nuzi demonstrate.[1] Nevertheless, it is incredible that Esau entered into such a transaction, with all of its ramifications in the light of the Abrahamic covenant. His decision shows how immoral and "godless" he was, according to the evaluation of Hebrews 12:16, whose author was amazed at Esau's willingness to sell his own birthright "for a

1. See C. H. Gordon in *The Biblical Archaeologist Reader, 2*, ed. D. N. Freedman and E. F. Campbell, Jr. (Garden City, N.Y.: Doubleday Anchor, 1964), 23–24.

single meal." In so doing, Esau showed that he "despised" his birthright (Gen. **25:34**).

The story as a whole serves as an example of the dangers of materialism, of allowing one's appetites to become the most important things in life.

Of course, both men were in the wrong. Jacob sinned by taking advantage of Esau during a moment of weakness. And Esau sinned by falling for Jacob's ridiculous offer and by succumbing to his own hunger pangs. But Esau's sin was the greater of the two, and it would have far-reaching future consequences.

Miscellaneous Episodes (26:1–35)

The inspired writer's attention shifted back to Isaac in Genesis 26, and we can now see how lackluster was Isaac's personality and how very ordinary were his activities. Isaac's character strikes us as being bland and passive in comparison to his father Abraham's. He had a hard act to follow, of course; he was destined to live in the shadow of his father's greatness. But he was so unimaginative that he did almost nothing original or on his own. In fact, just about his only claim to fame is his longevity: He lived to be 180 years of age (35:28), five years longer than Abraham's age.

Famine descended on the land of Canaan (**26:1**), just as it had in the days of Abraham (12:10). In this case Isaac and Rebekah did not go all the way down to Egypt, as Abraham and Sarah had done. The Lord appeared to Isaac (**26:2**), as he had so many times before to Abraham, and specifically told him and Rebekah not to go to Egypt. Instead he told them to go to Gerar, where Abraham and Sarah had gone after the destruction of Sodom and Gomorrah. There, in the land of the Philistines, God would prosper Isaac and confirm the Abrahamic covenant to and through him. He would do this because of Abraham's obedience, a fact that once again emphasizes the conditional nature of those covenant blessings (**26:5**).

How gracious God is! Memories of past divine favor and love seem to fade quickly. Yet when they do, God is always ready and able to give his children continued reassurances of his concern and reminders of his promises.

The king of the Philistines at that time was Abimelech (**26:1**). He was probably the son, or even the grandson, of the Abimelech who ruled over Gerar in Abraham's time (20:2). It was not unusual in those days for kings to adopt the names of their predecessors, whether recent or remote—a practice that has continued right down to the present.

Isaac lied to his Abimelech, just as Abraham had lied to the earlier one, and he did so for the same reason as Abraham. The results were also the same: The lie was discovered, and Isaac was rebuked by a pagan king. What a sad example of "Like father, like son"!

And yet, so amazing is God's grace that in spite of everything he blessed Isaac (**26:12**). His crops were bountiful and his flocks were huge, prompting Abimelech to expel him from Philistia. Isaac was becoming far too wealthy and powerful for Abimelech (**26:16**). When God decides to do so, he blesses his children in spite of themselves because his grace is greater than their sin.

Driven away from Gerar by Abimelech, Isaac set up camp in a nearby ravine. There he emptied the debris out of some wells that had been dug originally by Abraham and later plugged up by the Philistines. The redug wells did not supply Isaac's family and flocks with enough water, however, so his servants dug another well. But the herdsmen of Gerar quarreled with Isaac's herdsmen and claimed the water from that well for themselves, so it was named Esek (which means "dispute"). When Isaac's servants dug another well, it too became a bone of contention, so it was named Sitnah (i.e., "opposition"). Finally, Isaac moved some distance away and dug another well. This time no one quarreled over it, so it was named Rehoboth ("plenty of room").

Eventually Isaac left the region of Gerar entirely and went to Beersheba. There the Lord appeared to him again and said to him, "Do not be afraid, for I am with you" (**26:24**). God's promise to be with us is repeated often in the Bible (see, e.g., **26:3**; 28:15; 31:3; Matt. 28:20; Acts 18:10). When we are at our spiritual best, we want that kind of relationship with him. And he desires such fellowship with us also. When Jesus appointed his twelve disciples, the first reason given for that appointment was "that they might be with him" (Mark 3:14). The joy of love is to be with those we love.

The Lord told Isaac that his presence with him would enable him to live without fear (Gen. **26:24**). Freedom from fear, an agelong hope of people everywhere from time immemorial, was one of the late Franklin D. Roosevelt's highly publicized "Four

Freedoms." Isaac was told that true freedom from fear comes only in having a personal relationship with God. For today's believer, such a relationship can be found only in Jesus Christ (John 14:1–6).

At Beersheba, Isaac was again reminded of God's promise to Abraham, and in gratitude for the Lord's faithfulness he built an altar there. Meanwhile, Isaac's servants dug another well (Gen. **26:25**), which was named Shibah ("oath"; **26:33**) because of a covenant signed there between Abimelech and Isaac (**26:26–31**). Even though Abimelech had earlier sent Isaac away from Philistia, he recognized that God was with him and therefore wanted him as a friend rather than an enemy.

Beersheba ("well of the oath") had been given its name originally because of a significant event in the life of Abraham that had occurred there (21:25–31). Now its name was confirmed because of a similar event in Isaac's life. This is only one of many instances in Genesis 26 demonstrating that Isaac essentially repeated what his father had done rather than striking out in new directions. Living in the shadow of Abraham's greatness made it difficult for Isaac to assert his own originality and independence.

As Isaac had married at forty years of age (**25:20**), so did his son Esau (**26:34**; forty may be a round number for a generation in these verses, as often elsewhere in the OT; see, e.g., Num. 32:13). But while Isaac had married one Aramean girl and had done so according to God's specific will, Esau married two Hittite girls who made life miserable for his parents and who also made Rebekah determined not to allow Jacob to make the same mistake (**26:34–35; 27:46**). We recall that Hittites were in control of at least part of Canaan in those days (see Gen. 23), a fact referred to by Ezekiel when he spoke of Jerusalem's origins (Ezek. 16:3, 45).

Blessing for Jacob and Esau (27:1–46)

Before the rise of modern medicine, blindness and near blindness were common afflictions of elderly people (see Gen. 48:10). This is why Moses' good vision at the end of his life was so noteworthy (Deut. 34:7). Isaac's weak vision in his old age forms the backdrop of Genesis 27.

Isaac did not know that Esau had sold his birthright to Jacob, so he made preparations to bless his firstborn son Esau (**27:1–4**). Possession of the birthright was tantamount to receiving the blessing of the firstborn (see Heb. 12:16–17), even though Esau would later try to separate the two (Gen. **27:31–38**).

Isaac told Esau to go out and hunt some game and then to prepare a tasty meal for him, so that after Isaac had eaten he could bless him. A document from Nuzi attests to the ancient practice of an ailing father making a solemn oral statement to his son—a statement that, though not in written form, nevertheless had legal validity (see also Gen. 48–49).

Meanwhile Rebekah, who had been eavesdropping on the conversation, went and told Jacob about it. She then instructed him to go and get two young goats, which she would prepare into a tasty meal. The full tragedy of this instance of parental favoritism (see **25:28**) gradually unfolds as the story proceeds. Emphasized throughout the account is the phrase "just the way [Isaac] likes it" (**27:4, 9, 14**). It stresses the fact that Rebekah and Jacob were taking advantage of Isaac's appetite for a certain kind of food to trick him.

Another aspect of their trickery was to take advantage of Isaac's blindness by dressing Jacob in Esau's clothes and putting the goatskins on Jacob's hands and neck to make him smell and feel like Esau (**27:15–16**). Jacob, the "deceiver" par excellence, was tutored well by his equally deceitful mother.

Later, there would be divinely-ordained legislation prohibiting such deception of helpless people (Lev. 19:14; Deut. 27:18). But for now Rebekah simply brushed aside Jacob's fears and scoffed at the general revelation of God's will mediated to her through her conscience. And she did it with relish: "My son, let the curse fall on me" (Gen. **27:13**). We are reminded of the awful cry of the people of Jesus' day when Pontius Pilate offered to release him: "Let his blood be on us and on our children!" (Matt. 27:25). Greedy people will sometimes even shake their fists in the face of God to get what they want.

Jacob followed his mother's instructions to the letter and then went into his father's room, pretending to be Esau (Gen. **27:19**). Isaac was suspicious from the start, and his suspicions remained right to the end. He wondered how his son could have returned from the hunt so quickly (**27:20**); he wanted to touch his skin (**27:21**); he thought he recognized Jacob's voice (**27:22**); he asked the young man a second time to identify himself (**27:24**). And throughout the entire charade, Jacob lied again and again and again.

If the scene has a single redeeming feature, it is perhaps this: Jacob was reluctant to call Isaac's God his own. He said, "The LORD *your* God gave me success" (**27:20**). Apparently Jacob did not want to become personally involved with God's name while engaged in the act of deceiving his father.

But the crowning touch was the traitor's kiss (**27:26–27**). Jacob had become his father's Judas.

Finally, when Isaac smelled the clothes Jacob was wearing (they were Esau's clothes, of course), he gave him the blessing of the firstborn (**27:27–29**). He made Jacob the ruler of his brothers (present and future), he asked God to prosper him, and he confirmed to him a section of God's call to and blessing on Abraham (see 12:3).

Thus Isaac's five senses all played a crucial role in the success of the deceptive plot hatched by Rebekah and Jacob: (1) his weak eyesight (**27:1**) made it impossible for him to see that it was Jacob, not Esau, who was before him; (2) his taste for savory food (**27:4, 7, 9, 14, 17**) provided the backdrop for Jacob's pretense; (3) his sense of touch (**27:12, 21–22**) was deceived by the goatskins that covered Jacob's hands and neck; (4) when he smelled Esau's clothes, which were being worn by Jacob, he naturally thought Esau was present (**27:27**); and (5) his hearing—though not quite fooled by Jacob's voice (**27:22**)—did not provide him with enough confidence to overturn the evidence of the rest of Jacob's stellar performance.

No sooner had Jacob departed when Esau arrived back from hunting. Esau too brought in a tasty meal and asked Isaac to bless him. In a clipped echo of his earlier question to Jacob (**27:18**), Isaac asked, "Who are you?" When Esau identified himself, Isaac trembled violently from head to toe because he realized that he had already blessed the wrong person. Then he rhetorically asked who it was that he had blessed—blessed with a blessing that could not be revoked or retracted (**27:33**), so powerful and sacrosanct was every word spoken in formal solemnity in ancient times (see, e.g., Josh. 9:19–20).

Of course, both men knew who the deceiver had been. Then Esau commented on the appropriateness of the meaning of Jacob's name ("deceiver") and stated that Jacob had deceived him with respect both to his blessing and his birthright. Just as the Hebrew words for "birthright" (*bĕkōrâ*) and "blessing" (*bĕrākâ*) play on each other, so possessing the birthright implied receiving the blessing (Heb. 12:16–17).

Esau continued to beg his father for at least one blessing, and then he broke down and wept bitterly (27:38). It was too late for him to receive the main blessing, however (Heb. 12:17). The best he could hope for was a pitiful shadow or reflection of what Jacob had already received. And that is all Isaac could give him. Comparing the watered-down and essentially negative wording of Genesis 27:39 with the very similar but thoroughly positive wording of 27:28, it becomes immediately evident that the former is a grotesque parody of the latter. A hint of the later hostility between the Edomites (descendants of Esau) and Israelites (descendants of Jacob) can be seen in 27:40. (See especially 2 Kings 8:20–22, an instance in which Edom did indeed "throw off the yoke" of Israel from their necks.)

Needless to say, Esau hated Jacob because of his deception and trickery, and he resolved to kill him after Isaac's death. When Rebekah heard about it, she told Jacob about Esau's plans. At the time of Sarah's death, Isaac had "comforted" himself by getting married (Gen. 24:67). Now, Esau hoped to "console" himself by killing his brother Jacob (27:42). To Esau, murder was apparently just as valid a way to comfort oneself as marriage was.

Rebekah sternly warned Jacob that he should flee to Haran (where her brother Laban was living) until Esau had calmed down. She said to Jacob, "Do what I say" (27:43)—a command that had gotten him into trouble before (27:8, 13) but that was eminently sensible advice this time. She told Jacob to stay with Laban for "a while" (27:44), which eventually lengthened into a period of twenty long years (31:38, 41).

But Rebekah's fears for Jacob's safety were entirely justified. She knew that Isaac's death would soon bring on Jacob's death at the hands of Esau, and she did not want to have to mourn the loss of two members of her family at the same time (27:45).

This story—full of greed, deceit, scheming, lying, jealousy, and murderous intent—is indeed sordid. Jacob's early life shows him to have been something less than a worthy grandson of Abraham. Because of a situation of his own making, he was forced to run away from home to escape his brother's anger.

Fortunately for Jacob, God had a better idea for his future—an idea that began to take shape in Genesis 28.

20

Jacob's Years in Paddan Aram (28:1–30:43)

Jacob's Dream at Bethel (28:1–22)

Jacob's Marriage (29:1–30)

Fertility in Family and Flock (29:31–30:43)

$\mathbf{A}$s we have already seen, the real reason for Jacob's trip to Haran was to escape Esau's anger (27:43–45). But Rebekah, apparently not wanting to alarm Isaac, gave him the excuse that she did not want Jacob to marry a Hittite girl (27:46) as Esau had done (26:34–35). She preferred to conceal her real reason for doing what she did by offering an excuse in its place.

Jacob's Dream at Bethel (28:1–22)

Excuse or not, Isaac shared Rebekah's fears concerning Jacob's future wife. So he sent Jacob off to Paddan Aram ("the plains of Aram"; see also 25:20), another name for northwest Mesopotamia, where his grandfather Bethuel and his uncle Laban lived.

Using words similar to the ones Abraham had spoken to his servant on a parallel occasion (24:3–4), Isaac told Jacob to marry one of Laban's daughters (**28:2**). He also prayed that God Almighty would give Jacob "the blessing given to Abraham" (**28:4**; see 12:1–3), a blessing that we who are Gentile Christians have eventually come to share (see esp. Gal. 3:14). While our share is spiritual, in Jacob's case the physical aspect of the blessing was dominant, emphasizing (as always) descendants and land.

When Esau heard that Jacob, with Isaac's benediction and blessing, had left for Mesopotamia to find a non-Canaanite wife, he decided to try to please his father by acting in a similar way. So, in addition to the Hittite wives he already had, he married an Ishmaelite girl (Gen. **28:9**). That decision served only to stress the fact that Esau was not a spiritually discerning member of the covenant family.

Meanwhile Jacob had left Beersheba (**28:10**), where the family had been living (26:23), and he had departed for Haran. One evening he stopped for the night in a rock-strewn field and used one of the rocks as his pillow. To this very day, the area where Jacob slept presents a landscape characterized by outcroppings of rock with loose boulders and stones lying everywhere. In fact, he may have found it difficult to locate a rock-free place for his head even if he had wanted to. But however uncomfortable it may seem to us, Jacob used a rock for a pillow probably by choice rather than by necessity. In those days headrests were often quite hard, sometimes even made of metal.[1]

After falling sound asleep, Jacob had a dream in which he saw a "stairway" (**28:12**; it was not a "ladder," which, in the modern sense at least, is a device with rungs). It was standing on the ground with its top reaching into the sky. The image in the dream was that of the sloping, stepped side of a particular type of Mesopotamian temple tower known technically as a *ziggurat*.

The tower of Babel (11:1–9) was probably just such a ziggurat. In fact, the description of Jacob's staircase "with its top reaching to heaven" (**28:12**) reminds us very much of 11:4, where we are told that the builders were trying to erect a tower "that reaches to the heavens." While the tower of Babel came to symbolize confusion because of human arrogance (11:9), Jacob's staircase came to symbolize communion and fellowship with God, as we shall see (**28:15**). In Jacob's dream, the angels of God were ascending the

1. See, e.g., C. Aldred, *The Egyptians* (New York: Frederick A. Praeger, Inc., 1961), Plate 8; P. Montet, *Eternal Egypt* (New York: New American Library of World Literature, Inc., 1964), Plate 90.

staircase to bring Jacob's needs and prayers to the Lord and descending to bring the Lord's blessings and answers to Jacob.

The motif of the ascending and descending angels was referred to by Jesus in a memorable interview with Nathanael, one of his disciples. Jesus said to him, "You shall see heaven open, and the angels of God ascending and descending on the Son of Man" (John 1:51). In making that statement, our Lord was picturing himself as the true bridge between heaven and earth. Jesus Christ is the real ziggurat, the ultimate staircase, the only genuine mediator "between God and men" (1 Tim. 2:5). Jacob's dream of the staircase was fulfilled in Jesus.[2]

As I pointed out in chapter twelve, at the top of the ancient Mesopotamian ziggurat the builders often set up a small shrine that they sometimes painted with blue enamel to make it blend in with the color of their god's celestial home. They believed that their deity would dwell in the shrine temporarily as he came down to meet with his people. The worshiper, then, would climb the outside staircase of the ziggurat all the way to the top, hoping to enjoy communion and fellowship with the god who would condescend to meet him in the little chapel.

Similarly, in Jacob's dream God himself stood at the top of the staircase (Gen. **28:13**). To Jacob he renewed the blessing of Abraham and Isaac, again promising him the land of Canaan and numerous descendants. This time the patriarchs' descendants were compared to the number of the specks of dust on the surface of the earth (**28:14**).

We can observe a striking progression in the figures of speech that God used to help the patriarchs visualize how many descendants they would have. They were to be as numerous as the stars in the sky (15:5), of which many thousands can be seen with the naked eye on a typical Near Eastern night. More than that, they were to be as numerous as the grains of sand along the seashore (22:17), a number difficult to comprehend, reaching certainly into billions upon billions and beyond. That might still turn out to be a theoretically manageable number, however, because (as someone might argue) the coastlines of the earth, however vast, are nevertheless limited. But to have as many descendants as there are speaks of dust on the earth (**28:14**)? Incredible! Who

2. R. Youngblood, *Special-Day Sermons: Outlines and Messages*, 2d ed. (Grand Rapids: Baker, 1989), 31–40.

could possibly conceptualize that? A God who could afford to be so extravagant with his blessings must be infinitely great indeed. Dust, dust, dust—stretching in every direction, far beyond what the eye could see or the mind conceive—what an image to help the ancient Israelite understand how our God fulfills his promises!

Pagan religions in those early days taught that gods were merely local deities who would protect their people only if those people stayed within the borders of their own tribal territories. But Jacob was assured by the God of the patriarchs that he himself was not merely a tribal god. In fact he promised to be with Jacob wherever he went, even if he left Canaan (**28:15**). Realizing that God never leaves his children has been a source of comfort and strength to believers throughout the centuries (see again 26:3, 24; 31:3; Matt. 28:20; Acts 18:10).

When Jacob awoke from his sleep, he realized that God must have been there even though he had been unaware of his presence at first. His frightened response was that the place was awesome indeed, and he described it as "the house of God" and "the gate of heaven" (Gen. **28:17**). Since "Babel" literally means "gateway to a god" and since the tower of Babel was known at certain periods of its history as "The House of the Foundation-Platform of Heaven and Earth," Jacob's description serves to connect the staircase of his dream with the Mesopotamian ziggurats. But his description also functions as a transition to renaming the town near which his dream had occurred.

Jacob's pillow now became a pillar. He took the rock he had used as a headrest and set it up as a stone monument. After pouring oil on top of it to consecrate it (see Exod. 30:25–29), he gave the name "Bethel" to the town that had been formerly known as Luz (Gen. **28:19**). The new name commemorated Jacob's experience there, since Bethel means "house of God" (**28:17**).

Finally, Jacob made a vow that had several conditions attached to it. He promised that if God would indeed be with him, and if he would protect him while he was traveling, and if he would supply him with the basic necessities of life so that he would be able to return home safely (**28:21**; see also 33:18), then the Lord would be Jacob's God, the pillar would be God's house (in the sense that it would commemorate Jacob's meeting with God at Bethel), and, last but not least, Jacob would give to the Lord a tenth of everything he owned (**28:22**; see 14:20). The last half of

28:22, directed personally to God himself, is Jacob's first recorded prayer.

In summary, Jacob was promising God his life, his worship, and his possessions. Meeting God at Bethel was a critical stage in Jacob's relationship with him.

We might even call it Jacob's conversion.

Jacob's Marriage (29:1–30)

After his remarkable experience at Bethel, Jacob set out on foot and eventually reached the territory where the people of Qedem lived. An Egyptian story dating from the time of Egypt's Dynasty XII tells of how a man named Sinuhe, on voluntary exile from Egypt, arrived in the land of "Qedem,"[3] a word that means simply "east" (Gen. **29:1**). In Jacob's case, it referred to the region near Haran (**29:4**).

A well was located there, and it had a large stone covering its mouth. In fact, so huge was the stone that the local shepherds were apparently reluctant to roll it away unless there happened to be enough thirsty sheep and goats nearby to make the effort worthwhile.

Jacob asked the shepherds who were there if they were acquainted with Laban, Nahor's grandson (**29:5**). They told him they were, and then they pointed to Laban's daughter Rachel ("Rachel" means "ewe," an appropriate name for a shepherdess), who was just arriving to give water to her father's sheep.

When Jacob saw her, he went over and singlehandedly rolled the stone from the well's mouth (**29:10**), clearly a feat of unusual strength. Then he kissed her and wept with joy—obviously a case of love at first sight! Jacob told Rachel that he was related to her father through Rebekah. When she heard that, she ran and told Laban of Jacob's arrival, and then Laban in turn ran to greet him and bring him into his home.

After Laban had heard everything Jacob told him, he said to him, "You are my own flesh and blood" (**29:14**). Translated literally, his actual words were "Surely you are my bone and my flesh." As such, the words were reminiscent of Adam's exclamation concerning Eve at the time of her creation (2:23): "This is now bone of my bones and flesh of my flesh." (Blood kinship was a matter not taken lightly in ancient times.) Once again,

---

3. See J. A. Wilson in *Ancient Near Eastern Texts*, ed. J. B. Pritchard, 2d ed. (Princeton: Princeton University Press, 1955), 19.

although the fact is not made explicit in the text, God had brought a descendant of Abraham to the right bride (see 24:48).

When Jacob had stayed with Laban for a month, Laban asked him to continue working for him for mutually agreeable wages. By now Jacob had fallen deeply in love with Rachel, who was more beautiful than her older sister Leah (which means "cow"). So he told Laban that he would work seven years in exchange for the hand of Rachel in marriage.

Laban agreed immediately, and Jacob began to fulfill his unusual seven-year labor contract. Under such circumstances we might guess that seven years would crawl along at a snail's pace. In this case, however, "they seemed like only a few days to him because of his love for her" (29:20).

Unfortunately, Laban had secretly decided to give Jacob Leah instead of Rachel. Maybe he had tried unsuccessfully to marry her off earlier, and now he saw his chance. His plan was deceptively simple. At the end of the seven years, Jacob said to Laban, "Give me my wife" (29:21). Those carelessly expressed words would cost him dearly. If Jacob had simply used Rachel's name, the canny Laban would not have been able to substitute Leah. As it was, Laban prepared the customary wedding feast honoring the new bride. Then, after dark, he sent Leah into Jacob's tent. It was not until morning that Jacob realized he had been tricked. By that time it was too late to do anything about it, because he had already consummated the union with Leah.

How could Laban's scheme have turned out so successfully? Was Jacob unable to distinguish between the two girls because of the darkness? Did Leah's veil (see 24:65) conceal her identity? Had Jacob become intoxicated by the wine served at the wedding feast? Or was it a combination of these and perhaps other factors?

Whatever the reason, Jacob had obviously met his match in Laban: The deceiver had been deceived. Jacob had deceived Esau, and now Laban had deceived Jacob. "A man reaps what he sows" (Gal. 6:7).

Understandably, Jacob was upset and disgusted. He had worked hard for seven years and still had not won the hand of Rachel, so he asked Laban for an explanation. Laban pleaded local practice as his excuse: "It is not our custom here to give the younger daughter in marriage before the older one" (Gen. 29:26). Then he generously agreed to give Rachel to Jacob in exchange for another seven years of work!

Having no recourse under the law, at least to his knowledge, Jacob consented. The seven days of Leah's wedding feast were concluded as originally intended (29:28; see also Judg. 14:17). Jacob then received Rachel as his second wife, and seven more years of work began. Taking everything into consideration, it is no wonder that Jacob "loved Rachel more than Leah" (Gen. **29:30**).

Fertility in Family and Flock (29:31–30:43)

Because Leah was less loved than Rachel, the Lord took pity on her and gave her a son, Jacob's firstborn. Genesis 29:31–30:24 tells the story of the birth of eleven of Jacob's sons. The Hebrew love of punning is evident in the individual accounts of why each son was given a particular name. (The wordplays also help to fix each name firmly in the memory of the hearer or reader.)

Reuben was Jacob's firstborn son. His name means "See, a son!" and is related to Leah's observation that God had "seen" her misery (**29:32**). Similarly, Ishmael (which means "God hears") had been so named because God had "heard" Hagar's cry of affliction (16:11).

Likewise *Simeon* (which probably means "one who hears"), Jacob's second son, was given his name because the Lord had "heard" that Leah was unloved (**29:33**) by her husband.

Levi was born next. His name perhaps means "attachment" and reflects Leah's desire that now her husband would become "attached" to her because she had borne him three sons (**29:34**).

It is noteworthy that these first three boys were given names that mirror Leah's unhappy relationship with Jacob, a situation that was not of her own making.

Judah ("praise") was so named because when he was born Leah said, "I will praise the LORD" (**29:35**). In this case no comment is made about Leah's relationship to Jacob, perhaps in anticipation of the fact that in later years Judah gained in prominence and eventually became one of the two most important of Jacob's twelve sons.

Meanwhile, Rachel began to envy Leah's fertility. She wanted very much to have children of her own (**30:1**; see also **30:24**) and said to Jacob in a fit of jealousy, "Give me children, or I'll die!" (Her words were ironically and tragically prophetic, because she died in labor when Jacob's twelfth son, Benjamin, was born; see 35:18.)

But Jacob replied, "Am I in the place of God?" Joseph would respond similarly in a different situation years later (50:19). Both men were reminding their listeners that God is sovereign, that he does as he pleases, and that we cannot overrule his purposes.[4]

Rachel sheepishly realized that she had blamed Jacob for something that was not his fault. So she then told him to cohabit with her servant girl Bilhah and produce a son through her (**30:3**). Jacob's grandmother Sarah had made a similar suggestion to Abraham many years before (16:2). As I pointed out earlier (see chapter fifteen), the legal sanction behind such proposals has been amply illustrated by contract documents found at Nuzi—but the morality of Rachel's demand is no less questionable than Sarah's had been.

Bilhah, said Rachel, was to bear the child "for me" (lit. "on my knees"; **30:3**), a phrase symbolic of adoption procedure (see 48:5, 12) and indicating that Rachel intended to adopt the newborn child as her own. Jacob consented to Rachel's request, and Bilhah became his concubine (35:22) for the purpose of bearing children.

So *Dan* was born to Jacob and Rachel through Bilhah. His name means "He has vindicated," since God had, in effect, argued Rachel's case by hearing her plea and vindicating her cause (**30:6**).

The sixth son, *Naphtali* ("my struggle"), was also born to Bilhah. He was so named because Rachel had "had a great struggle" with her sister Leah and had won the battle (**30:8**).

As Rachel had given her servant girl Bilhah to Jacob as a concubine, so Leah now gave her servant girl Zilpah to him. Through Zilpah the seventh son, *Gad*, was born. His name, meaning "good fortune," reflects Leah's joyful cry at his birth: "What good fortune!" (**30:11**).

Asher ("happy") was also born to Zilpah. He was given that name because at his birth Leah exclaimed, "How happy I am! The women will call me happy" (**30:13**).

Jacob's firstborn son Reuben, now old enough to play in the fields, found some mandrake plants there one day and brought them to his mother Leah. "The peculiar shape of the large, fleshy, forked roots, which resemble the lower part of the human body, gave rise to a popular superstition that the mandrake would

4. See R. Youngblood, *The Heart of the Old Testament* (Grand Rapids: Baker, 1971), 17–26.

induce conception."[5] Rachel, who at this stage of her life probably believed that superstition, asked Leah for some of Reuben's
mandrakes.

Leah agreed, but only if Rachel would allow Jacob to sleep
with Leah that night. (Apparently Rachel, as Jacob's favorite wife,
had the questionable privilege of deciding which of Jacob's wives
or concubines he would sleep with on any given night.) Out of
this arrangement, tainted by superstition and sordidness, came
the next son.

Issachar, Leah's fifth son, was Jacob's ninth. His name perhaps
means "reward" because, as Leah said, "God has rewarded me
for giving my maidservant to my husband" (**30:18**). She had also
told Jacob earlier that she had "hired" him (another possible
meaning of Issachar) in exchange for Reuben's mandrakes (**30:16**).

Leah's sixth son was Jacob's tenth. Leah was sure that Jacob
would now "honor" her because she had borne him six sons, so
she named the newborn baby *Zebulun* (which probably means
"honor").

Jacob's eleventh child was actually a daughter named Dinah,
but since daughters were considered less important than sons in
those days, nothing more is said of her here (**30:21**). Instead we
are told that God now "remembered" (**30:22**) Rachel in her distress, just as he had remembered Noah in his (8:1) and would
later remember Hannah in hers (1 Sam. 1:19–20). To "remember"
in such situations did not mean to recall something that had
been temporarily forgotten. It meant, rather, to "pay special attention to" or "lovingly care for" someone. So God remembered
Rachel, paid attention to her needs, and gave her a son of her
own. The newborn baby was named *Joseph*, meaning "may he
add," because of Rachel's plea that God would add yet another
son to her (**30:24**).

The fulfillment of that plea would result in Rachel's death
(35:16–18). In the meantime, however, Jacob had become the
father of eleven sons and one daughter through four different
wives. His family had become fertile indeed, and God was blessing them lavishly.

God's blessings of fertility on Jacob's family were matched by
similar blessings on Jacob's flocks, a subject that occupies the
remainder of Genesis 30. Now that Rachel had given birth to a

5. *Fauna and Flora of the Bible* (London: United Bible Societies, 1972), 139.

son, Jacob felt that it was about time for him to begin the trip back to Canaan. So he asked Laban to allow him to leave with his wives and children.

The crafty Laban, however, could see that he had a good thing going for him. He had observed that God was blessing Jacob (**30:27**). Similar observations had been made by other men concerning Abraham (21:22) and Isaac (26:28) in former years. Jacob's prosperity is an illustration of the fact that when a man of God's choice is doing a good job, his employer will usually want to keep him around for as long as possible.

So Laban asked Jacob to name his wages and stay in Mesopotamia. Jacob finally agreed, requesting as his wages only the speckled and spotted animals in Laban's flocks. Laban readily consented to Jacob's request, but then he secretly removed all such animals from his flocks without telling Jacob he was doing so.

Nevertheless, Jacob had apparently already formulated his own plans for breeding animals with speckled or spotted markings. He went and gathered some "poplar" and other branches and cut "white" stripes in them, exposing some of the "white" wood of the branches (**30:37**). The Hebrew words for "poplar" and "white" are puns on the name Laban, which means "white." Jacob's scheme was saying, in effect, "I'll give Laban some of his own medicine!"

Jacob had tricked his brother Esau (Edom, "red") by offering him some red stew; he would now attempt to trick his uncle Laban ("white") by making use of white branches. He placed the branches in conspicuous positions near the watering troughs that Laban's animals were accustomed to using. The stronger female sheep and goats would see the branches when they came to drink, and Jacob superstitiously hoped that they would then produce speckled young because they had seen speckled wood.

In many ways, Jacob and Rachel were two of a kind. She had bargained for some mandrakes, superstitiously hoping that by eating them she would become pregnant (**30:14–15**). God honored her desire—but in spite of, not because of, her foolish superstition (**30:22–23**). Similarly, God honored Jacob's desire for large flocks, but—again—in spite of his superstitious maneuvering and not because of it (31:4–10). Like his grandfather (13:2) and father (26:12–13) before him, Jacob became very wealthy (**30:43**).

21

Jacob's Return Home (31:1–37:1)

Jacob's Departure from Laban (31:1–55)

Jacob's Meeting with Esau (32:1–33:20)

The Rape of Dinah (34:1–31)

Jacob's Return to Bethel (35:1–29)

The Edomite Genealogy (36:1–37:1)

By this time, Jacob had been living in Mesopotamia for twenty years (**31:38, 41**). He had married two wives, acquired two concubines, and become the father of eleven sons and one daughter. He had also accumulated a great amount of wealth.

Surely the time was now ripe for him to go back to Canaan.

Jacob's Departure from Laban (31:1–55)

Several factors made Jacob decide to return home. First, Laban's sons were complaining that Jacob had become wealthy at their father's expense (**31:1**). This meant that their own inheritance had been severely reduced. So it was likely that they

227

would become angry with Jacob, and their anger could easily erupt into violence.

Second, Laban himself had begun to look at Jacob with disfavor. Jacob could tell that things were not the same between them as they had been before in happier days (**31:2, 5**).

Third, Rachel and Leah felt that their father Laban had cheated them out of their own share of the family inheritance by stupidly allowing Jacob to take it over bit by bit. They came to the conclusion that their future security lay elsewhere, with Jacob, and so they encouraged him to leave Laban and take them along with him (**31:14–16**).

Finally, and overriding every other consideration, it was God's will for Jacob to leave Mesopotamia and return to Canaan. Circumstances may seem to be compelling us to undertake a certain course of action, but before we act we should be as sure as we can that God is in it.

In Jacob's case, the Lord specifically told him that he was to go back to Canaan (**31:3, 13**). As before, so also now God promised to accompany Jacob with his protecting presence (**31:3**; see also **31:5**). Jacob told his wives that Laban had cheated him by changing his wages ten times (**31:7**; see also **31:41**) but that in spite of Laban's deceit God had stepped in and made Jacob prosperous (**31:7–9**). (Even Jacob's own superstitious attempts to increase the size of his flocks as recorded in 30:31–43 were successful only because God overruled, as Jacob himself finally seemed to realize; see **31:9**.) Clinching his decision to return to Canaan was a dream in which Jacob heard the angel of the Lord, who spoke in the name of the God of Bethel, command Jacob to go back home (**31:11–13**).

So every signal Jacob was receiving—from Laban, from Laban's sons, from Jacob's own wives, from God himself—indicated to him that the time was ripe for him to go home and that he should prepare to leave as soon as possible (**31:17–18**).

But two clouds hung over the scene of Jacob's potential departure.

First, Jacob had deceived Laban by not telling him that he was leaving (**31:20**). Jacob had already crossed the Euphrates (the "River" of **31:21**; see also 15:18) and was headed for Gilead (a territory northeast of the Sea of Galilee) before Laban found out he had left. Laban took some men with him and set out in pursuit, but one night during the chase God warned Laban not to harm Jacob (**31:24**).

When he finally overtook Jacob, Laban scolded him for deceiving him. He told Jacob that he would have liked to have given him and his family a royal farewell. "Why did you run off secretly?" he asked (**31:27**). Jacob's only response was that he was afraid Laban would have taken his daughters away from him by force (**31:31**).

Second, and to complicate matters even further, Rachel had stolen Laban's *teraphim* (household idols) while Laban had been away from home shearing sheep (**31:19**). Why she had done so is debatable. Many scholars have felt that possession of a man's household idols was tantamount to possessing the rights to his estate after his death. Contract tablets from Nuzi have been used to support this idea[1] (for information about Nuzi, see chapter thirteen). But it is more likely that the Nuzi custom implied deliberate bequeathal by the owner of the idols and that therefore stealing them would not legitimize the thief's claim.[2] Rachel probably took the idols either hoping they would protect her en route or simply to have objects of worship from that day onward. We know that similar practices were current in the Near East hundreds of years later.[3] After all, Rachel was probably not yet completely free of her polytheistic background and beliefs (see Josh. 24:2 and esp. Gen. **35:2**).

At any rate, Laban became angry when he found out his "gods" (**31:30**) had been stolen. He asked Jacob why he had taken them, apparently feeling that Jacob was the most likely thief. Obviously, Laban had come to know Jacob fairly well by this time.

But Jacob did not know that Rachel had taken the idols. So he told Laban that if he could find them among the belongings of anyone in Jacob's party, that person would be put to death (**31:32**). Such a vow, even made in all innocence, can be very

1. See, e.g., E. A. Speiser, "Nuzi," in *The Interpreter's Dictionary of the Bible*, ed. G. A. Buttrick (Nashville: Abingdon, 1962), 3:573–74.

2. See, e.g., M. J. Selman, "Nuzi," in *The Illustrated Bible Dictionary*, ed. J. D. Douglas (Wheaton, Ill.: Tyndale, 1980), 2:1103; see also B. L. Eichler, "Nuzi," in *The Interpreter's Dictionary of The Bible: Supplementary Volume*, ed. K. Crim et al. (Nashville: Abingdon, 1976), 635.

3. See Josephus, *Antiquities* XVIII, 9, 5; see also R. Youngblood, "Teraphim," in *Wycliffe Bible Encyclopedia*, ed. C. F. Pfeiffer et al. (Chicago: Moody, 1975), 1685.

dangerous, as Joseph's brothers were to discover years later (44:6–12).

Jacob told Laban to go ahead and look around if he wanted to. Laban did so, but he could not find the idols because Rachel had hidden them in her camel saddle and was sitting on them. She apologized to her father for not getting up to pay him the respect due him, stating that she could not get up because she was having her monthly period (**31:35**). In later generations the law of Moses would stipulate that a woman in that condition was ritually unclean (Lev. 15:19), and that may have been true even here.

We must not miss the humor of this scene and its contrast with the majesty and power of the one true God. False gods like Laban's are so small and so helpless that they can be hidden in a camel saddle, there to be rendered unclean by a menstruating woman (see Lev. 15:20)!

Now it was Jacob's turn to become angry. He scolded Laban for what he thought was a false accusation. He then pointed out to him that Laban had gotten the better of the deal in every way during the twenty years of their business relationship (Gen. **31:36–41**). He ended his tirade by saying, "If the God of my father, the God of Abraham and the Fear of Isaac, had not been with me, you would surely have sent me away empty-handed" (**31:42**).

Jacob had referred to God as "the God of my father" also in **31:5**, and Laban, speaking to Jacob, had spoken of "the God of your father" in **31:29**. Here in **31:42** Jacob identified him more specifically as "the God of Abraham and the Fear of Isaac" (see also **31:53**).

If the word "Fear" is correctly translated here and is intended as a title for God, we should probably understand it in the sense of "revered one." But it has also been suggested that it means "kinsman."[4] If the former is the right translation, the title refers to God's holiness, his aloofness, his transcendence. But if the word means "kinsman," the reference would be to God's closeness, his nearness, his immanence. Although we cannot be certain of the correct translation, the latter would fit in well with the intimate relationship the patriarchs enjoyed with their God.

Laban did not back down from his claims of ownership over

---

4. W. F. Albright, *From the Stone Age to Christianity*, 2d ed. (Baltimore: Johns Hopkins Press, 1957), 248.

his daughters, grandchildren and flocks. But he recognized that his daughters had every right to accompany their husband Jacob back to Canaan if they wished to do so (**31:43**). So Laban proposed that he and Jacob make a covenant between them, a covenant to be solemnized by offering a sacrifice (**31:44**; see also 15:9–11, 17–18; Exod. 24:5–8) and sharing a meal (Gen. **31:46**; see also Exod. 24:11). The covenant they entered into was a nonaggression pact in which Laban and Jacob promised not to deceive each other or trespass on one another's territory (Gen. **31:50, 52**).

To mark the boundary between them, Jacob set up a rock as a pillar. He also had his men gather stones and pile them up into a mound. Each man gave the mound a name in his own language: Laban the Aramean (see **31:24**) called it Jegar Sahadutha (Aramaic for "witness heap"), while Jacob the Hebrew called it Galeed (Hebrew for "witness heap"; for the later naming of an altar in a similar way, see Josh. 22:34).

It was also called Mizpah ("watchtower") because Laban said to Jacob, "May the Lord keep watch between you and me when we are away from each other" (Gen. **31:49**). This statement is sometimes called the "Mizpah Benediction" and is well known and beloved among many Christian groups. But Laban and Jacob were in no mood to wish each other well or to ask God to protect them while they were separated from each other. The context indicates that Laban's statement should be understood to mean something like this: "May the Lord keep an eye on you and me while we're separated from each other"—to keep each man from cheating or deceiving the other. So the so-called Mizpah Benediction turns out to be a malediction, or at least a negative benediction.

The mound and pillar were set up as boundary markers between the northern territory where Laban lived and the territory to the south where Jacob would once again live (**31:52**). They were set up in the hill country of Gilead (**31:25, 54**). (Jacob's name for the mound, "Galeed," is a pun on "Gilead.")

Each man took a solemn oath to abide by the terms of the covenant. On the one hand, Laban's oath seems to intentionally reflect his polytheism, his belief in many so-called gods. The verb in **31:53** is plural, and his oath can be translated, "May the god(s) of Abraham and the god(s) of Nahor, the god(s) of their father, judge between us." In other words, Laban took his oath in the name of Terah's god or gods (see Josh. 24:2). On the other hand, Jacob took his oath in the name of the one true God, the God of his father Isaac (Gen. **31:53**), the God whom Jacob had met and worshiped at Bethel twenty years earlier (28:13).

The two men had now finally made their decision to separate, apparently never to see each other again. The next morning Laban kissed his daughters and grandchildren goodbye and then went home (**31:55**). (The Hebrew word for "bless" often means simply "say hello" or "say goodbye"; see esp. 47:7, 10.)

Jacob's Meeting with Esau (32:1–33:20)

Before he could return confidently and safely (**33:18**) to Canaan, Jacob would have to settle accounts with his brother Esau, whom he had cheated out of his birthright and blessing (27:36). When Jacob had left Canaan, his life had been tainted with treachery and deceit. But since then he had had a profound spiritual experience, so his relationship with Esau would have to be made right. Our fellowship with God can never be complete until we become reconciled with people we have wronged. In Jacob's case, even before meeting Esau again he would meet God again, as we shall see.

After leaving Laban, Jacob continued on his way accompanied by the angels of God (**32:1**). Their presence no doubt reminded Jacob that God had promised to be with him always (28:15; see also 28:12; **31:11, 13**).

When he saw the angels, Jacob exclaimed, "This is the camp of God!" (**32:2**). In commemoration of his vision, the place where Jacob saw them was named Mahanaim, which means "two camps" or "two armies." Its location is uncertain, but it was situated somewhere in Gilead east of the Jordan River and north of the Jabbok River. The name anticipated also the "two groups" into which Jacob would soon divide his household and herds (**32:7, 10**).

The presence of the angels must have comforted and reassured Jacob, at least to some extent. As a psalmist of a later generation said, "The angel of the LORD encamps around those who fear him, and he delivers them" (Ps. 34:7).

But Jacob realized that Esau might still be angry with him, so he decided to take the necessary precautions. He sent messengers on ahead of him to Esau (Gen. **32:3**). When they arrived, they were to refer to Esau as Jacob's "lord" and to Jacob as Esau's "servant" (**32:4, 5**; see also **32:18, 20**) in order to stress Jacob's humility.

When the messengers returned, they told Jacob that Esau was coming to meet him with an army of 400 men. Greatly frightened by this news, Jacob divided his household and animals into two groups. This would allow one group to escape if Esau attacked the other group (**32:6–8**).

He also sent a large number of animals to Esau as a gift. He divided them into three separate herds to be presented to Esau at intervals, hoping to calm him down gradually before Jacob himself arrived (**32:13–21**).

But before he sent the animals, in his second recorded prayer (for his first, see 28:22) Jacob prayed to God for mercy, reminding him that he had advised him to go back to Canaan (**32:9**; see **31:13**) and that he had promised to give him a large number of descendants (**32:12**; see 28:14). Jacob was acting on the important truth that when a believer gets into a difficult situation, he should go to God in prayer immediately and not do so only as a last resort.

That same night, Jacob sent the members of his immediate family across the Jabbok River (today called the Wadi Zerqa, a stream flowing westward into the Jordan River about twenty miles north of the Dead Sea). Left alone, Jacob suddenly found himself wrestling with "a man" (**32:24**) in a struggle that lasted till daybreak. Hosea 12:3–4 identifies Jacob's opponent as God himself in the person of a divine messenger, an angel.

This strange wrestling match ended in a draw. The angel managed to dislocate Jacob's hip (**32:25**), causing him to walk with a limp after that time (**32:31**). Jacob's injured tendon (probably the sciatic muscle) is the basis of a later Israelite dietary prohibition (**32:32**).

But Jacob refused to let the angel go until the angel agreed to bless him (**32:26, 29**). The angel changed Jacob's name from Jacob ("deceiver") to Israel ("God struggles" or "he struggles with God") because he had struggled with God and emerged victorious, at least to some extent (**32:28**). God would later confirm Jacob's change of name (**35:10**), and the fact that "Jacob" had become "Israel" would often be recalled in later generations (1 Kings 18:31; 2 Kings 17:34). Jacob's little family would eventually grow and become the mighty nation of Israel.

In turn, Jacob asked the angel what his name was, but he refused to tell him (Gen. **32:29**). He indicated that there was no need for Jacob to know that fact (see the similar refusal expressed by the angel of the Lord in another situation recorded in Judg. 13:17–18).

To commemorate the wrestling match and its consequences, Jacob named the place where it happened Peniel (Gen. **32:30**), elsewhere always spelled "Penuel" (see, e.g., **32:31**; both words mean "the face of God"). The exact location of the site is unknown, but it would not have been too far from the Jabbok River. Like Hagar before him, Jacob thought he had seen God face to face and was therefore surprised that he was still alive (**32:30**; see 16:13; see also Exod. 33:20, 23). Similar situations are also recorded in Judges 6:22; 13:22.

Such cases simply reinforce the fact that the angel of God was not God himself. No one can see God's face and remain alive (Exod. 33:20). It is possible to see only his "back" (Exod. 33:23) or "feet" (24:10) or "form" (Num. 12:8) or the like, and even then only in a symbolic or figurative or visionary sense. God is spirit (John 4:24) and therefore has no physical characteristics as such.

This is why idolatry was considered to be the supreme blasphemy in ancient Israel. Any attempt to represent God in a sculpture, painting, or any other art form is bound to result in a misrepresentation of him (see esp. Deut. 4:15–18). It will make him appear infinitely less than what he really is.

As Jesus reminded us, "No man has seen God at any time" (John 1:18). In other words, no one has ever seen the invisible God, whose essence is spiritual. Only in the person of Jesus himself, God the Son, can we discover the character of God (Heb. 1:1–3).

Jacob's experience at Penuel is a fine example of persistence in faith and prayer.[5] Fearless in his struggle "with God [at the Jabbok] and with men [e.g., with Laban in Mesopotamia]" (Gen. **32:28**), he now had nothing to fear from Esau. Genesis 33 displays Jacob's courtesy toward his brother but is completely silent about the fear he had shown earlier. Similarly, our lives will be spiritually vital only as we strengthen them with persistent prayer.

When Jacob saw Esau coming with his 400 men, he divided his wives and children into three groups in the order of their importance in his eyes. He then lined up the groups, one behind

---

5. G. Vos, *Biblical Theology* (Grand Rapids: Eerdmans, 1948), 111–14.

the other, keeping the most important group (Rachel and Joseph) in the rear (**33:1–2**). He himself led the way, bowing down to the ground seven times as he approached Esau (**33:3**). This was a sign of total and abject humility, as certain fourteenth-century-B.C. documents found at Tell el-Amarna in Egypt demonstrate.[6]

But Esau ran forward to meet him, and the two brothers enjoyed a tearful reunion (**33:4**). As he had instructed his messengers to do (**32:3–5, 17–20**), Jacob himself also referred to himself as Esau's "servant" and to Esau as his "lord" (**33:5, 8, 13–15**). But Esau generously insisted on calling Jacob his "brother" (**33:9**), obviously willing to let bygones be bygones.

After Jacob had introduced his family to Esau (**33:5–7**; cf. **48:9**), he insisted that Esau accept the gift of animals he had offered him. Then, not wanting to go to Seir, Esau's homeland, Jacob told Esau to go on ahead. He gave him the excuse that his children and animals were weak and that he did not want to delay Esau (**33:12–16**).

When Esau had left, Jacob went on to a place called Succoth (which means "shelters"). There he built a house for himself and shelters for his animals (**33:17**). We cannot say for certain where Succoth was located, but it was east of the Jordan River and on an approximately direct line between Penuel (**32:31**) and Shechem (**33:18**).

At long last, Jacob crossed the Jordan and arrived at Shechem, a city founded during the patriarchal period and located near the center of the land (see Judg. 9:34–39). The Lord had answered Jacob's prayer of twenty years earlier that he might return to his homeland "safely" (**33:18**; see 28:21). Although Rebekah had expected Jacob to live in Mesopotamia only "for a while" (27:44), his stay there had stretched into many long years. But God in his own good time had now brought Jacob home. Our prayers are always answered, even if not always in the way we expect them to be.

The plot of ground where Jacob pitched his tent near Shechem he purchased for a hundred "pieces of silver" from the sons of Hamor the Hivite. Since Hamor means "donkey," it is possible that Hamor and his sons were donkey caravanners, as the patri-

---

6. See, e.g., W. F. Albright in *Ancient Near Eastern Texts*, ed. J. B. Pritchard, 2d ed. (Princeton: Princeton University Press, 1955), 483–90; see also R. F. Youngblood, *The Amarna Correspondence of Rib-Haddi, Prince of Byblos (EA 68–96)* (Ann Arbor: University Microfilms, 1972), 15–18.

archs themselves may have been (see chapter thirteen). The word translated "pieces of silver" (Heb. *qĕśîtâ*) is found only twice elsewhere and always in patriarchal contexts (Josh. 24:32; Job 42:11).

Jacob (or his men) dug a well near Shechem. Mentioned also in John 4:5–6, "Jacob's well" can still be visited at the present time. It is one of the few clearly authentic ancient sites to be seen in the Holy Land today. The well is deep, and its water is cold and delicious.

At Shechem, Jacob built an altar and named it El Elohe Israel (lit. "God, the God of Israel") in gratitude to God for bringing him safely home. In so doing, Jacob was following a practice begun by his grandfather Abraham, who had a habit of building altars at places where he had significant spiritual experiences (Gen. 12:7; 13:18; 22:9). Jacob's response to God was the correct one. God had answered his prayer, and so Jacob worshiped him with heartfelt thanks **(33:20)**.

The Rape of Dinah (34:1–31)

The title of this section could just as easily be "The Rape of the City of Shechem."

Genesis 34 is one of the most sordid chapters in the entire Bible. It tells a story of rape, anger, deceit, greed, murder, violence, and selfishness. God's name appears twice in the place-name that ends Genesis 33, and God's name begins Genesis 35—but it is no wonder that the name of God does not appear even once in all of Genesis 34.

The city of Shechem had its namesake in one of the sons of Hamor the Hivite **(33:19; 34:2)**. The young Shechem was the most honored (and perhaps pampered) member of his family **(34:19)**. He was no doubt accustomed to getting just about anything he wanted. So when he saw and desired Jacob's only daughter Dinah, he seized her and raped her.

It often happens that after a man has committed the sin of rape, his desire turns to disgust. This is what took place, for example, after David's son Amnon had raped his half-sister Tamar (2 Sam. 13:10–15).

The reverse was true in the case of Shechem, however. After he had raped Dinah, he fell in love with her (Gen. **34:3**). In both instances the act of rape was disgraceful and vile **(34:7;** 2 Sam. 13:12). And in Dinah's case, her brothers were enraged when they heard about it.

Meanwhile, Shechem had told his father Hamor that he wanted to marry Dinah (Gen. **34:4**). Hamor was pleased with the idea, so he told Dinah's father and brothers that intermarriage between their two families would be mutually beneficial. As for Shechem, he offered to bring as large a bridal price and gift as Jacob and his sons wanted (**34:12**).

What Dinah's brothers really wanted, however, was revenge. So, as true sons of Jacob, they deceitfully agreed to the marriage of Shechem and Dinah. This would take place, however, only on the condition that all the males in the city of Shechem agreed to be circumcised, just as all the males in Jacob's family had been (**34:15**). Jacob's sons had obviously learned a few dirty tricks from their father's previous example in his own moments of sinful weakness. Now they were about to use the holy ceremony of circumcision—the sign of the Abrahamic covenant—as a tool to further their wicked plans. Few sins are more despicable than pressing the sacred into service for profane use.

Hamor and Shechem were completely duped by the suggestion of Jacob's sons. So they made a formal proposal to all the male Shechemites at the gateway of the city, the normal forum for legal activity and discussion in ancient times (**34:20**; see also 23:10). The ulterior motive of greed entered into their decision, since they felt that they would gain in wealth at the expense of the Israelites (**34:23**). So the fateful circumcision took place.

Men weakened by pain and loss of blood are no match for strong, healthy, angry men. Two of Jacob's sons, Simeon and Levi—apparently the ringleaders, since they (like Dinah) were Leah's offspring—counted on that fact. And they were fiendishly correct: They were easily able to kill all the male Shechemites and retrieve Dinah from Shechem's house. The sons of Jacob then came and plundered the city of all its wealth, taking its women and children captive as well.

The vengeance they meted out was terrible indeed. Even though a woman had been raped—and that was the only excuse Simeon and Levi had (**34:31**)—the punishment far exceeded the crime. At any rate, two wrongs never make a right, nor does might make right.

And all Jacob could think of was his own reputation. Never mind the fact that his daughter had been raped, or that every male citizen of Shechem had been slaughtered, or that the city itself had been plundered, or that its women and children had been taken captive, or that Jacob's sons had degraded and dehumanized themselves by committing acts of unspeakable wickedness. Jacob's ego had now been hurt, and he thought only of his lowered standing among the local inhabitants. His selfish response to the violence and bloodshed his sons had perpetrated is highlighted by his use of "me," "my," and "I" no less than six times in **34:30**.

As for Simeon and Levi, Jacob's deathbed blessing would turn out to be a curse for them (49:5–7). Their descendants would be scattered far and wide because of the terrible crime at Shechem.

A sordid chapter indeed, Genesis 34 remains a solemn example of how deep people can sink in sin.

Jacob's Return to Bethel (35:1–29)

We are not told how much time elapsed between the events of Genesis 34 and those of Genesis 35. But sooner or later God told Jacob to leave Shechem and go southward to Bethel. There he was to build an altar to the Lord, who had appeared to him at Bethel more than twenty years before (**35:1**; see 28:13).

Jacob wanted to make sure that the members of his household were not ritually unclean when they made the trip. So he told them, among other things, to get rid of their "foreign gods," the idols that Rachel and perhaps others had brought along with them (**35:2**; see **31:19, 30, 34**). Included were "the rings in their ears" (**35:4**)—items of jewelry that were often used as amulets or charms and therefore had pagan religious connotations (see Hos. 2:13). After gathering the idols together, Jacob buried them under a large tree near Shechem (Gen. **35:4**).

As always, God was with Jacob (**35:3**) just as he had promised he would be (28:15), and the fear of him protected Jacob and his household as they traveled (**35:5**). When he arrived at Bethel, he built the altar that God had commanded him to build (**35:7**) and he named it El Bethel ("the God of Bethel").

At about the same time Deborah, Rebekah's nurse who had accompanied her all the way from Mesopotamia (24:59) and may even have outlived her (the last reference to Rebekah alive is 29:12), died and was buried under an oak tree near Bethel. The mourning and weeping that took place at her death gave rise to the name Allon Bacuth ("oak of weeping") for that spot (**35:8**).

God "again" appeared to Jacob and confirmed to him his new

name, Israel (**35:9–10**; see **32:28**). As he had revealed himself to Abraham as "God Almighty" when telling him that he would be the ancestor of numerous descendants who would occupy the land of Canaan (17:1–8), so he now did to Jacob (**35:11–12**). By himself Jacob could not possibly succeed in producing descendants or conquering the land, but with God Almighty on his side Jacob could not possibly fail in doing so.

In gratitude for God's continued promise of help, Jacob again set up a pillar and consecrated it at the very place he had earlier named "Bethel" (i.e., "house of God"; **35:14–15**; see 28:18–19). In so doing he renewed his vows of commitment to the Lord.

Jacob and his household then left Bethel and continued southward. Rachel was in the last stages of pregnancy, and she began to have severe labor pains while the group was traveling. The midwife assisting her told her not to be afraid, assuring her that she was going to have another son (**35:17**). Her words to Rachel were strangely reminiscent of Rachel's own plea when Joseph had been born (30:24). Sadly enough, she died in childbirth (**35:18**) in ironic and tragic fulfillment of another earlier plea she had made (30:1).

Just before Rachel died, she named Jacob's newborn son Ben-Oni (which means "son of my trouble"). Jacob, however, soon renamed the boy Benjamin, which means "son of the right hand" or "son of the south." These two possible translations of the name are related, since one set of ancient Hebrew terms for indications of direction was based on facing toward the east, in which case south was the direction to the right. Benjamin was the ancestor of one of the Israelite tribes that eventually settled in southern Canaan. During the patriarchal period itself, a Semitic tribe with a name very similar to that of Benjamin was located in a region situated to the south of certain other tribes, according to the Mari letters (see chapter thirteen).[7]

Rachel was the only wife of the three patriarchs Abraham, Isaac, and Jacob who was not buried in the cave of Machpelah at Hebron alongside her husband (see 49:29–32). Instead, she was buried beside the road leading to Ephrath (the older name for Bethlehem; see the great messianic prophecy in Mic. 5:2, where the two names are combined as "Bethlehem Ephrathah"; see also Ruth 1:2).

7. See W. F. Albright, *Yahweh and the Gods of Canaan* (Garden City, N.Y.: Doubleday, 1968), 78–79.

Jacob marked Rachel's grave with a tombstone (Gen. **35:20**), and its location was still known in Samuel's time (1 Sam. 10:2). Even today a site near Bethlehem called "Rachel's Tomb" is pointed out by guides and visited by tourists, although in this case we cannot be sure of its authenticity.

Jacob settled down in that general area for a time. While the family was there, Reuben cohabited with his father's concubine Bilhah on at least one occasion (**35:22**). Although he was Jacob's firstborn (**35:23**), he lost his preeminent position because of his sin (49:3–4; 1 Chron. 5:1).

The birth of Benjamin, Jacob's twelfth son, now made the roster of Jacob's sons complete, so they are conveniently listed in the record at this point (Gen. **35:22–26**). Then, still continuing southward, Jacob finally arrived at his father's home in Mamre or Kiriath Arba (older names for Hebron). Isaac died at the age of 180 and was buried by his sons Esau and Jacob (**35:28–29**).

Abraham and Isaac were now off the scene. Although Jacob still had twenty-seven years of life ahead of him, he was already 120 years old at the time of Isaac's death (see 25:26; 47:28). Jacob was suddenly left without three of the people who were dearest to him: his father, his mother, and his favorite wife. The old order was rapidly disappearing, and the focus of attention was about to shift from the older patriarchs to the younger ones and from Canaan to Egypt.

The Edomite Genealogy (36:1–37:1)

Helping us to catch our breath as we move from the old order to the new is Genesis 36, another section of "connective tissue." An earlier example had to do with Ishmael's descendants (25:12–18), while this one is concerned with the descendants of Esau.

Genesis 36 begins and ends with the information that Esau was the ancestor of the Edomites. "Edom" means "red" (see also 25:30), and the territory of the Edomites was located southeast and south of the Dead Sea where reddish-hued rock formations are a conspicuous feature of the landscape.

The names of Esau's wives in **36:2–3** differ somewhat from those in 26:34 and 28:9. The easiest solution to the discrepancies is to assume that errors crept into the text as it was copied and recopied from generation to generation. It is equally possible, however, that Esau's wives had alternate names (after all, Esau himself was also known as Edom), or even that Esau had more than three wives.

The land of Edom was also called "Seir" (**36:8**; see also **32:3**), which means "hairy." We are reminded that "Esau" also may mean "hairy" (see 25:25). Esau apparently drove out the original Horite (Hurrian) inhabitants of Seir (14:6), whose family tree is recorded in **36:20–30**.

A total of twelve Edomite tribes is listed in **36:11–14** (five in **36:11**, four in **36:13**, and three in **36:14**). The frequently recurring pattern of twelve tribes is believed by some scholars to be related to the supposed practice of each tribe supplying the needs of their central sanctuary for one month of the year.[8] We have already observed the pattern in the case of the descendants of Nahor (22:20–24), Ishmael (25:13–16), and Jacob himself (**35:22–26**). Incidentally, "son" in Genesis 36 could in some cases mean "grandson" or, more broadly, "descendant," in accord with general Hebrew usage elsewhere in the OT.

As Genesis 14:14 apparently contains a later editorial touch in its mention of Dan (long before the town in question was called by that name), so also Genesis **36:31** seems to imply a later editorial touch in the way in which it mentions Israelite kings (long before the time of the Israelite monarchy).[9] Since other OT books, like the Psalms, were compiled over a period of centuries, such editorial updating to help later readers should not alarm or even surprise us.

Our doctrine of inspiration is not affected at all by such observations. The same God who inspired the original author (or authors, in the case of a book like Proverbs) of an OT book also inspired its compilers and editors (if any). The final product, the completed Word of God, is just as inspired and infallible and authoritative as each individual word and verse and chapter and book that entered into its compilation. And we should be grateful for whatever God's people in ancient times, "moved by the Holy Spirit" (2 Pet. 1:21), did to clarify that Word for us.

8. See, e.g., M. Noth, *The History of Israel*, rev. ed. (New York: Harper and Brothers, 1960), 85–91.

9. See, e.g., D. Kidner, *Genesis* (Downers Grove, Ill.: Inter-Varsity Press, 1967), 15–16, 178.

22

Joseph's Migration to Egypt (37:2–41:57)

JOSEPH SOLD INTO SLAVERY (37:2–36)

THE JUDAH-TAMAR EPISODE (38:1–30)

JOSEPH EMPLOYED AND IMPRISONED (39:1–40:23)

JOSEPH EXALTED (41:1–57)

For the tenth and final time, we meet the phrase "This is the account of . . ." (Gen. **37:2**). It marks off the last main section of Genesis, a section that is fourteen chapters in length (chaps. 37–50). It focuses more on Joseph than on Jacob, more on Egypt than on Canaan.

We can most conveniently discuss the section in three separate segments: chapters 37–41, chapters 42–47, and chapters 48–50. The time span of chapters 37–41 is at least twenty years (see **37:2; 41:46; 41:53–54**).

Joseph Sold into Slavery (37:2–36)

At the age of seventeen, Joseph was helping his brothers in their task as shepherds. He worked along with all ten of his older brothers, but more specifically he assisted the four who were the sons of Bilhah and Zilpah (**37:2**; see 35:25–26). On at least one occasion, Joseph brought a bad report about them (doubtless all ten of them, as the later context indicates) back to his father Jacob.

Joseph and Benjamin, Jacob's eleventh and twelfth sons and therefore his youngest, had been born to his favorite wife, Rachel. Though younger than Joseph, Benjamin was probably still only a small child at this time, too young as yet to be Jacob's favorite. So of all his sons, Jacob preferred Joseph as one of the two who had been born when Jacob was an old man.

In recognition of Joseph's favored status, Jacob made him a beautiful garment. We do not know exactly what it looked like, but it was probably either a "richly ornamented robe" (**37:3**)—the "coat of many colours" of the King James Version rendering—or a full-length robe, possibly with long sleeves. In any event, it was the kind of robe also worn by children of royalty in ancient times (see 2 Sam. 13:18). It was probably made of expensive materials, and it was certainly a badge of honor. It was also a clear sign of favoritism, however, and it caused Joseph's brothers to become jealous of him (Gen. **37:4**).

In the course of time, Joseph had two dreams that strained the relationship between himself and his brothers even further, because he naïvely told them what he had dreamed.

The first dream portrayed all the brothers out in the fields at harvest time, tying up stalks of grain. Suddenly Joseph's bundle stood upright and all the other bundles gathered around it and bowed down to it (**37:7**). The dream would in fact come true years later (see 42:6; 43:26; 44:14). But for now, Joseph's brothers were understandably indignant that the young Joseph implied that some day he would rule over them. As it turned out, however, in God's providence Joseph would indeed become "the prince among his brothers" (Deut. 33:16; see also 1 Chron. 5:2).

The second dream portrayed the sun, the moon, and eleven stars bowing down to Joseph (Gen. **37:9**). When Jacob heard about it, he scolded Joseph for implying that Jacob, Leah (Joseph's "mother" now that Rachel was dead; see 35:19), and Joseph's eleven brothers (including Benjamin) would eventually bow down to him (**37:10**). Jacob himself was to be preeminent (27:29), not Joseph—or at least that is what Jacob thought!

Because of his dream, Joseph's brothers now hated him all the more. But Jacob kept in mind what Joseph had said (**37:11**). Centuries later Mary, the virgin mother of Jesus, would demonstrate a similarly thoughtful response to the remarkable events surrounding the birth and boyhood of her firstborn son (see Luke 2:19, 51).

Some time after Joseph had told his brothers about his dreams, they were grazing their father's flocks near Shechem. Jacob decided to send Joseph northward from the family estate at Hebron to find out how the men were getting along. When he arrived at Shechem, he was told that his brothers had moved the flocks farther north to the region near Dothan.

As soon as Joseph's brothers saw him coming in the distance, they began to make plans to kill him. They scornfully referred to him (Gen. **37:19**) as "that dreamer" (lit. "master of dreams" or "dream expert"). Their intention was to kill him, throw him into a pit, and claim that a wild animal had eaten him up.

But Reuben, Jacob's firstborn, felt responsible for Joseph's safety. He warned the other brothers not to take Joseph's life and told them simply to throw him into the pit. (He hoped to return later, rescue Joseph, and take him back home to Jacob.) Many years later, when the tables had been turned and the brothers found themselves in an extremely difficult situation, Reuben would remind them of his earlier warning and would tell them that now they would all have to pay for their crime against Joseph (42:22).

When Joseph finally came to where his brothers were, they stripped him of his robe (**37:23**), that hated symbol of parental favoritism (**37:3**), and threw him into the pit (an empty water cistern, perhaps similar to the rectangular, ten-foot-deep cisterns that still dot the landscape near the ancient site). With callous indifference to his cries for help, they then sat down to have lunch.

As they did so, they spotted a caravan of Ishmaelites coming from Gilead and heading for Egypt. The camels in the caravan were loaded down with balm and other spices (**37:25**; Jer. 8:22 indicates that Gilead was noted for its balm). The Ishmaelites are also referred to in Genesis 37 as "Midianites" (**37:28**) and as "Medanites" (Hebrew text of **37:36**). But this is not surprising in light of the fact that Midian and Medan were sons of Abraham through his concubine Keturah (25:2) and were therefore half-brothers of Ishmael (see also Judg. 8:22, 24, 26).

Judah, reflecting on Reuben's warning (Gen. **37:22**) not to shed Joseph's blood (**37:26**), suggested to his brothers that they sell Joseph to the Ishmaelites. After all, the brothers would not want to have his blood on their hands, would they? Judah's proposal represents quite a contrast to Cain's insensitive attitude toward his brother Abel (see 4:9–10).

The brothers agreed. They pulled Joseph up from the pit and sold him to the Ishmaelites. The subject of "pulled" and "sold" in **37:28** is the brothers of **37:27**, according to Joseph's later statement in 45:4. (Stephen understood the story in the same way; see Acts 7:9.)

The price the brothers received was twenty shekels of silver (Gen. **37:28**). That was still the monetary value of a male servant of Joseph's age in the time of Moses (Lev. 27:5). After selling Joseph, the brothers then left the area of the pit, as the context implies.

Meanwhile, Reuben had apparently been away tending the flocks while Joseph was being sold. When he returned to the pit (alone, perhaps to rescue Joseph; see Gen. **37:22**), he was shocked to discover that Joseph was not there. So he tore his clothes as a sign of mourning (see **37:34**) and then went to tell the other brothers (who, of course, already knew).

The men dipped Joseph's robe in goat's blood (**37:31**)—the second time a slaughtered goat was used in an act of betrayal (27:8–17)—and brought it back to their father Jacob. They cynically asked him whether it was Joseph's. Jacob identified it and came to the conclusion that a wild animal must have devoured Joseph (**37:33**)—which is what most of the brothers had planned to tell Jacob anyhow (**37:20**).

Jacob's response to the sight of the blood-spattered robe was to tear his own clothes, put on sackcloth, and mourn the loss of his son. His other sons and daughters tried to comfort him, but to no avail. The mention of Jacob's "daughters" (**37:35**) probably is intended to include daughters-in-law (see **38:2** for an example), since as far as we know Jacob had only one daughter (see 30:21).

Jacob refused to be comforted and said that he would continue to mourn until he reached sheol, where his son was (**37:35**). The term "sheol" is often used in the OT as a synonym for "grave." But it is also sometimes used as a more general reference to the "realm of death" (Deut. 32:22), the shadowy netherworld that served as a dwelling place for the departed spirits of the dead.[1]

In line with the principle of progressive revelation, not every doctrine is fully developed or crystal clear in the OT. God often revealed his truth in stages, one step at a time. The doctrine of immortality is an excellent case in point. It does not spring full-blown from the pages of the OT, and for a very good reason. Only in the resurrection of Jesus Christ did immortality move from fond hope to glorious assurance. It is he "who has destroyed death and has brought life and immortality to light through the gospel" (2 Tim. 1:10).

Jacob, whose understanding of the afterlife could only be partial, preferred mourning to being comforted. Even as he did so, his favorite son Joseph was being sold by the Ishmaelites to Potiphar, one of the Egyptian pharaoh's officials, the captain of the guard (Gen. **37:36**; see Ps. 105:17).

Genesis 37 is a story of naïveté and latent pride on the part of Joseph. It is also a story of hatred, murderous intent, and deception on the part of most of his brothers. In addition, favoritism and insensitivity on Jacob's part lurk in the background. They were undesirable qualities that brought him and his sons to grief, leading Jacob from joy to sorrow, Joseph from freedom to slavery, and the brothers from contentment to jealous rage and violence.

And so it is with us. When we allow our emotions and desires to lead us into sinful acts (James 1:14–15), we ourselves become miserable and everyone around us suffers.

The Judah-Tamar Episode (38:1–30)

Judah's prominence in Genesis 37 (see **37:26–27**) serves as a natural transition to Genesis 38. Judah's unsavory affair with Tamar in Genesis 38 also contrasts sharply with Joseph's rebuff of Potiphar's wife in Genesis 39.

Genesis 38 forms a sad and sorry interlude in Joseph's story, just as Genesis 34 did in Jacob's story. Like Genesis 34, it tells a tale of lustful desire and its unfortunate consequences.

---

1. For a concise discussion, see D. K. Innes, "Sheol," in *The Illustrated Bible Dictionary*, ed. J. D. Douglas (Wheaton, Ill.: Tyndale, 1980), 3:1436; for a detailed defense of the meaning "grave," see R. L. Harris, "Why Hebrew *She'ol* Was Translated 'Grave'" in K. L. Barker, ed., *The NIV: The Making of a Contemporary Translation* (Grand Rapids: Zondervan, 1986), 58–71.

Genesis 38, however, has a happy ending. It describes the birth of a boy who would continue the promised line of Abraham's descendants.

The position of Genesis 38 in the book as a whole indicates that its events occurred shortly after Jacob learned about Joseph's reputed death. Judah went to visit a man of Adullam (**38:1**), a town located southwest of Jerusalem. There Judah met and married a Canaanite woman, and that was the start of his troubles. She bore him three sons (**38:3–5**), and in due course two of the boys reached marriageable age.

In accord with the custom of those times (see, e.g., 21:21; 24:4), Judah chose a wife for his firstborn son Er. The young man was wicked, however, and the Lord put him to death before his wife Tamar became pregnant.

Again in accord with ancient custom, Judah told his second son, Onan, to cohabit with Tamar, his deceased brother's widow. The purpose of such a practice was to produce offspring who could perpetuate the deceased man's name and estate.

For all practical purposes, Onan had no choice in the matter; it was his legal duty to do as Judah demanded (**38:8**; see esp. Deut. 25:5–6, a passage referred to in Matt. 22:24). The custom itself is known as "levirate marriage" (Lat. *levir*, "husband's brother") and explains why Boaz had to get legal permission from Naomi's and Ruth's nearest male relative before Boaz himself, next in line, could marry the widow Ruth (see Ruth 3:12–13; 4:1–6).

Onan, however, knew that Tamar's offspring would not be his own. So he spilled his semen on the ground when he lay with her. His action displeased the Lord, who then put Onan to death also (Gen. **38:9–10**).

Just as the sinfulness of the men of Sodom (see 19:4–9) gave rise to the word "sodomy" (a synonym for "homosexuality"), so also Onan's sin gave rise to the word "onanism," a synonym for "coitus interruptus" (now widely used as a means of birth control). Yet the Lord did not judge Onan simply for practicing coitus interruptus. He did so because Onan refused to perform his levirate duty and continue Judah's line. (Incidentally, the names of Er and Onan appear as tribal designations in documents of the early second millennium B.C.)[2]

---

2. See W. F. Albright, *Yahweh and the Gods of Canaan* (Garden City, N.Y.: Doubleday, 1968), 79–80.

After Onan's death Judah told Tamar to go back to her father's house and live there as a widow until Shelah, Judah's third son, reached marriageable age. Actually, Judah had no intention of giving Shelah to Tamar as a husband. Directly or indirectly she had caused the death of Judah's first two sons, and he was afraid that Shelah also might die because of her (**38:11, 14**). Some time later, Judah decided to go to Timnah (a place of uncertain location) to shear his sheep. His wife had recently died, and the period of mourning for her was over (**38:12**).

When Tamar heard that Judah was going to Timnah, she took off her widow's clothes and dressed herself like a prostitute (see Prov. 7:10), including covering her face with a veil to avoid recognition. She then stationed herself at a certain place on the road (Gen. **38:14**), apparently a customary procedure for prostitutes in ancient times (see Jer. 3:2). She obviously intended to prey on Judah's loneliness and weakness for her own ends, however commendable they might have been.

En route to Timnah, Judah saw her and was overpowered by his own desires. He agreed to pay her a young goat in exchange for her services (Gen. **38:17**). Because the veil concealed her identity, he did not recognize her. She demanded collateral until a goat could be sent to her. The collateral in this case consisted of Judah's personal seal[3] (which he used to sign and seal documents), the cord on which it hung from his neck, and his shepherd's staff (**38:18**).

Judah agreed to her terms and cohabited with her, after which she left the area and changed back into her widow's clothes. When he later sent his Adullamite friend with the goat in order to retrieve his personal items, the woman was nowhere to be found. So Judah decided to drop the matter (**38:20–23**).

About three months later, however, Judah's affair returned to haunt him. He learned that his daughter-in-law Tamar had become illegitimately pregnant. Later Mosaic punishment for

---

3. Probably a cylinder seal, a small, delicately carved (and often inscribed) cylinder made of hard semiprecious stone, drilled through lengthwise so that it could be worn on a cord around the neck. Such seals were often rolled on damp clay, leaving the impression of a "signature" that could be used as a personal means of attestation, legal or otherwise. For examples, see J. B. Pritchard, *The Ancient Near East in Pictures Relating to the Old Testament* (Princeton: Princeton University, 1954), plate 240; D. J. Wiseman and A. R. Millard, "Seal, Sealing," in *The Illustrated Bible Dictionary*, 3:1406–07.

extramarital intercourse was death by stoning (Deut. 22:20–24; see also John 8:4–5), although in certain cases the prescribed penalty was death by burning (Lev. 21:9). Judah ordered the latter for Tamar.

When she was led out for formal sentencing and execution, however, she brought with her Judah's seal, cord, and staff, claiming them to be the possessions of the man who had made her pregnant. Judah recognized them immediately and then praised Tamar for being more righteous than he was. He conceded that Tamar's present condition was his fault, since she had been reduced to a desperate course of action to protect Er's inheritance simply because Judah would not allow the now-fully-grown Shelah to enter into levirate marriage with her (Gen. **38:26**).

The time of Tamar's delivery eventually arrived. Like Rebekah, Er's great-grandmother, Tamar also gave birth to twin boys (see 25:21–24). As she was about to deliver, one of the twins reached out his hand, so the attending midwife tied a scarlet thread around his wrist to mark him as the firstborn (**38:28**). But he withdrew his hand back into the womb, and then his brother was born ahead of him. The surprised midwife said, "So this is how you have broken out!" That is why the boy was named Perez, which means "breaking out."

The baby with the scarlet thread on his wrist was then born. He was named Zerah, the meaning of which is uncertain. Some scholars have related it to a similar word meaning "sunrise," from which they have deduced "scarlet" or "brightness," while other scholars have related it to a word meaning "braided," from which they have deduced "thread."

Though born of an adulterous relationship, Perez became the ancestor of David (Ruth 4:18–22) who in turn became the ancestor of Jesus Christ (see esp. Matt. 1:1–6). Of the four OT women listed in the Matthean genealogy, Tamar, Bathsheba ("Uriah's wife," 1:6) and Rahab (assuming her to be the prostitute of Josh. 2:1) participated in immoral sexual relationships, while Ruth (Matt. 1:5) was a Moabitess (Ruth 1:4) and therefore not a member of the covenant family by birth. Obviously, such irregularities did not automatically disqualify them from becoming ancestresses of our Lord.

Joseph Employed and Imprisoned (39:1–40:23)

The scene now shifts back to Egypt, and the first verse of Genesis 39 reviews the information found in the last verse of Genesis 37 in order to get us back on the track of Joseph's story. We are reminded again that Joseph had become a servant of Potiphar, a high Egyptian official.

Genesis 39 stresses the fact that God was with Joseph (**39:2, 3, 21, 23**), an emphasis noted by Stephen in his review of Israel's history (see Acts 7:9). Joseph's master observed that fact as well (Gen. **39:3**), just as Abimelech had done in Abraham's case (21:22) and a later Abimelech had done in Isaac's case (26:28).

Everything Joseph did was successful (**39:3**). He may have been the prototype of the righteous man described in Psalm 1:3. The Lord blessed the Egyptian official's household for Joseph's sake (Gen. **39:5**), as he had blessed Laban for Jacob's sake (30:27). In summary, Joseph's master learned that he could entrust anything to him, so he put everything he owned in Joseph's care (**39:6**).

But Joseph possessed more than spiritual qualities and administrative abilities. He was also handsome and well-built (**39:6**)—so much so that his master's wife "took notice of" (lit. "lifted up her eyes at") him (**39:7**). That ancient phrase meant "to look with desire or lust at," as our context demonstrates and as section 25 of Hammurapi's famous code of laws shows (see chapter thirteen).[4]

The woman asked Joseph to come to bed with her, but he refused. He told her that to do so would be to betray his master's trust and confidence in him. He also informed her that if he did what she wanted him to do, he would be sinning against God himself (**39:9**).

An important theological point is being made here: Our sin is never private. Every time we sin, we sin against God. And in a certain sense our sin is always against him alone (Ps. 51:4).

The woman was persistent, however. Finally one day, when no one else was around, she grabbed Joseph by the clothes and again begged him to come to bed with her. But he wisely left his clothes in her hand and ran away (Gen. **39:12**). One of the best

---

4. See T. J. Meek in *Ancient Near Eastern Texts*, ed. J. B. Pritchard, 2d ed. (Princeton: Princeton University Press, 1955), 167.

ways for us to keep from sinning is to flee from temptation whenever it begins to work on us (2 Tim. 2:22).

Angry by now, the woman called out to the men of her household. She told them Joseph had tried to rape her (Gen. **39:14**), and she showed them his clothing as proof of her claim. She referred to him as a "Hebrew" (**39:14**), a term of reproach when used by an Egyptian. When her husband returned home she told him the same story, this time demeaning Joseph even further by calling him a "Hebrew slave" (**39:17**).

Potiphar, understandably enraged, put Joseph into the prison house where the pharaoh's prisoners were held (**39:20**). Potiphar's anger (**39:19**) may have been directed not so much against Joseph as against the fact that he felt compelled to believe his wife's story and therefore to imprison his trusted steward. In any event, once again the Lord was with Joseph and blessed him. God gave him favor in the sight of the prison warden, who in turn gave him important responsibilities even while he was in jail. The warden placed the same kind of confidence in Joseph that his former master had placed in him. Joseph was a worthy son of Jacob: The Lord was with both men wherever they went (see 28:15).

(The so-called Story of Two Brothers is an ancient Egyptian tale that is similar to the biblical account of Potiphar's wife's attempted seduction of Joseph.[5] It provides the closest lengthy external parallel to any section of the entire Joseph cycle—but its folkloristic style and mythological elements are worlds apart from the sober dignity of the Genesis account. Written primarily for purposes of entertainment, the Egyptian story is devoid of ethical or moral value, while Genesis 39 begins and ends by stating that the Lord was with Joseph and gave him success in whatever he did.)

While Joseph was in prison, the pharaoh's chief cupbearer and chief baker wronged or offended the pharaoh in some way. So the men were arrested and turned over to Potiphar, who put them in the same prison where Joseph was confined. Joseph was assigned to be their servant (**40:1–4**). After the two new prisoners had been in custody for some time, one night each of them had a dream.

The next morning, Joseph could tell by looking at their faces

---

5. See J. A. Wilson in *Ancient Near Eastern Texts*, 23–25.

that they were dejected (**40:6–7**; see also **41:8**). (Centuries later
Nehemiah, another cupbearer, was similarly unhappy, as his
master could tell by looking at him; see Neh. 2:2.) Joseph asked
them what was wrong, and they said that they had had dreams
but that there was no one available to interpret them (Gen. **40:8**).
Belief in the importance of having significant dreams interpreted
was widespread in the ancient Near East.[6]

Joseph told the men that only God can interpret dreams properly and precisely. He would say much the same thing to the
pharaoh two years later (**41:16, 25, 28**), and Daniel would speak
in a similar way to Nebuchadnezzar of Babylon (Dan. 2:27–28).
The careers of Joseph and Daniel, God's men who eventually
came to occupy prominent positions in foreign courts, were very
much alike even though separated by hundreds of years. Other
resemblances between the experiences of these two men will be
pointed out as we proceed.

Joseph asked the pharaoh's officials to describe their dreams.
After the cupbearer had spoken, Joseph interpreted his dream for
him (Gen. **40:12–13**). In the light of what Joseph had said earlier
(**40:8**), his interpretation implied that he was attuned to God's
wisdom. Within three days, Joseph said, the pharaoh would lift
up the head of the cupbearer and restore him to his former
position. To "lift up the head" in that context meant to "graciously release from prison," as a comparison of the Hebrew text
of 2 Kings 25:27 and Jeremiah 52:31 shows.

Then Joseph requested that the cupbearer put in a good word
for him to the pharaoh. After all, Joseph had already been subjected to the indignities of being kidnapped, sold as a slave, and
imprisoned even though innocent (Gen. **40:14–15**).

Next, the baker described his dream, which Joseph then interpreted. Within three days, Joseph said, the pharaoh would lift up
the head of the baker. Up to that point, the interpretation of the
baker's dream was the same as that of the cupbearer's dream. But
now to "lift up the head" took on ominous and grisly tones: In
the baker's case, it meant to "lift off the head." The baker, said
Joseph, would be beheaded and then his body would be impaled
on a stake as a warning to others who might be plotting crimes
against the pharaoh (**40:19**). (Ancient drawings and inscriptions

6. See esp. A. L. Oppenheim in *Transactions of the American Philosophical Society*
46/3 (1956): 179–353.

indicate that "impale on a stake" is the most likely meaning of the phrase "hang on a tree" in the OT.)[7]

Since God had given Joseph the interpretations, they both came true as predicted. The third day was the pharaoh's birthday, so he threw a party for all his servants (**40:20**). The chief cupbearer was restored to his former position, and the chief baker was beheaded.

The Bible does not mention many birthdays, but another famous one resulted in the same tragic consequences. The birthday of Herod the tetrarch was the occasion of the beheading of John the Baptist (Matt. 14:6–11).

The chief cupbearer, back on the job, was relieved and happy—so much so that he completely failed to remember Joseph's request. Genesis 40 ends with the simple, sad observation that the cupbearer "forgot him."

But God did not forget—and two years later Joseph's seemingly hopeless situation would be totally and miraculously changed.

Joseph Exalted (41:1–57)

After those two full years had passed, the pharaoh himself had a couple of disturbing dreams. In the first dream, he watched as seven ugly, emaciated cows devoured seven sleek, fat cows. In the second, he saw seven thin, scorched heads of grain swallowing up seven full, healthy heads of grain (**41:1–7**).

The next morning, the pharaoh's mind was troubled by what he had dreamed. As in the case of his chief cupbearer and chief baker (**40:6**), the pharaoh was worried because he did not know what his dreams meant (see also Dan. 2:1, 3). Worst of all, the pharaoh's "magicians" (probably priests who claimed to have occult powers) also could not interpret them (Gen. **41:8**; see also Dan. 2:8–11). Egyptian magicians were intelligent and clever (Exod. 7:11, 22; 8:7), but even they could not do some things (8:18).

The unusual flurry of activity in the pharaoh's court finally jogged the memory of the chief cupbearer. He apologized to the pharaoh for not telling him about the "young Hebrew" who had

---

7. It was a common means of execution and subsequent public humiliation. The conspicuously displayed corpse would also serve as a warning to other potential traitors or criminals. For graphic portrayals of impaled victims see, e.g., Pritchard, *The Ancient Near East in Pictures Relating to the Old Testament*, plates 362, 368, 373.

correctly interpreted two other dreams two years earlier (Gen. **41:12**).

So the pharaoh sent for Joseph (see Ps. 105:20), who shaved himself and changed his clothes before coming into the pharaoh's presence (Gen. **41:14**). When the pharaoh asked him if he had the ability to interpret dreams, Joseph said that he could not do so apart from God's help (**41:16**; see also **40:8**; Dan. 2:27–28, 30).

Joseph's complete dependence on God was one of his most admirable characteristics. We, too, should always recognize and acknowledge that all we are and have comes from God (2 Cor. 3:5).

When he described his dreams to Joseph, the pharaoh added a detail or two about which we had not been previously informed. He said that the emaciated cows looked worse than anything he had ever seen in his life (Gen. **41:19**). He also said that even after they had devoured the fat cows, they were still as emaciated as before (**41:21**). Although the pharaoh did not yet know what his dreams meant, he obviously sensed that something terrible was about to happen.

Joseph then told the pharaoh that his two dreams had only one meaning: Seven years of great abundance would be followed by seven years of severe famine throughout the whole land of Egypt. Such seven-year famines were not uncommon elsewhere (see 2 Kings 8:1), but they almost never occurred in Egypt because of the dependable regularity of the annual overflow of the waters of the Nile River. Rare examples of lengthy famines were not entirely unknown in Egypt, however.[8]

Joseph went on to tell the pharaoh that his dream had been repeated in two forms because the matter had been firmly decided by God and because God would waste no time in bringing it to pass (Gen. **41:32**; see **37:5–9**; Amos 7:1–6, 8; 8:2). Recent scholarship has seen in this verse a clue to the repetitions that appear so often in the first five books of the OT: They are there for emphasis, and they describe events in which the hand of God is clearly demonstrated.[9]

In any event, Joseph recommended that the pharaoh put a

8. See J. A. Wilson in *Ancient Near Eastern Texts*, 31–32.
9. U. Cassuto, *The Documentary Hypothesis*, trans. I. Abrahams (Jerusalem: Magnes Press, 1961), 83.

wise and intelligent man in charge of Egypt to oversee the storage of surplus food during the years of abundance so that the people would not starve during the years of famine.

The pharaoh readily agreed to Joseph's proposal. In fact he decided that Joseph himself should be that man (see Acts 7:10), since it was quite obvious that Joseph possessed "the spirit of God" or "the spirit of the gods" (Gen. **41:38**). It is also possible to translate that phrase "the Spirit of God," but such a translation would be out of character in a statement coming from the lips of a pagan, polytheistic ruler. (The same observation applies to the similar phrases found in Dan. 4:8–9, 18; 5:11, 14.)

So the pharaoh formally appointed Joseph to be second in command throughout Egypt (Gen. **41:40**; see also Ps. 105:21–22). Joseph would ride in a chariot second only to that of the pharaoh himself (Gen. **41:43**), probably occupying the position of vizier (in 45:8, Joseph is called "father to Pharaoh"; "father" was a title of honor often given to viziers). He would wear the pharaoh's personal signet ring (see Esther 3:10), he would be dressed in the finest clothing (see Esther 6:11), and he would wear a gold chain around his neck (see Dan. 5:7, 16, 29). The pharaoh would make sure that Joseph had all the trappings of royalty, including the homage of the people, who were required to stand at attention whenever Joseph made his appearance (Gen. **41:43**).[10]

Renamed Zaphenath-Paneah (an Egyptian phrase of uncertain meaning), Joseph was given a wife named Asenath (which probably means "she belongs to [the goddess] Neith"). She was the daughter of Potiphera, priest of On (which means "city of the pillar" in reference to its many obelisks).

We must carefully distinguish Potiphera from the Potiphar (a name of uncertain meaning) of Genesis **37:36; 39:1** who was Joseph's earlier master. The name Potiphera means "he whom Ra has given." It was an appropriate name, since Potiphera was the priest of On, a city where the sun god Ra was especially honored. The ruins of the city are located ten miles southeast of modern

---

10. See T. O. Lambdin in *Journal of the American Oriental Society* 73 (1953): 146, where Hebrew *'abrēk* (NIV "make way") is translated "stand at attention." It is also possible, however, that the word is related to Akkadian *abarakku*, "steward" (see, e.g., W. G. Lambert, *Babylonian Wisdom Literature* [Oxford: Clarendon, 1960], 259 line 8), as well as to Phoenician *hbrk*, "vizier," in the first line of an inscription excavated in 1946–47 at Karatepe in Turkey (see the translation of E. Lipiński in *Near Eastern Religious Texts Relating to the Old Testament*, ed. W. Beyerlin [Philadelphia: Westminster, 1978], 241, n. o).

Cairo, and the ancient Greeks called it "Heliopolis" ("city of the sun"; see also Jer. 43:13; Ezek. 30:17).

Now thirty years old (Gen. **41:46**), Joseph had lived in Egypt for thirteen years (see **37:2**) by the time he became second in command in that land. Seven years of abundance came, just as he had predicted. During those years his wife Asenath bore him two sons. The firstborn was named "Manasseh" ("he causes to forget") because God had made Joseph "forget" all his previous loneliness and misery (**41:51**). The second son was named "Ephraim" ("twice fruitful") because God had made Joseph "fruitful" in the land of his distress (**41:52**). Implied also in the name is the fact that God had given Joseph "two" sons (see **41:50**).

Again as Joseph had predicted, the seven abundant years ended and were followed by seven years of famine (**41:54**; see also Acts 7:11). Joseph's foresight, however, made it possible for Egypt to feed not only its own people (**41:55–56**) but also the people from all the surrounding regions (**41:57**).

Genesis 37–41 has told us the story of how God was with Joseph and of how he made him prosperous in everything he did. Joseph found favor in the eyes of his father (**37:3**), in the eyes of Potiphar (**39:4**), in the eyes of the prison warden (**39:21**), and in the eyes of the pharaoh himself (**41:38**).

And in everything that happened, God's perfect plan was at work to fulfill his purposes in the lives of Joseph, his brothers, and his father Jacob.

23

Jacob's Migration to Egypt (42:1–47:31)

JACOB'S SONS GO TO EGYPT DURING THE FAMINE (42:1–44:34)

THE BROTHERS ARE RECONCILED TO JOSEPH (45:1–28)

THE WHOLE FAMILY MOVES TO EGYPT AND SETTLES THERE (46:1–47:31)

Genesis 37–41 describes how and why Joseph went down to Egypt, and Genesis 42–47 tells us how and why Jacob did the same.

Neither man went willingly. Joseph was sold into slavery and then imprisoned, rising to prominence only later. Jacob went to Egypt only after a long and complex series of events compelled him to make the move. But it is those events that give Genesis 42–47 its drama and suspense and that make it one of the most absorbing sections in all of Genesis.

Within the past fifty years, two distinct but equally profound treatments of the relationship between Joseph and his brothers (see Gen. 42–45) have been written. In what is surely one of the great literary achievements of our time, Thomas Mann essentially defends the traditional view of the narrative: that Joseph gently and carefully orchestrated his brothers' journeys back and forth from Canaan to Egypt in a way that would convince the aged Jacob that Joseph was still alive and that it would be eminently worth his while to make the trip himself in order to see his son again.[1] On the other hand, Maurice Samuel, in a much shorter treatment, pictures Joseph as a vengeful and calculating tyrant who, though anxious to see his father, manipulates the emotions and actions of his brothers in order to torment them.[2]

As is so often the case in such matters, the truth probably lies somewhere between the two opposing viewpoints. It is entirely understandable that Joseph would take a certain delight in witnessing the scene of his brothers bowing down before him, respectfully calling him "my lord" and cravenly referring to themselves as "your servants," again and again—all in fulfillment of his dreams twenty years before. At the same time, it is equally understandable that Joseph would want to make absolutely certain that his ten brothers were telling him the truth when they informed him that Benjamin and Jacob were still alive. Joseph's complicated plan to induce Jacob's entire family to pull up stakes in Canaan and settle in Egypt took its emotional toll on Joseph as well: He wept, again and again.

Jacob's Sons Go to Egypt During the Famine (42:1–44:34)

The same famine that had struck Egypt had also descended on the neighboring territories, including Canaan. When Jacob learned that grain was available in Egypt, he told his eleven sons to stop staring at each other and to go to Egypt to buy some food. Only in that way would the family be able to remain alive.

Jacob permitted only ten of the brothers to make the trip. He did not want to send Benjamin along because he was afraid harm might overtake him (**42:4**). After all, Joseph and Benjamin were the only two sons that Rachel had borne to Jacob. And since Rachel, now dead, had been Jacob's favorite wife, he did not want to lose Benjamin as he had lost Joseph.

Unknown to Jacob and his family, Joseph had become a high official in Egypt (**42:6**), second only to the pharaoh himself

---

1. *Joseph and His Brothers* (New York: Knopf, 1948).
2. *Certain People of the Book* (New York: Knopf, 1955), 299–350.

(41:40, 43). So when the brothers arrived in Egypt, they were obliged to buy grain directly from Joseph. They also had to bow down to him (**42:6**)—just as he had dreamed they would some day (37:7, 9).

Joseph had been a teenager when his brothers had last seen him (37:2). He was now at least thirty-seven years old (41:46, 53, 54), wearing Egyptian clothes, speaking the Egyptian language (**42:23**), and in a position of authority, so his brothers failed to recognize him (**42:8**). But they had already become adults when he had last seen them. Their appearance had evidently not changed much, because he recognized them immediately (**42:7**).

Remembering the dreams he had had (**42:9**), Joseph treated his brothers harshly at first. He pretended not to know them, accused them of being spies, and put them all in prison for three days (**42:7–17**). About twenty years earlier he had described his dreams to his brothers, and they had scoffed at the possibility that he would some day rule over them (37:8). But now here they were, calling him "my lord" and referring to themselves as his "servants" (**42:10**).

On the third day of their incarceration, Joseph went to see his brothers. He told them he was going to keep one of them in prison until the others had gone back home and brought their youngest brother to Egypt.

The brothers came to the conclusion that their present calamity was the result of the sin they had committed against Joseph many years before (**42:21**). Reuben then reminded them that he had warned them not to harm Joseph but that they had failed to listen to him (**42:22**; see 37:21–22).

As they discussed their plight, Joseph was listening to what they said. But they did not know he could understand them, because they thought he was an Egyptian. After all, he had been using an interpreter (**42:23**).

The entire scene, however, was too much for Joseph. He left the room to weep and release his pent-up emotions. Then he came back and bound Simeon as the others watched (**42:24**). Although Simeon was Jacob's second son, Joseph bound him instead of Reuben, Jacob's firstborn, probably because Reuben had earlier tried to save Joseph (37:21–22).

After Simeon had been locked up in the prison, Joseph gave his men orders to fill the grain sacks of the other brothers. His men were also told to put each brother's money back in his sack and then to send them on their way to Canaan.

When the brothers stopped for the night and one of them opened his sack to get feed for his donkey, he saw his money and immediately told the others. They trembled at the sight of it, wondering what God was doing to them.

After they arrived in Canaan, the brothers told their father Jacob the whole story. Then when the other sacks were opened and each man's money was found in his sack, the men were frightened all the more.

Jacob, who had already mourned the loss of Joseph and had now lost Simeon as well, did not want the other brothers to take Benjamin to Egypt. Even Reuben's generous offer of his own two sons as collateral for Benjamin's safety (**42:36–37**) did not change Jacob's mind. He was still afraid, as he had been earlier (**42:4**), that harm would come to Benjamin. And if that should happen, the other brothers would be guilty of sending their father to an early grave because he would grieve over his youngest son (**42:38**; see also 37:35).

The famine became more and more severe, however. So when Jacob and his family had used up all the grain the brothers had brought from Egypt he again told his sons to go back there for more food (**43:2**). Judah said they were willing to go, but only if Jacob would agree to send Benjamin along, since otherwise the trip would be of no avail.

This time Judah offered himself as collateral, assuring Jacob that he would take full responsibility for Benjamin's safety (**43:9**). Judah stated that if Benjamin did not accompany the others to Egypt the whole family—Jacob, his children, and his grandchildren—would die of hunger (**43:8**).

Judah, Jacob's fourth son, had now become the spokesman for all the brothers. He had begun to assume that role many years earlier (37:26–27), and he would continue to speak for his brothers in the future as well (**44:14–34; 46:28**). Judah's tribe would eventually become preeminent among the twelve tribes of Israel (see 49:8–12), and he himself would be an ancestor of the Messiah (Matt. 1:2, 17; Luke 3:23, 33).

Judah's persuasive arguments finally convinced Jacob to allow his sons to return to Egypt and take Benjamin with them. He advised them to take samples of some of the best products of

Canaan as gifts for the Egyptian official. He also told them to take twice as much money as they needed. If they did so they would be able to return the money they had found in their sacks, which Jacob hoped had been put there by mistake (Gen. **43:12**).

Jacob prayed that God Almighty, the God of the patriarchs (17:1; 28:3; 35:11; see esp. Exod. 6:3), would exert his power and grant Jacob's sons mercy in the official's eyes (Gen. **43:14**). In any event, Jacob was resigned to his fate: "If I am bereaved . . . , I am bereaved" (**43:14**). Hundreds of years later, Queen Esther would utter a similar statement of resignation: "If I perish, I perish" (Esther 4:16).

After the brothers arrived in Egypt and Joseph saw that Benjamin was with them, he ordered his steward to prepare a feast. When the steward took the men to Joseph's house, they were afraid that it was because of the money they had found in their sacks. They felt that now they would be enslaved and their donkeys would be confiscated. So they took the steward aside and explained to him that they had brought back the money found in their sacks. They further told him that they had brought other money also with which to buy food (Gen. **43:19–22**).

The steward assured them there was no need to worry. He told them that their God must have put the money in their sacks, since he himself had received money for the food they had bought earlier. Simeon was then released from prison, and all the brothers were provided with the same kind of hospitality for themselves and their animals (**43:24**) that Laban had given to Abraham's servant and animals many years before (24:32).

When Joseph came into the house, the brothers brought their gift to him. Once more they bowed down before him (**43:26**), as they would do later on as well (**43:28**)—fulfilling Joseph's earlier dream again and again (37:7, 9).

Joseph inquired about the health of their father, and then he took a closer look at Benjamin. The narrator at this point has emphasized the special status of Benjamin by referring to him as "his own [i.e., Joseph's] mother's son" (**43:29**). Joseph said to Benjamin, "God be gracious to you" (**43:29**). The essence of that phrase would become well known and loved in benedictions and prayers of later years (Num. 6:25; Ps. 67:1).

Once again, the experience was beyond Joseph's powers of self-control. His heart was so stirred by the sight of his brother

Benjamin that he left the room to weep (Gen. **43:30**). If Jeremiah can justly be called the "weeping prophet," surely Joseph can justly be called the "weeping patriarch" (see **42:24; 45:2, 14–15; 46:29**). He must have been a tenderhearted and sensitive person.

After washing his face and regaining control of his emotions (**43:31**)—something he was not always successful in doing (**45:1**)—he returned and ordered food to be brought in. He was served in one place and his brothers in another place. His Egyptian guests were served in still another place, because Egyptians would not eat together with Hebrews, perhaps for ritual reasons (**43:32**; see also Exod. 8:26). The Egyptian avoidance of shepherds (Gen. **46:34**), on the other hand, was probably not for ritual but for social reasons.

As the brothers were being given places at the table in the correct order of their ages, from the oldest to the youngest, they looked at each other in amazement, wondering how an Egyptian official could possibly know who was who (**43:33**). Portions of food were then distributed to them from Joseph's table, with Benjamin receiving five times as much as any of the others (**43:34**; see also **45:22**).

After the meal, Joseph told his steward to fill up his visitors' sacks with food, put each man's money back into his sack, and put Joseph's own silver cup into Benjamin's sack. The brothers were then escorted out of the city the next morning. When the men had gone only a short distance from the city, Joseph sent his steward to overtake them and accuse them of repaying good with evil by stealing his silver cup. The steward caught up with them and repeated Joseph's words to them (**44:4–6**).

Not knowing that the cup was in Benjamin's sack, the brothers said indignantly, "If any of your servants is found to have it, he will die, and the rest of us will become my lord's slaves" (**44:9**). Their retort was similar to what Jacob, equally unsuspecting, had said years before to Laban concerning the latter's household idols (31:32).

The steward agreed to the men's proposal, but he softened the potential penalty to slavery for the guilty brother and freedom for the others (**44:10**). The suspense of the story builds as we read that the sacks were searched, beginning with the one belonging to the oldest and ending with the one belonging to the youngest. And there in Benjamin's sack, as previously planned by Joseph, the silver cup was found. Sensing that all was now lost, the brothers tore their clothes as a sign of mourning and despair (**44:13**; see also 37:29, 34) and went back to the city with the steward.

When the men arrived at Joseph's house, they threw themselves to the ground before him (**44:14**), again in fulfillment of his earlier dream (37:7, 9). Joseph—doubtless with tongue in cheek—asked them how they could possibly have expected to trick a man with the occult powers he possessed (**44:15**).

Judah once again became the spokesman for the others (see **43:3**). He readily admitted their collective guilt and indicated that they would all resign themselves to becoming Joseph's slaves (**44:16**). But Joseph responded as his steward had: Only Benjamin would become Joseph's servant, and the others were free to go back to their father.

At this point in the story, Judah made one of the most eloquent pleas to be found anywhere in the Bible (**44:18–34**). Consistently referring to Joseph as "my lord" and to himself, his brothers, and their father as "your servants" (once again, see 37:8), Judah begged Joseph for a hearing and continued by reviewing the entire affair in a highly emotional way.

He flattered Joseph by claiming him to be like the pharaoh himself (**44:18**). He pointed out that Benjamin was the only one of his mother's sons left and was therefore beloved by his father (**44:20**). He asserted that Jacob had already lost one of his wife's two sons and would die heartbroken if he lost the other (**44:27–29**). Employing the same Hebrew phrase that would later be used of David's relationship to Jonathan (see 1 Sam. 18:1), Judah indicated that Jacob's life was bound up in Benjamin's life so closely and completely that the loss of Benjamin would kill Jacob and the brothers would then be responsible (Gen. **44:30–31**).

Finally, Judah pleaded with Joseph to enslave him rather than Benjamin (**44:33**). He said that he could not possibly go back to his father unless he took Benjamin with him, because he could not bear to see the misery and despair that would overcome Jacob. So Judah ended his earnest request by offering himself as a substitute for his brother. Are we not reminded of an infinitely greater offering, nearly two thousand years later, by an infinitely greater Substitute (John 10:11–18)?

The Brothers Are Reconciled to Joseph (45:1–28)

By this time Joseph had seen so much remorse and repentance and unselfishness in his brothers that he could no longer control his own emotions (Gen. **45:1**; see **43:31**). So he sent all the other people out of the room and then revealed his identity to his brothers (**45:1**; Acts 7:13). His joyful sobbing was so loud that Egyptians in other sections of the palace could hear it.

Joseph exclaimed to his brothers, "I am Joseph!"

They were so surprised at hearing him speak to them in their own language, and were so afraid at learning that he was still alive, that they were unable to answer him (Gen. **45:3**). They had not seen Joseph for twenty-two years (see 37:2; 41:46, 53; **45:6**), so they probably thought that by now he had died in slavery. Seeing him alive was quite a shock.

So Joseph tried to reassure them and calm their fears. This time he said, "I am your brother Joseph" (**45:4**), stressing the fact that at least from his own standpoint he still cherished that brotherly relationship. He did not overlook the fact that it was they who had sold him into slavery in Egypt, of course. But he emphasized God's sovereign will behind what had taken place (**45:5, 7–8**). Because God had made Joseph the pharaoh's advisor, Jacob's entire family would now be saved from starvation. (Stephen stressed that point also; see Acts 7:9–10.)

Joseph then told his brothers to hurry back home and bring his father and the rest of the clan to Egypt right away. Again the narrator stresses God's hand in Joseph's rise to power (Gen. **45:9**). On their arrival, Jacob and his family would be settled in Goshen (**45:10**) in the eastern delta, the best part of the land of Egypt (**45:18**), and all their needs would be cared for.

Apparently noticing their reluctance to believe him, Joseph again assured them of his identity. He reminded them that he was speaking to them in their own language, not through an interpreter (**45:12**). After repeating his desire that they hurry on to Canaan and bring Jacob and the other members of the family back as soon as possible, he enjoyed a tearful reunion with Benjamin and then with his other brothers.

When the pharaoh learned that Joseph's brothers had come to Egypt, he was delighted. He told Joseph to order his brothers to take carts full of supplies with them to Canaan. They were then to bring Jacob and their families back to Egypt.

The pharaoh's command underscored what by now had become Joseph's fondest desire: Jacob's entire clan would be reunited once again. The pharaoh's promise that they would eat "the fat of the land" (**45:18**) was reminiscent of Isaac's blessing on Jacob (see 27:28) and should be viewed as at least a partial fulfillment of it.

Jacob's sons agreed to Joseph's proposal. Among the supplies Joseph gave to each of them was a set of clothes. To Benjamin, however, Joseph gave five sets (**45:22**; see also **43:34**) as well as an additional present of 300 shekels of silver. Plenty of other provisions were sent along with them also.

As they departed, Joseph, with a twinkle in his eye, told them not to fight or quarrel with each other during the trip (**45:24**). He knew his brothers' weaknesses all too well!

After the men had arrived at their father's home, Jacob listened to their story in stunned disbelief. But when they told him everything Joseph had said, and when he saw the carts Joseph had sent, his spirit revived. He was now convinced that Joseph was still alive, and he became determined to make the long journey to Egypt. "I will go and see him," he said, "before I die" (**45:28**).

The Whole Family Moves to Egypt and Settles There (46:1–47:31)

Jacob was apparently living on the patriarchal estate at Hebron at this time (see 35:27). So his trip to Egypt took him and his family westward to Beersheba, where he stopped briefly in order to worship the Lord (**46:1**) as his father Isaac (26:23–25) and grandfather Abraham (21:33) had done before him.

While at Beersheba, Jacob had a night vision similar to that of Isaac in the same place years earlier. Even the words that God spoke to each man were similar (see 26:24; **46:3**). The Lord spoke Jacob's name twice, expressing the same sense of urgency as he had to Abraham at Moriah and eliciting the same response: "Here I am" (**46:2**; see 22:11).

God told Jacob not to be afraid. Before Jacob and his family left the promised land to go down to Egypt, God spoke to him and reaffirmed the promise of posterity originally given to Abraham (**46:3**; see 12:2). The Lord's prophecy would be abundantly fulfilled (Exod. 1:7).

God also promised to accompany Jacob to Egypt and bring him

(in the person of his descendants) back to Canaan again (Gen. 46:4)—a prediction of the exodus (see also 15:16). The Lord's promise to be with Jacob at all times had first been spoken many years earlier at Bethel (28:15) and had followed him throughout his life (31:3). A final promise to Jacob was that the hand of his own son Joseph would close Jacob's eyes at the time of his death (46:4).

After the divine confirmation of his decision to visit Joseph, Jacob set out westward from Beersheba with his family, his cattle, and his goods, eventually arriving in Egypt (46:5–7).

Genesis 46:8–27 is another section of "connective tissue" (see 22:20–24; 25:12–18; 36:1–43). In this case, however, the genealogy is very interesting in its own right.

A question immediately arises: How is the number "seventy" to be understood (46:27; see also Exod. 1:5; Deut. 10:22)? The section itself demands a literal understanding of the number, since thirty-three (Gen. 46:15) plus sixteen (46:18) plus fourteen (46:22) plus seven (46:25) equals seventy.

Now we face a second question: How does the "seventy" of 46:27 relate to the "sixty-six" of 46:26? Let me attempt a reconstruction based on the data before us.

One problem is that the number of names in 46:8–15 is thirty-four, not thirty-three. We cannot exclude the name of Jacob's daughter Dinah (46:15) because the text explicitly states that thirty-three was the total of the "sons and daughters" listed here, and Dinah's name is the only clearly female name in the list. The only other possibility readily available for exclusion is the name "Ohad" (46:10), which does not appear in the parallel lists in Numbers 26:12–14 or 1 Chronicles 4:24. Although Ohad does appear also in Exodus 6:15, both there and in Genesis 46:10 its Hebrew form looks very much like that of the nearby name "Zohar." Perhaps, then, Ohad was added accidentally by a scribe engaged in copying the text. A comparison of Genesis 46:8–25 and Numbers 26:4–57 demonstrates that scribal omissions, additions, variations in spelling, and so forth, are rather frequent in genealogical lists.

Another problem is the fact that although the names of Er and Onan were included in the total listing of seventy, those two men had already died in Canaan (Gen. 46:12). We observe, however, that 46:26 states: "All those who went to Egypt with Jacob—

those who were his direct descendants, not counting his sons' wives—numbered sixty-six persons." So from the total of seventy we must subtract the names of Er and Onan—and we must also subtract the names of Manasseh and Ephraim, Joseph's sons who had been born in Egypt (**46:20, 27**).

The "seventy" of **46:27**, then, is the ideal, complete number of Jacob's descendants who would have been in Egypt if Er and Onan had not sinned and been punished with death (38:7–10). Although other reconstructions of who it was that constituted the seventy members of Jacob's family who arrived in Egypt at one time or another have been attempted, the one outlined above seems to account best for all the textual evidence that we have.[3]

When Jacob reached the Egyptian frontier, he sent Judah ahead of him to lead the way to Goshen (Gen. **46:28**). Judah's importance is again emphasized by the narrator, as we observed earlier (see 37:26–27; **43:3–10; 44:14–34**). After the family had arrived in Goshen, Joseph came out in his chariot to meet his father. The meeting between Joseph and Jacob was highly charged emotionally (**46:29**). Jacob's lonely years had ended, and he declared that he was ready to die.

But Joseph apparently felt that everyone still had a lot of living to do. He told Jacob's family that he would now announce their arrival to the pharaoh and forewarn him that they were shepherds by trade. For their part, they were advised to tell the pharaoh that shepherding was a long and honorable tradition in their family. Only then would they be able to settle down in Goshen, because the Egyptians tended to look down their noses at shepherds. In fact, under ordinary circumstances they refused to associate with them (**46:34**).

Joseph then went in and made the announcement to the pharaoh, introducing five of his brothers to him. The pharaoh told Joseph to allow Jacob and his family to live in the eastern delta of Lower Egypt, "the best part of the land" (**47:11**), as fertile then as now. Furthermore, the most able men among them were to be put in charge of the pharaoh's livestock (**47:1–6**). Even in

---

3. Jacob himself cannot be included in enumerating the seventy since Exod. 1:5 clearly states that it was his "descendants" who numbered seventy. The figure of seventy-five given in Stephen's speech in Acts 7:14 includes additional sons of Joseph, presumably born after Jacob's arrival in Egypt. In fact, the Septuagint, the Greek translation of the OT from which Stephen perhaps quoted, reads "seventy-five" in both Gen. 46:27 and Exod. 1:5.

times of economic instability there are usually worthwhile tasks for able people to perform.

When Joseph introduced his father Jacob to the pharaoh, the pharaoh asked him how old he was. Jacob replied that his wanderings had so far lasted for only a few miserable years—a mere 130, to be exact (**47:9**)! They had been brief, he continued, in comparison to those of his forefathers. (Abraham, after all, had lived for 175 years, Isaac for 180; see 25:7; 35:28.) Again we observe the patriarchs' evaluation of themselves as wanderers, strangers, exiles (see also Heb. 11:13).

Jacob "blessed" the pharaoh at the beginning and the end of their conversation (Gen. **47:7, 10**). But that probably means no more than that he said "hello" and "goodbye" to him. The Hebrew word *shālôm* (lit. "wholeness," "well-being," "peace") is universally used in the same senses today.

And so it was that Joseph settled his father and brothers in Goshen, called "the region of Zoan" (Ps. 78:12, 43) and "the district of Rameses" (Gen. **47:11**; see also Exod. 1:11). Since the "Rameses" mentioned was probably Rameses II, who ruled Egypt centuries after Joseph's time, the reference to the land of Rameses in Genesis **47:11** is doubtless a later editorial touch.

As the famine continued and became more and more severe, the Egyptians finally used up all their money to buy the grain that Joseph had stored up during the years of abundance (**47:13–15**). They soon found it necessary to trade their cattle for Joseph's grain (**47:16–17**), then their lands, and finally themselves (**47:18–20**). In this way all the land in Egypt became in fact what it had always been in theory: the personal property of the pharaoh. Only the land that belonged to the priests was not turned over to the pharaoh. He had traditionally given them a regular allowance to live on, so they did not have to exchange their land for grain (**47:22, 26**).

Genesis **47:21** presents something of a problem to the reader, but it seems to mean that the Egyptian people were ordered to move into the cities temporarily until seed for planting could be efficiently distributed to them (**47:23**). They were then to plant the seed on the pharaoh's land. When the harvest came in, they were to give one-fifth of it to the pharaoh and keep four-fifths for themselves and their households (**47:24–25**). This was simply an extension of a practice that had already begun in an initial way during the seven years of abundance (41:34). The difference was that during the abundant years the people had continued to own their own land, while now all the land belonged to the pharaoh by legal status (**47:26**).

Meanwhile Jacob's family, soon to become the people of Israel, continued to live in Goshen. There they became wealthy and increased their numbers by leaps and bounds (**47:27**)—an asset that would eventually be transformed into a liability when "a new king, who did not know about Joseph, came to power in Egypt" (Exod. 1:7–8). The "people" aspect of the Abrahamic covenant (Gen. 12:2; 13:16; 15:5; 17:2, 4–6, 16; 22:17; 26:4, 24; 28:3, 14; 35:11) was now beginning to gain momentum. The God of Abraham, Isaac, and Jacob would once again demonstrate his faithfulness to his people.

Jacob lived in Canaan and Mesopotamia for 130 years (**47:9**) and in Egypt for seventeen years (**47:28**). He had now reached his 147th year, the year of his death. So he summoned Joseph and told him to take an oath: "Put your hand under my thigh" (**47:29**). It was the same command that Abraham had given to his servant who was going out to search for a bride for Isaac (24:2). The action accompanied an especially solemn form of oath, with the hand of one person being placed near the organ of generation of another. In this case it was used because Jacob insisted on being buried not in Egypt but in Canaan, where his forefathers had been buried (**47:29–30**). In both cases, ties of family kinship were strongly emphasized (see 24:3–4). Abraham had wanted Isaac to be joined with his relatives in life; Jacob wanted to be joined with his relatives in death.

After Joseph had taken the oath, Jacob "worshiped as he leaned on the top of his staff" (**47:31**). If we pay attention to the vowels of the Hebrew text, however, we would read that Jacob "bowed down at the head of his bed" (see NIV footnote).

Hebrews 11:21 quotes this passage from the Septuagint, the ancient Greek translation of the OT, which reads "staff" instead of "bed" (the original Hebrew consonants of the word in question could be read either way, depending on the vowels that were pronounced along with them). So Hebrews 11:21 tells us also that Jacob "worshiped as he leaned on the top of his staff."

It is difficult to make a choice between the Genesis vocalic reading and the reading in Hebrews, because each has obvious merit. The Genesis **47:31** marginal reading, "bed," fits in well contextually with 48:1–2. On the other hand, the Hebrews 11:21 reading, "staff," is not out of place there and would work equally well in Genesis **47:31**. On balance, then, the reading "staff" is probably best for both passages.

24

The Last Days of Jacob and Joseph (48:1–50:26)

THE END OF JACOB'S LIFE (48:1–50:14)

THE END OF JOSEPH'S LIFE (50:15–26)

The story of how a loving father and his beloved son lived out their final years concludes our study of the text of the Book of Genesis.

Most of this three-chapter section details events that preceded Jacob's death. Only twelve verses are allotted to Joseph's last days.

The End of Jacob's Life (48:1–50:14)

Jacob had already expressed his willingness to die, now that he had seen Joseph for the first time after a long separation and now that the whole family was together again (46:30). But Jacob still needed to do a few things to put his house and affairs in order. For example, he needed to take care of bequeathing his estate to his heirs. In this case, bequeathal essentially amounted to pronouncing various blessings on Joseph's sons as well as on his own.

Blessing Joseph's Sons (48:1–22)

As soon as Joseph was told that his father had become ill, he decided to take his two sons, Manasseh and Ephraim, and go to visit him (**48:1**). When they arrived at Jacob's house, Jacob rallied his strength and sat up in bed (**48:2**). He then reminded Joseph of how God Almighty had appeared to him at Luz (later renamed Bethel) in Canaan and had renewed to him the twin promises of land and descendants (**48:3–4**; see 28:13–14 and esp. 35:11–12).

By using the name "God Almighty," Jacob was acknowledging that only an all-powerful God could have made such far-reaching promises with the assurance that they would be fulfilled (see also 17:1; 28:3; 35:11; 43:14). We are again reminded that God Almighty was the distinctive and characteristic name of God used by the patriarchs (Exod. 6:3).

Jacob now proceeded to adopt Joseph's two sons. Although Manasseh was Joseph's firstborn (Gen. 41:51), Jacob referred to the two boys as "Ephraim and Manasseh" (**48:5**). He spoke Ephraim's name first in anticipation of the fact that he would bless Ephraim first and Manasseh second (**48:14–20**).

Jacob went on to declare that Ephraim and Manasseh would now be his, just as Reuben and Simeon were his. In other words, Ephraim and Manasseh would enjoy equal status with Jacob's firstborn son (Reuben) and second son (Simeon; see 35:23). Although Jacob had twelve sons, Joseph's portion of Jacob's inheritance would be divided between Ephraim and Manasseh, making a total of thirteen tribal allotments. To reduce the number back down to twelve again, the territorial share belonging to Levi (Jacob's third son; see 29:34; 35:23) would be eliminated. The Levites would be given only a number of towns with their surrounding pasturelands (Josh. 14:4).

Jacob's adoption of Ephraim and Manasseh would make it necessary for Joseph's next two sons to move up and take their places as far as Joseph's eventual bequeathal of his own estate was concerned. They in turn would perpetuate the names of Ephraim and Manasseh for inheritance purposes (Gen. **48:6**).

Jacob's reminder to Joseph of his mother Rachel's untimely death on the way back from Paddan ("the plain"; the word is an abbreviation of Paddan Aram; see 25:20) as they approached

Bethlehem (**48:7**; see 35:16–19) was probably intended to justify Jacob's adoption of Ephraim and Manasseh. In effect, they took the place of other sons that Rachel might have been expected to bear if she had continued to live. By the same token Joseph, still young and virile, had plenty of time to father additional sons through one or more wives.

Apparently Jacob had not met Manasseh and Ephraim yet, so when Joseph brought them in to Jacob he wanted to know who they were (**48:8**). It is also possible that his question was due to the fact that he could not see them clearly because of poor vision (**48:10**). In any event, Joseph answered by saying that they were the sons that God had given him (**48:9**). Joseph used words that were reminiscent of Jacob's own words to Esau in response to a similar question years earlier (33:5). We, too, would do well to acknowledge our own children as gifts from a loving God whenever opportunity to do so presents itself.

Like Isaac in his old age (27:1), the elderly Jacob had weak eyes and was hardly able to see (**48:10**). So he asked Joseph to bring the boys closer to him in order that he might bless them. As they sat on Jacob's knees, he kissed and embraced them in an act probably symbolic of adoption procedures (**48:10–12**; see esp. 30:3). Jacob was thrilled at having the opportunity of seeing not only Joseph but also Joseph's sons (**48:11**).

After Joseph had lifted the boys down from Jacob's knees and bowed low in respect before him (**48:12**), he placed Ephraim in front of Jacob's left hand and Manasseh in front of Jacob's right hand (**48:13**). This was to make sure that Jacob would put his right hand on the head of Manasseh, Joseph's firstborn, as he blessed the two boys. But Jacob, who had other plans, crossed his arms as he performed the blessing, putting his right hand on Ephraim's head and his left on Manasseh's (**48:14**).

Then Jacob blessed the sons of Joseph. He invoked the name of God (**48:15**) in the person of the "Angel" (**48:16**) who had earlier blessed Jacob himself (32:29). Jacob's blessing depicts God as Companion, Shepherd, and Redeemer. As it was true of Jacob, so it is true of all believers: Our God is with us, he leads us, he saves us.

Jacob also prayed that his own name and the names of Abraham and Isaac would be perpetuated in the names of Ephraim and Manasseh. He further prayed that the boys would produce a multitude of descendants upon the earth (**48:16**).

Although by now it may be tedious to repeat it, I would once again call attention to the reference to land and descendants, the two main aspects of the Abrahamic covenant.

Joseph was displeased when he saw his father's right hand on Ephraim's head, so he took hold of the hand in order to shift it over to Manasseh's head. But Jacob refused to move his hand. He indicated that although Manasseh would also be greatly blessed, nevertheless the younger son would be greater than the older (**48:17–20**). Ephraim's descendants did become the most powerful tribe in the north during the time of the divided monarchy (931– 722 B.C.). In fact "Ephraim" was one of the names used by the prophets to refer to the northern kingdom (see, e.g., Hos. 9:13; 12:1, 8). Again we notice the tendency in Genesis (and throughout the OT, for that matter) to bypass the firstborn in deference to a younger son. God wanted to make sure that his people were not unduly restricted by the tenacious legal custom known as primogeniture.

Jacob told Joseph that he was about to die but that God would be with Joseph and bring him back to Canaan, the land of his forefathers (**48:21**). Years later, Joseph would echo those words to his brothers just before his own death (**50:24**). At the same time he would declare that they were to carry his bones back to Canaan with them (**50:25**). In similarly intricate ways are the promises of a faithful God transmitted from generation to generation in our lives.

Jacob also gave Joseph a preliminary gift before blessing all twelve brothers with blessings appropriate to each (**49:28**). Joseph was granted a mountain "ridge" or "shoulder" (**48:22**), the Hebrew word for which can also be read as the place-name "Shechem." Since Joseph was later buried at Shechem in a plot of ground that became the property of his descendants (Josh. 24:32; see also Gen. 33:19; John 4:5), Shechem was probably the reference intended in Genesis **48:22**.

Jacob said that he took the place from the Amorites in battle, a possible allusion to the plunder of Shechem by Jacob's sons (34:27–29). Needless to say, it could also be a reference to a battle otherwise unmentioned in the OT.

Blessing Jacob's Sons (49:1–28)

Genesis **49:2–27** is by far the longest poem in the Book of Genesis. Often entitled "The Blessing of Jacob" by modern scholars, it is one of the oldest poems of any length in the entire Bible.[1] It is also one of a series of poetic blessings in Genesis that includes those of Noah (9:26–27), Melchizedek (14:19–20), Isaac (27:27–29; 27:39–40), and another by Jacob himself (**48:15–16**).

Because of its length, its complexity, its age, and the fact that it is a poem, the Blessing of Jacob contains numerous rare words and unusual grammatical constructions. Such factors make it one of the most difficult chapters in Genesis to interpret in detail. In broad outline, however, its message and purpose are clear.

Shortly before his death, Jacob summoned his sons to gather around him. He wanted to tell them what was going to happen to them in the future (**49:1**). Not all of his prophecies would be fulfilled at the same time, of course. Some of the blessings turned out to be curses, while others were descriptions of character as well as predictions of future events.

After an introductory statement to set the stage and tone of the blessings (**49:2**), Jacob addressed each son individually, except for Simeon and Levi (who were two of a kind, birds of a feather). The order in which he addressed them was neither that of their birth (29:31–30:24; 35:16–19) nor that of the listing in 35:23–26. These two listings and the Blessing of Jacob do, however, mention the first four sons in the order of their birth.

Reuben, Jacob's firstborn, was initially described by Jacob as being supreme in honor and might because he was the firstfruits of Jacob's strength (**49:3**). But as we learned earlier, Reuben had cohabited with Bilhah, Jacob's concubine (35:22), perhaps on more than one occasion. He seems to have been a man of impulse and indecision (see Judg. 5:15–16), as "turbulent as the waters" (Gen. **49:4**). Because of his sinful activity, he would lose the supremacy due him as the firstborn. His birthright would be given to Joseph's descendants (1 Chron. 5:1). As the newly declared firstborn, Joseph was entitled to a "double share" (Deut. 21:17) of Jacob's property, ultimately the tribal territories of Ephraim and Manasseh after Joshua's conquest of Canaan.

Simeon and *Levi* were addressed together because they shared certain things in common: cruelty, anger, fierceness (Gen. **49:5–7**). As in the case of Reuben, Jacob's blessing turned into a curse (**49:7**) for Simeon and Levi because of their murder of the

---

1. See, e.g., W. F. Albright, *Yahweh and The Gods of Canaan* (Garden City, N.Y.: Doubleday, 1968), 19–20.

male citizens of Shechem years earlier (34:25–31). Piling crime upon crime, they had also crippled the oxen belonging to Shechem by cutting the tendons in their legs (**49:6**).

Jacob stated poetically that he did not want to associate with Simeon or Levi any longer (**49:6**). Then he indicated directly that some day their tribes would be dispersed and scattered throughout the other Israelite tribes (**49:7**).

And so it happened. Simeon became a part of Judah (Josh. 19:1, 9), eventually losing its identity by being absorbed into it. The so-called Blessing of Moses (Deut. 33), another very ancient poem containing predictions about and characterizations of the twelve tribes of Israel, does not even mention Simeon.

As for Levi, his descendants received no extensive territory of their own, as mentioned earlier. Forty-eight towns, together with the pasturelands surrounding them, were the Levites' only territorial inheritance (Josh. 14:4; 21:41–42; Num. 35:1–8), however honorable (Num. 18:21–24).

The blessing on *Judah* (Gen. **49:8–12**) rivals the one on Joseph (**49:22–26**) in length. Judah and Joseph would father the most powerful tribes in Israel (Judah in the south, Joseph in the north) and would compete for leadership in later generations, a fact reflected in 1 Chronicles 5:1–2.

Genesis **49:8** contains a double pun on Judah's name, since the Hebrew words for "praise" (see also 29:35) and "hand" resemble the word "Judah." The wording of **49:8** is also strongly reminiscent of Isaac's blessings on Jacob (see 27:29) and Esau (see 27:40), as well as of Joseph's memorable dreams (37:5–10).

The image of Judah (or Israel) as a lion (**49:9**) became common in later biblical literature (Num. 24:9; Mic. 5:8; Ezek. 19:1–7). In Revelation 5:5, Jesus is called "the Lion of the tribe of Judah" in demonstration of his conquering majesty. In the very next verse he is called the "Lamb" in demonstration of his meekness and his willingness to be sacrificed for the sins of the world (see also John 1:29, 36).

Genesis **49:10** is undoubtedly the most well-known and best-loved verse in the Blessing of Jacob. Jewish and Christian interpreters alike have seen in it a prediction of the coming Messiah. It may well contain such a prediction, although the verse is not easy to translate. If it is indeed messianic, however, the NT ignored that fact since it nowhere quoted the verse in whole or in part.

The crux of the problem is the word traditionally rendered as

"Shiloh." Elsewhere in the OT, the place-name Shiloh (a town in central Canaan) is never spelled like it is in the Hebrew text of this verse, nor is Shiloh ever elsewhere a name for the Messiah.

Many recent scholars prefer to vocalize the Hebrew text slightly differently from Jewish oral tradition and to read the crucial line something like this: "until tribute comes to him" (see also Isa. 18:7, where the word for "tribute" is translated "gifts"). Such a reading forms an excellent parallel to the final line of the verse and results in the following translation for the verse as a whole:

> The scepter will not depart from Judah,
> nor the ruler's staff from between his feet,
> until tribute comes to him
> and the obedience of the nations is his.

This solution has the advantage of making good sense out of a difficult verse. It also preserves the parallelism of successive lines so characteristic of Hebrew poetry in general and of this poem in particular.

When all is said and done, however, "until he comes to whom it belongs" is probably the best choice in the light of Ezekiel 21:27, where the phrase "until he comes to whom it rightfully belongs" occurs in a similarly messianic context.

In any event, whether messianic or not, Genesis **49:10** represents Judah's descendants as being powerful and conquering for generations on end. The scepter motif is also reflected in Numbers 24:17, another verse that has been traditionally considered messianic. Like Genesis **49:10**, however, it is never quoted or referred to in the NT.

Genesis **49:11–12** perhaps foresaw the time in the future when Judah would cease to be a wandering tribe and would settle down to a more tranquil life. It also hints at the prosperity Judah would some day enjoy.

The blessing on *Zebulun* (**49:13**) is perplexing, because his tribal territory (see Josh. 19:10–16) was landlocked by those of Asher and Manasseh. But it was close enough to the Mediterranean Sea to "feast on the abundance of the seas" (Deut. 33:19)— that is, to participate in seaborne commerce. Perhaps that is all Genesis **49:13** intended to say.

Issachar's blessing contains a rare word, "saddlebags" (**49:14**), that appears elsewhere only in Judges 5:16 and in a related form in Psalm 68:13. In all three cases it can be translated either "saddlebags" or "campfires," and recent scholarship is divided as to its meaning.

Fortunately, the total thrust of the blessing is unaffected by this minor difficulty. Issachar, though sturdy and strong, would be pressed into doing forced labor for another tribe or nation (Gen. **49:14–15**). For a possible fulfillment of this prophecy, see Judges 5:15.

Dan's descendants would "judge" their people (or "rule" them; the word is a pun on the name "Dan"). They would take their rightful place among Israel's tribes (Gen. **49:16**). Dan's characterization as a treacherous serpent (**49:17**) was entirely appropriate, as Judges 18:27 demonstrates.

Before proceeding to bless the rest of his sons, Jacob paused to catch his breath with the heartfelt prayer, "I look for your deliverance, O LORD" (Gen. **49:18**). An elderly man on his deathbed, Jacob begged for God's help as he continued his strenuous speech, a speech that must have taxed all his physical, intellectual and spiritual faculties.

Such a plea was entirely in character when voiced by God's people (see, e.g., Isa. 25:9). It can also serve as a model prayer for us today, because it demonstrates one man's patience as well as his confidence in the Lord's love and concern for him.

In *Gad*'s brief blessing (Gen. **49:19**) there are three puns on his name ("attacked," "raiders," "attack"). Located east of the Jordan River on the border of Moab (Josh. 13:24–28), the tribe of Gad was vulnerable to raids from its southern neighbor, as the ninth-century-B.C. Mesha inscription illustrates.[2]

Asher's coastal location (Josh. 19:24–31) and fertile farmlands would make them wealthy and enable them to produce delicacies fit for a king (Gen. **49:20**).

The characterization of *Naphtali* as a "doe set free" (**49:21**) probably refers to the independent spirit of that tribe. They were located in the hill country north of the Sea of Galilee (Josh. 19:32–39).

Jacob's blessing on *Joseph* (Gen. **49:22–26**) is about the same length as his blessing on Judah (**49:8–12**). It underscores the

---

2. See Albright in *Ancient Near Eastern Texts*, ed. J. B. Pritchard, 2d ed. (Princeton: Princeton University Press, 1955), 320.

importance of the tribes that would some day descend from Joseph's sons, Manasseh and Ephraim. It also illustrates, however incidentally, Jacob's insistence that Ephraim should be more powerful than Manasseh (**48:5, 14–20**) because it makes a pun on Ephraim's name (the Hebrew word for "fruitful," used twice in **49:22**, is similar to the word "Ephraim," which means "twice fruitful").

The tendency of Ephraim's descendants to expand their territory (**49:22**), their victories in battle (**49:23–24**), the fertility of their fields as God blessed their crops (**49:25–26**), and their supremacy over the other tribes, especially in the north (**49:26**)—all would be amply illustrated in Ephraim's later history (Josh. 16:5–10; 17:14–18; Judg. 8:1; 12:1; Isa. 7:1–2; Hos. 12:8; 13:1).

A striking feature of Joseph's blessing is the series of names by which Jacob referred to God (Gen. **49:24–25**). He called him "the Mighty One of Jacob" (see also Isa. 49:26), "the Shepherd" (see Gen. **48:15**; Ps. 23:1), "the Rock of Israel" (see, e.g., Ps. 18:2 and esp. 19:14), "the God of [Joseph's] father" (see Gen. 31:29, 42), and "the Almighty," the most characteristic patriarchal designation for God.

The series reminds us again of how numerous God's qualities and attributes are. No matter how serious our problems might seem, he has infinite resources to help us.

Among the descendants of *Benjamin*, Jacob's youngest son, were many who committed acts of lustfulness and savagery (see Judg. 19–21). So Jacob appropriately pictured Benjamin as a vicious wolf (Gen. **49:27**).

The Blessing of Jacob closes with a summary statement that stresses the suitability of the blessing that he had given to each of his sons (**49:28**). Later developments would prove his evaluation to be correct in every case, since God himself was the ultimate source of Jacob's ability to foresee the future destiny of his sons and their descendants.

Jacob's Death and Burial (49:29–50:14)

The Book of Genesis now draws rapidly to a close. After Jacob had blessed his twelve sons, he told them that he was about to join his ancestors in death. He made his sons promise to bury him in the cave of Machpelah where the other patriarchs and their wives, as well as his own wife Leah (but not Rachel; see

35:19), had been buried (**49:29–32**). Having given his sons that final command, Jacob died (**49:33**) at the ripe old age of 147 years (47:28).

Joseph, who showed his emotions more openly than his brothers did (see 42:24; 43:30; 45:14–15; 46:29; **50:17**), wept over his father (**50:1**). He then instructed the "physicians" to embalm Jacob (**50:2**). He may have deliberately avoided using the services of professional embalmers because of the accompanying pagan religious ceremonies such services would have entailed. The forty days required for the embalming and the seventy days the Egyptians mourned for Jacob (**50:3**) may have overlapped, but in any event the time periods were in general harmony with what we know of ancient Egyptian custom.[3]

After the days of mourning were over, Joseph asked for and received the pharaoh's permission to take Jacob's body to Canaan for burial (**50:4–6**). A large entourage of relatives and dignitaries, including Jacob's household and many prominent Egyptians, made the trip (**50:7–9**). En route, they stopped at the threshing floor of Atad (a place of uncertain location) near the Jordan River.

While there, the group held a seven-day ceremonial lamentation for Jacob. When the local Canaanite inhabitants observed it they renamed the place "Abel Mizraim." The name means both "mourning of Egypt" and "meadow of Egypt," so perhaps the designation was a deliberate pun (**50:10–11**).

The mourners then continued on their way and buried Jacob in Hebron. Afterwards they all returned to Egypt (**50:12–14**).

The End of Joseph's Life (50:15–26)

With Jacob now dead and buried, the last dozen verses of the Book of Genesis describe Joseph's final days.

Joseph Reaffirms His Forgiveness (50:15–21)

As soon as Joseph's brothers realized the full implications of Jacob's death, they became afraid that Joseph would now seek revenge against them for selling him as a slave (**50:15**). We remember that Esau had planned to take similar action against Jacob as soon as Isaac died (see 27:41).

So the brothers warned Joseph that Jacob had told them to

---

3. See J. J. Davis, *Mummies, Men and Madness* (Winona Lake, Ind.: BMH Books, 1972), 97–100.

plead for Joseph's forgiveness. Joseph wept when he received the message, perhaps partly because he felt that his brothers had falsely implicated Jacob in their story and was saddened by the lengths to which they would go to save themselves, perhaps partly at his own failure to have reassured them long before this (**50:16–17**). The brothers even offered to be Joseph's slaves (**50:18**), as—once again and finally—Joseph's youthful dreams (37:6–7, 9) received ironically unexpected fulfillment.

But Joseph assured the men that he would not play God by taking matters into his own hands (**50:19**). Indeed, he could not do so, any more than his father Jacob could have done so in other circumstances years before (30:2).

Joseph then gave his brothers an important lesson about the providence of God, who had planned everything that had happened so that only good would result. Genesis **50:20** is the OT equivalent of Romans 8:28.

Joseph's generosity, his spirit of forgiveness, his loving concern again expressed themselves. He told his brothers once more not to be afraid (Gen. **50:21**; see **50:19**). He also promised to provide them and their children with everything they needed.

What a beautiful illustration of our God, who calms our fears, assures us of his providence, and promises to supply all our needs "according to his glorious riches in Christ Jesus" (Phil. 4:19)!

Joseph's Death and Burial (50:22–26)

Even after his father had died, Joseph continued to make his home in Egypt. He lived to the age of 110 years (Gen. **50:22, 26**), which, as we noted earlier in our study (see chapter thirteen), was considered to be the ideal life span, according to ancient Egyptian records.

Joseph had the privilege of seeing his son Ephraim's children down to the third generation (**50:23**), an experience similar to those enjoyed by other patriarchs (see, e.g., Job 42:16). Joseph's firstborn, Manasseh, had a son named Makir, whose children were adopted by Joseph (Gen. **50:23**; see 30:3; **48:10–12**). Makir became the ancestor of a powerful nation (Josh. 17:1), and his name was used as a virtual synonym for "Manasseh" in Judges 5:14.

When the time came for Joseph to die, he told his brothers twice that God would surely come to their aid (Gen. **50:24–25**).

The Lord would not forget his promises to Abraham, to Isaac, to Jacob, or to their descendants. He would continue to express his loving concern for the people of Israel and would bring them back to Canaan.

And Joseph, of course, wanted to make that memorable trip, too. So he made his brothers promise to carry his bones along with them (**50:25**). Their descendants were able to keep the promise (Exod. 13:19), and when they arrived in Canaan they lovingly buried Joseph's remains at Shechem, on the plot of ground that Jacob had purchased from Hamor's sons (Josh. 24:32; see Gen. 33:19).

After his brothers had taken the oath that Joseph requested, he died, was embalmed, and was placed in a sarcophagus. To all intents and purposes the last of the patriarchs had now passed from the scene, and our story, in one sense, is over. The Book of Genesis, the book that began with the fragrance of life, concluded with the stench of death. It started "in the beginning" (1:1) and ended "in a coffin in Egypt" (**50:26**).

If that coffin had been the final curtain in the biblical drama, we of all people would be most miserable—but it was not, and we are not. Before Joseph died, he told his brothers: "God will . . . take you up out of this land to the land he promised on oath to Abraham, Isaac and Jacob" (**50:24**). In so doing, Joseph "spoke about the exodus of the Israelites from Egypt" (Heb. 11:22).

That, however, is another story.[4]

4. See, e.g., R. Youngblood, *Exodus* (Chicago: Moody, 1983).

25

The Patriarchs, Though Dead, Yet Speak

What the Patriarchs Tell Us about God's Relationship to Us

What the Patriarchs Tell Us about Our Relationship to God

What the Patriarchs Tell Us about Our Relationship to Each Other

Hebrews 11 is often referred to as the "Roll Call of the Faithful." The chapter as a whole contains forty verses and is well worth reading many times over. In cameo-like portraits, it depicts the essential characteristics and activities that made it possible for certain people from the OT to qualify for a place in a list of men and women who displayed unusually great faith.

The heart of the chapter is 11:4–32, a section that gets down to specific cases and actually names a number of people whose lives exemplified genuine faith in God. To the credit of the patriarchs, the author of Hebrews devoted more than half of those twenty-nine verses—fifteen, to be exact—to detailing the ways in which the patriarchs and their wives proved themselves to be men and women of faith (11:8–22).

The text says that Abel, the first person to be mentioned in the main section (11:4–32), because of his faith, "still speaks, even though he is dead" (11:4). We could say the same about the patriarchs as well. They all died, but through their faith they still speak to us today.

In fact, they give us a kind of patriarchal theology. To be sure, it is not laid out in orderly and systematic fashion. But it is none the less helpful for all that. The patriarchal narratives in Genesis 11:27–50:26 give us a wealth of practical information about God's relationship to us, our relationship to God, and our relationship to each other.

Our final study in this book will concentrate on several aspects of each of these three important subjects.

What the Patriarchs Tell Us about God's Relationship to Us

The story of the patriarchs is an exciting and absorbing account about actual people in actual situations.

Needless to say, however, the real hero of the patriarchal narratives is God himself (as noted at the beginning of chapter fourteen). Even when he does not occupy center stage in the story, he is at least nearby, waiting to relate himself to his people in one way or other. In fact he is eager to come to the aid of all who need him. The God of the patriarchs is our God as well, the God who seeks, the God who acts.[1]

He takes the initiative in acting on behalf of his people. Even when we are not particularly looking for him, even when we are not aware of his presence, he is there. He reveals himself to us in various ways: in nature, through conscience, in his Word, through the witness of the Holy Spirit in our lives. And he revealed himself to the patriarchs in various ways as well: in dreams (Gen. 28:12–15), in visions (15:1), in the person of the angel of the Lord (22:11).[2]

God also made himself known to the patriarchs in a way more difficult to define than these. We are told often that he "appeared"

---

1. For a careful treatment of the theme of God in action, see G. E. Wright, *God Who Acts* (London: SCM, 1952).

2. See esp. G. Vos, *Biblical Theology* (Grand Rapids: Eerdmans, 1948), 82–89.

to them (e.g., 17:1), which literally means that God "allowed himself to be seen" by the patriarchs. This does not imply that they saw him in all the fullness of his splendor and glory, but rather that they experienced his spiritual presence in an intimate and personal way. They enjoyed communion and fellowship with him to an exceptional degree.

The names that God gave to himself or by which he allowed himself to be called are another indication of his willingness to disclose his plans and purposes to the patriarchs.

El Elyon was a name by which both Abraham and Melchizedek referred to God (14:18–20, 22). It means "God Most High" and stresses the fact that the one true God is God par excellence, that he occupies the supreme position in the universe over all other so-called gods, whether real or imagined. In that same context where Abraham and Melchizedek appear together, God is also called "Creator of heaven and earth" (14:19, 22; see also 24:3). This name emphasizes the fact that everything that exists owes its origin and continued existence to him.

El Shaddai (see, e.g., 17:1) was the divine name most characteristic of the patriarchal period (Exod. 6:3). While its literal meaning was probably something like "God, the Mountain One," for all practical purposes the traditional translation "God Almighty" gets at the functional significance of the name. "God Almighty" was a designation that stressed the omnipotence of God in the lives of the patriarchs. God Almighty, because he is all-powerful, had the power to help them overcome all their difficulties. He was able to protect them when they were traveling (even in foreign countries), to supply them with all the food and clothing and shelter they needed (even to make them wealthy), to help them produce children (even when they were beyond the age of childbearing), and to give them success in whatever they attempted to do (even when naïveté and superstition were their only native resources). In short, God Almighty (see also the name "the Mighty One of Jacob" in Gen. 49:24) was the God whose strength was made perfect in their weakness (see 2 Cor. 12:9).

God is also the "Judge" of the whole earth (Gen. 18:25). He dealt with the patriarchs, and deals with us, in perfect justice. He destroyed Sodom, Gomorrah, and the other towns in the plain because their inhabitants were sinful beyond recall. At the same time, however, "he rescued Lot, a righteous man," (2 Pet. 2:7) "out of the catastrophe" (Gen. 19:29). As the Judge of us all, God is eminently able to distinguish between his own children and the children of Satan. His holiness often delivers, but it also disciplines.

El Olam (21:33), another name by which God was known during the patriarchal period, means the "Eternal God" and stresses his everlasting nature. Implicit in the name is continuity, the fact that although our lives are brief at best God has always existed and always will exist. He and his promises are dependable. They continue on from generation to generation, because time is for him not an obstacle but an opportunity. In referring to "the God of my father" (31:5, 42), Jacob could do so with the confidence that the God who had been Isaac's God and Abraham's God would also be his own God and his children's God and their children's God throughout endless ages.

"The Fear of Isaac" (31:42) is a phrase that is doubtless another title for the God of the patriarchs. If correctly translated, it highlights the fact that God wants his people to worship him, to respect him, to honor him, to hold him in awe. In other words, it emphasizes God's transcendence, his aloofness, his otherness, his distance from us. But if it means "the Kinsman of Isaac," as some scholars contend, it emphasizes God's immanence, his cordiality, his similarity to us, his nearness to us.

How can God be both far away and close at hand at the same time? His omnipresence (as it has traditionally been called) is certainly one of the mysteries of his being. Although I plan to ask him for a detailed explanation when I get to heaven, in the meantime I must be content with observing that the Bible teaches both his distance and his nearness. Indeed, there is an impressive statement of both in Isaiah 57:15, the first three lines of which focus on Godıs transcendence and the last three on his immanence:

> For this is what the high and lofty One says—
> he who lives forever, whose name is holy:
> "I live in a high and holy place,
> but also with him who is contrite and lowly in spirit,
> to revive the spirit of the lowly
> and to revive the heart of the contrite."

Two final names of God that were used during the patriarchal period and that deserve special mention are "the Shepherd" and "the Rock of Israel" (Gen. 49:24). Both arc found iıı the same line of the same verse, even though they appear at first to be unrelated to each other.

Closer examination, however, reveals that both names have to do with God as Protector of his people. Like a shepherd, our God watches over us, expresses his concern for us, and cares for our needs. Like a fortress made of stone and rock, our God shields (see 15:1) us from the onslaughts of Satan and shelters us from the storms and stresses of life that threaten to overwhelm us. Whether in the symbolism of lambs protected by the strong arm of a shepherd or of birds protected in the crevice of a rocky cliff, he gives us the assurance that our problems and difficulties do not have to defeat us.

The patriarchs must have learned a great deal about the nature of their God just by thinking through the implications of his many names.

But God's relationship to them was expressed in countless other ways as well. His continuing concern for them was a reflection of other attributes of his that we have not yet mentioned in this chapter.

Every time God told one of the patriarchs about something that was going to happen in the future, he was giving tangible expression to his omniscience. Only a God who knows everything dares to make such far-ranging and far-reaching predictions.

Every time God confirmed his covenant with the patriarchs, he was expressing his love and faithfulness to them and their descendants. Covenants were not entered into lightly in ancient times, and God seemed to derive special delight from taking oaths in his own name (22:16; see Heb. 6:13).

Every time God made one of the patriarchs wealthy or successful, he was demonstrating his providence in a special way. He was reminding them that all they could ever hope to have or be depended on his goodness and grace.

Every time God rescued the patriarchs from danger, he showed them that he was merciful (see esp. Gen. 19:16). And his mercies are without limitation; as Lamentations 3:23 puts it, "they are new every morning."

Every time God—but perhaps we have already given enough examples. We could comment on his sovereignty, his elective purpose, his patience, his incredible willingness to bless and strengthen and give to people who were often unwilling to bless and strengthen and give in return.

Although for the patriarchs Calvary could have been only the dimmest of hopes two thousand years in the future, their God maintained a warm and cordial relationship toward them. The more spiritually perceptive among them must have been supremely grateful for the depth of that relationship.

Should not we, who live two thousand years after Calvary, be infinitely more grateful for the additional blessings God has showered down on us through our Lord Jesus Christ?

What the Patriarchs Tell Us about Our Relationship to God

By definition, a relationship is always a two-way street. As God related himself to the patriarchs in various ways, so they related themselves to him in various ways.

It has become a commonplace in our time to assert that Moses was the first OT figure to embrace monotheism, the belief that there is only one God.[3] Theoretical monotheism has been observed by recent scholars in such passages as Deuteronomy 4:35, 39; 6:4; 32:39. But it should be pointed out that the ancient Hebrew people tended to be short on theory and long on practice. In other words, they were not theologians or philosophers so much as they were servants and worshipers. This evaluation applies to Moses as well: He was much more a practical monotheist than a theoretical monotheist.

The same can be said of the patriarchs. In their better moments, each of them loved the Lord with all his heart and soul and mind and strength. Although their ancestors had been polytheists (Josh. 24:2), there were times of deep spiritual significance in their own lives when they got rid of the other gods, real or imagined, that they had been accustomed to worshiping (Gen. 35:2–4). At such times the one true God so monopolized their attention and experience that they had no time or opportunity for other loyalties. In other words, the patriarchs were practical monotheists. God slowly, surely, firmly weaned them away from the worship of all that was unworthy. And they learned to love him for it.

The means that God used to assure that the patriarchs would give him their undivided loyalty was the covenant. By its very

3. See, e.g., W. F. Albright, *From the Stone Age to Christianity*, 2d ed. (Baltimore: Johns Hopkins Press, 1957), 271–72.

nature, entering into a covenant tends toward an exclusive relationship that brooks no rivals. "I will be their God, and they will be my people" (Jer. 31:33; see also Gen. 17:7) became a characteristic phrase throughout the OT expressing the covenant relationship. As the ancient Israelites were to worship God alone because of their covenant relationship to him, so also the true Christian is to refer only to Jesus Christ as "Lord" (Rom. 10:9).

The Abrahamic covenant was solemnized by sacrifice, the slaughter and offering of animals to the Lord (Gen. 15:9–10). The patriarchs often built altars at places where they had significant spiritual experiences. The best known of these is doubtless the one at Moriah, where the two basic principles of OT sacrifice were strikingly exemplified: sacrifice as the gift of life (Isaac) to God, and sacrifice as the substitution of life (the ram; see 22:9–13).

The mention of sacrifice helps us recall the importance of the shedding of blood to pave the way for man's proper relationship to God throughout the Bible. "The life of a creature is in the blood," and "it is the blood that makes atonement for one's life" (Lev. 17:11). The principle that shedding blood was a prerequisite for the removal of sin is not clearly expressed in the patriarchal narratives. But circumcision as the sign of the Abrahamic covenant reminds us, at the very least, that a general covenant becomes individually effective only as the individual relates himself in a personal way to a ceremony involving the shedding of blood.

That principle is important for us as well. We can become members of the covenant people of God only by confessing that "Christ died for our sins according to the Scriptures" (1 Cor. 15:3) and that "the blood of Jesus," God's Son, "purifies us from all sin" (1 John 1:7).

Believing in God's covenant provisions for them made it possible for the patriarchs to enjoy communion and fellowship with him. Over and over again the Lord promised to be with them wherever they went, as we have already observed.

The constant presence of God in their lives might well have had the effect of teaching them that their God was the God of other people and nations also. The patriarchs do not seem to have been conscious of that fact to the extent that they were overcome by a strong zeal to witness to their faith in the one true God, with the possible exception of the Abraham-Melchizedek encounter. But opportunities and incentives to witness to people of other nations were there for those who had the eyes to see them. Canaan, after all, was the crossroads of the ancient world, and providentially so. People from the surrounding nations often had to travel through Canaan while going from one place to another. Separated from their own temples and priests by long distances, they could have become prime objects of witness on the part of the patriarchs and their descendants. Had the patriarchs been more zealous in buying up the opportunities, one aspect of God's call to Abraham would have begun to be fulfilled even in those early days: "All peoples on earth will be blessed through you" (Gen. 12:3). Universal faith in the one true God would have been well on its way.

But while the faith of the patriarchs may not have been mission-minded, it was none the less fervent for all that. They worshiped the Lord in numerous ways, and they did so openly and unashamedly. They made promises and vows of various kinds to him (see 28:20–22). They prayed long and loudly and often to him, giving us enviable examples of persistence (18:22–33; 32:26). They paid tithes to him or to his representatives in gratitude for his goodness (14:20; 28:22). In short, they expressed their love to God in every way that was available to them.

This is not to say that the patriarchs were perfect either in their worship or their conduct. One of the commendable qualities of Scripture that make it so eminently readable is that it does not gloss over the sins and frailties of even its greatest heroes. In the case of the patriarchs, the Bible presents them to us as they really were, warts and all.

It is not necessary for us to dwell again on their sins of violence, deceit, murder, rape, theft, and so forth. We have already commented on them at length, perhaps even giving more time and attention to them than they warrant. We simply observe once again that the patriarchs were real people with real problems and that they committed real sins that were really judged by the living God. The patriarchs were tempted in all points just as we are, and they often succumbed.

But their failures are not what the NT writers remembered them for. They were recalled, fondly and frequently, for their deep and abiding relationships to God, the most important of which was their faith that God could do the impossible. When they were closest to the center of his will, the quality of their faith was such that it could be compared favorably with our faith in the resurrection of Christ (Rom. 4:19–25).

And as the NT writers remembered the patriarchs most often for their faith in God, so also should we.

What the Patriarchs Tell Us about Our Relationship to Each Other

"Faith without deeds is dead" (James 2:26). Dependence on God must be coupled with the willingness to act on that dependence if its genuineness is to be proven.

Needless to say, well-meaning activities can be the outgrowth of sin rather than of faith. When Sarah suggested to Abraham that it might be a good idea for him to sleep with Hagar in order to produce a son who would fulfill God's promise (Gen. 16:2), that was an example of sinful impatience rather than of confident faith. And when Abraham agreed to Sarah's proposal, that was an example of carnal weakness rather than of patient dependence on God and his promises.

Such examples, however, are of value to us only in showing us what not to do in analogous situations. The patriarchs have much to teach us positively in the complex matter of our relationships with other people, whether inside or outside the household of faith.

In his classic treatment of the beliefs, feelings, and aspirations of the patriarchs,[4] J. Strahan spends considerable time in discussing the moral and ethical standards to which they adhered, some of which were part and parcel of their culture and others of which were the direct result of their personal relationship to a loving God. We can learn much, even today, from the positive ideals that the patriarchs tried to emulate in their own lives.

The prompt courtesy that the patriarchs showed to their guests is a noteworthy characteristic that recurs again and again throughout the narratives (18:2–7; 19:1–3; 24:28–32; 29:12–13). The hospitality the patriarchs provided for their visitors made them feel right at home. They seemed to take special delight in entertaining guests as lavishly as their resources would allow.

Patriarchal generosity was expressed in other ways as well. A particularly fine example is to be found in Abraham's offer to Lot

---

4. J. Strahan, *Hebrew Ideals*, 4th ed. (Edinburgh: T. & T. Clark, 1922).

(13:9). In effect, Abraham told Lot that he could make use of whatever section of the Jordan Valley region he desired, and that Abraham would content himself with what was left.

Springing from Abraham's generosity was also a commendable spirit of self-sacrifice. Risking life and limb, he dashed off to the north country to rescue his ungrateful nephew Lot from a band of marauding kings. Then, after saving Lot and his friends and after retrieving the plunder the kings had taken, he refused to keep any of the plunder for himself (14:14–16, 21–24).

Strong ties of blood kinship developed in the patriarchs a sense of loyalty to each other, another quality demonstrated in Genesis 14. Such loyalty can be seen throughout the Book of Genesis, especially in the many descriptions of patriarchal marriages that took place within the tribe or clan.

Times of joy and laughter, though not mentioned frequently in the patriarchal accounts, must have occurred often in their experience. They had a great deal to be thankful for and happy about, as passages such as 21:6 and 31:27 imply. Sharing joy always doubles it, and the patriarchs doubtless had many opportunities to prove that fact.

But while they knew how to laugh with each other, they also knew how to weep with each other. Like their later countrymen, they knew that "there is a time for everything, and a season for every activity under heaven: . . . a time to weep and a time to laugh" (Eccles. 3:1, 4). In fact the patriarchs, along with other people in the ancient Near East, developed mourning and grieving into a fine art. When calamity or death struck, they tore their clothes (Gen. 37:29), dressed themselves in sackcloth (37:34), and wept uncontrollably, often for many days (37:34; 50:3, 10).

The display of emotion, whether laughter or weeping or anger or any one of a number of others, still tends to be much more demonstrative and open in Eastern countries than in the West. We have already noted how often Joseph wept as first his ten older brothers, then Benjamin, and finally Jacob arrived in Egypt, a series of events that brought the whole family back together again. The account of that gradual reunion underscores Joseph's difficulty in controlling his emotions (42:24; 43:30–31; 45:1).

As laughter can be evoked by ties of kinship, so also can weeping. Jacob and Esau wept as they saw each other for the first time after long years of separation (33:4). The tears were probably a mixture of joy and remorse, but they strengthened the ties of brotherhood that had been strained to the breaking point. In fact, Esau insisted on calling Jacob "my brother" on that occasion (33:9). Jacob had wronged Esau, but never mind—they were still brothers. Similarly, Joseph's brothers had wronged him, but never mind, said Joseph: "I am your brother!" (45:4).

In these incidents we see something of the spirit of forgiveness that also characterized the patriarchs during moments of high moral and ethical sensitivity. Another example that comes readily to mind occurred near the end of Joseph's life. A touching scene full of forgiveness and selflessness appears in 50:15–21. Here Joseph told his brothers that even their crimes against him found their place in the perfect will of a God who never makes mistakes. Although they had sold Joseph into slavery in Egypt, God eventually used him to save his whole family. Joseph's compassion and his depth of spiritual understanding on that occasion would be hard to parallel elsewhere in Scripture.

The patriarchs, though dead, yet speak. Like Joseph, they sob with rejoicing when most of us would scream with rage. Like Abraham, they rush to do God's will while most of us rationalize or refuse to do what we know he desires. And like Jacob, they love deeply and with infinite patience (29:20) while our love often tends to be shallow and perfunctory. Although not perfect by any means, the lives of the patriarchs frequently put ours to shame by comparison.

These were all commended for their faith, yet none of them received what had been promised. God had planned something better for us so that only together with us would they be made perfect. Therefore, since we are surrounded by such a great cloud of witnesses, let us throw off everything that hinders and the sin that so easily entangles, and let us run with perseverance the race marked out for us. Let us fix our eyes on Jesus, the author and perfecter of our faith . . .

(Heb. 11:39–12:2)

Select Bibliography

(Inclusion of a book in the following lists does not necessarily indicate wholesale approval of the author's viewpoint or methodology.)

Commentaries

Aalders, G. Ch. *Genesis*. 2 vols. Grand Rapids: Zondervan, 1981.

Boice, J. M. *Genesis: An Expositional Commentary*. 3 vols. Grand Rapids: Zondervan, 1982, 1985, 1987.

Brueggemann, W. *Genesis*. Atlanta: John Knox, 1982.

Cassuto, U. *A Commentary on the Book of Genesis. Part I: From Adam to Noah*. Jerusalem: Magnes, 1961. *Part II: From Noah to Abraham*. Jerusalem: Magnes, 1964.

Davis, J. J. *Paradise to Prison: Studies in Genesis*. Grand Rapids: Baker, 1975.

Driver, S. R. *The Book of Genesis*. 8th ed. London: Methuen, 1911.

Griffith Thomas, W. H. *Genesis: A Devotional Commentary*. Grand Rapids: Eerdmans, 1946.

Kidner, D. *Genesis: An Introduction and Commentary*. Downers Grove, Ill.: InterVarsity, 1972.

Plaut, W. G. *The Torah: A Modern Commentary. Genesis*. New York: Union of American Hebrew Congregations, 1974.

Ross, A. P. *Creation and Blessing: A Guide to the Study and Exposition of the Book of Genesis*. Grand Rapids: Baker, 1988.

Sarna, N. M. *Understanding Genesis*. New York: Schocken, 1970.

Schaeffer, F. A. *Genesis in Space and Time*. Downers Grove, Ill.: InterVarsity, 1972.

Speiser, E. A. *Genesis*. Garden City, N.Y.: Doubleday, 1964.

von Rad, G. *Genesis: A Commentary*. Philadelphia: Westminster, 1961.

Westermann, C. *Genesis: A Commentary*. 3 vols. Minneapolis: Augsburg, 1984, 1985, 1986.

Ancient Near Eastern Backgrounds

Albright, W. F. *Archaeology and the Religion of Israel.* 4th ed. Baltimore: Johns Hopkins, 1956.

_____. *From the Stone Age to Christianity.* 2d ed. Baltimore: Johns Hopkins, 1957.

_____. *Yahweh and the Gods of Canaan.* Garden City, N.Y.: Doubleday, 1968.

Beyerlin, W., ed. *Near Eastern Religious Texts Relating to the Old Testament.* Philadelphia: Westminster, 1978.

Finegan, J. *Light from the Ancient Past.* 2d ed. Princeton: Princeton University, 1959.

Heidel, A. *The Gilgamesh Epic and Old Testament Parallels.* 2d ed. Chicago: University of Chicago, 1949.

_____. *The Babylonian Genesis.* 2d ed. Chicago: University of Chicago, 1951.

Kitchen, K. A. *Ancient Orient and Old Testament.* Chicago: Inter-Varsity, 1966.

_____. *The Bible in Its World.* Downers Grove, Ill.: InterVarsity, 1978.

Lambert, W. G., and A. R. Millard. *Atra-Ḥasīs: The Babylonian Story of the Flood.* Oxford: Oxford University, 1969.

Parrot, A. *The Tower of Babel.* New York: Philosophical Library, 1955.

Pritchard, J. B., ed. *Ancient Near Eastern Texts Relating to the Old Testament.* 2d ed. Princeton: Princeton University, 1955.

_____, ed. *The Ancient Near East in Pictures Relating to the Old Testament.* 2d ed. with supplement. Princeton: Princeton University, 1969.

_____, ed. *The Ancient Near East: Supplementary Texts and Pictures Relating to the Old Testament.* Princeton: Princeton University, 1968.

Schoville, K. N. *Biblical Archaeology in Focus.* Grand Rapids: Baker, 1978.

Thomas, D. W., ed. *Documents from Old Testament Times.* New York: Harper, 1961.

_____, ed. *Archaeology and Old Testament Study.* Oxford: Oxford University, 1967.

Thompson, J. A. *The Bible and Archaeology.* 3d ed. Grand Rapids: Eerdmans, 1982.

Walton, J. H. *Ancient Israelite Literature in Its Cultural Context.* Grand Rapids: Zondervan, 1989.

Wiseman, D. J., ed. *Peoples of Old Testament Times.* Oxford: Oxford University, 1973.

Genesis and Science

Cameron, N. M. de S. "Genesis and Evolution." *Themelios* 7 (1982): 28–31.

Coulson, C. A. *Science and Christian Belief.* London: Collins, 1958.

Gillispie, C. C. *Genesis and Geology.* New York: Harper, 1959.

Hummel, C. E. *The Galileo Connection.* Downers Grove, Ill.: InterVarsity, 1986.

Maatman, R. W. *The Bible, Natural Science, and Evolution.* Grand Rapids: Reformed Fellowship, 1970.

Ramm, B. *The Christian View of Science and Scripture*. Grand Rapids: Eerdmans, 1954.

Creation and Flood

Bonhoeffer, D. *Creation and Fall*. New York: Macmillan, 1959.

Bright, J. "Has Archaeology Found Evidence of the Flood?" In *The Biblical Archeologist Reader*, edited by G. E. Wright and D. N. Freedman, 32–40. Garden City, N.Y.: Doubleday, 1961.

Filby, F. A. *The Flood Reconsidered*. Grand Rapids: Zondervan, 1971.

Fretheim, T. E. *Creation, Fall, and Flood*. Minneapolis: Augsburg, 1969.

Hyers, C. *The Meaning of Creation*. Atlanta: John Knox, 1984.

Kikawada, I. M., and A. Quinn. *Before Abraham Was*. Nashville: Abingdon, 1985.

Kornfield, W. J. "The Early-Date Genesis Man." *Christianity Today*, June 8, 1973, 7–10.

Longacre, R. "The Discourse Structure of the Flood Narrative." *SBL Seminar Papers* (1976), 235–62.

Moore, J. R. "Charles Lyell and the Noachian Deluge." *Journal of the American Scientific Affiliation* 22 (1970): 107–15.

Morris, H. M., and J. C. Whitcomb, Jr. *The Genesis Flood*. Philadelphia: Presbyterian and Reformed, 1961.

Newman, R. C., and H. J. Eckelmann, Jr. *Genesis One and the Origin of the Earth*. Grand Rapids: Baker, 1981.

Parrot, A. *The Flood and Noah's Ark*. London: SCM, 1955.

Pember, G. H. *Earth's Earliest Ages*. New York: Revell, n.d.

Rehwinkel, A. M. *The Flood*. St. Louis: Concordia, 1957.

Renckens, H. *Israel's Concept of the Beginning*. New York: Herder and Herder, 1964.

Ridderbos, N. H. *Is There a Conflict Between Genesis 1 and Natural Science?* Grand Rapids: Eerdmans, 1957.

Schmeling, W. A. *Creation Versus Evolution? Not Really!* St. Louis: Clayton, 1976.

Vos, Geerhardus. *Biblical Theology*. Grand Rapids: Eerdmans, 1948.

Whitcomb, J. C., Jr. "Did the Flood Cover the Earth?" *His*, May 1958, 37–40.

_____. *The Early Earth*. Winona Lake, Ind.: BMH, 1972.

Wiester, J. *The Genesis Connection*. Nashville: Thomas Nelson, 1983.

Yamauchi, E. "Is That an Ark on Ararat?" *Eternity*, February 1978, 27–32.

Youngblood, R. "Moses and the King of Siam." *Journal of the Evangelical Theological Society* 16 (1973): 215–22.

_____, ed. *The Genesis Debate: Persistent Questions About Creation and the Flood*. Grand Rapids: Baker, 1991.

Zimmerman, P. A., ed. *Darwin, Evolution, and Creation*. St. Louis: Concordia, 1959.

Patriarchs

Clarke, E. G. "Jacob's Dream at Bethel as Interpreted in the Targums and the New Testament." *Studies in Religion* 4 (1974–75): 367–77.

Fokkelman, J. P. *Narrative Art in Genesis.* Assen/Amsterdam: Van Gorcum, 1975.

Gaubert, H. *Abraham, Loved by God.* New York: Hastings House, 1968.

Greengus, S. "Sisterhood Adoption at Nuzi and the 'Wife-Sister' in Genesis." *Hebrew Union College Annual* 46 (1975): 5–31.

Hunt, I. *The World of the Patriarchs.* Englewood Cliffs, N.J.: Prentice-Hall, 1967.

Lowenthal, E. I. *The Joseph Narrative in Genesis.* New York: Ktav, 1973.

McCarthy, D. J. "Three Covenants in Genesis." *Catholic Biblical Quarterly* 26 (1976): 179–89.

Mendenhall, G. E. "Mari." In *The Biblical Archaeologist Reader. Volume 2,* edited by E. F. Campbell and D. N. Freedman, 3–20. Garden City, N.Y.: Doubleday, 1964.

Pfeiffer, C. F. *The Patriarchal Age.* Grand Rapids: Baker, 1961.

Redford, D. *A Study of the Biblical Story of Joseph (Genesis 37-50).* Leiden: Brill, 1970.

Smith, R. H. "Abram and Melchizedek (Gen. 14:18–20)." *Zeitschrift für die Alttestamentliche Wissenschaft* 77 (1965): 129–53.

Strahan, J. *Hebrew Ideals.* 4th ed. Edinburgh: T. & T. Clark, 1922.

Vos, Geerhardus. *Biblical Theology.* Grand Rapids: Eerdmans, 1948.

Weeks, N. "Man, Nuzi, and the Patriarchs: A Retrospect." *Abr-Nahrain* 16 (1975–76): 73–82.

Wiseman, D. J. "Abraham in History and Tradition." *Bibliotheca Sacra* 134 (1977): 123–30, 228–37.

Wright, G. E. *Shechem: The Biography of a Biblical City.* New York: McGraw-Hill, 1965.

Youngblood, R. *The Heart of the Old Testament.* Grand Rapids: Baker, 1971.

General Index

Scripture Index

(An asterisk [*] indicates where a specific scriptural passage receives its primary treatment in the commentary.)